LITHUANIANS IN THE UNITED STATES: SELECTED STUDIES

LEO J. ALILUNAS, EDITOR

San Francisco, California
1978

Published By

R&E Research Associates, Inc.
4843 Mission Street
San Francisco, California 94112

Publishers
Robert D. Reed and Adam S. Eterovich

Library of Congress Card Catalog Number
77-081018

I.S.B.N.
0-88247-487-1

CONTENTS •

In recent years there has been a development of what ethnic scholars call the "new pluralism." The passage by Congress of the Ethnic Heritage Studies Program Act made available $2.5 million for projects involving ethnic and racial minorities. A federally financed survey in 1973 indicated that 135 colleges and universities offered 315 courses dealing with a wide variety of American cultural groups. Institutions such as Wayne State University, City University of New York and others have organized courses concerned with formerly neglected ethnic groups, such as the Polish-Americans, Slavic-Americans and Italian-Americans.

The new ethnic studies movement has even begun to penetrate the public schools. An increasing number of publishing companies and multi-media production companies are marketing paperback materials, records, tape cassettes and filmstrips on various groups such as the Czechs and Slovaks, the Hungarians, the Irish, the Italians, the English, the French, the Dutch, the Russians, the Scotch and Scotch-Irish, the Swedes, the Norwegians, the Germans, the Finns, the Greeks and the Poles. But the Lithuanians in the United States have continued to be a neglected people in both school and scholarly publications dealing with ethnic studies.

The sociologist, Harold J. Abrahamson, in his recent book, Ethnic Diversity in Catholic America, points out that Lithuanians in the United States, whom he estimates at 1,300,000, have been neglected, along with such other ethnics as Armenians, Greeks, Ukrainians and Finns. He believes research on these groups in terms of their structure, their cultural values, and their social mobility and status is essential.

Specialists in American immigration history such as Oscar Handlin, Carlton C. Qualey and others have indicated the need for significant studies of the coming of the Baltic peoples to the United States. Lithuanians and other Baltic peoples have been consistently neglected in well known American immigrant writings such as George M. Stephenson, A History of American Immigration, 1870-1924 (1926), Louis Adamic, From Many Lands (1940), Marcus Lee Hansen, The Immigration in American History (1942), Oscar Handlin, Race and Nationality in American Life (1948), Maldwyn A. Jones, American Immigration (1960), Carl F. Wittke, We Who Built America. The Saga of the Immigrant (1964), and Philip A. Taylor, The Distant Magnet: European Emigration to the U.S.A. (1971). There is only one book the editor has found in this category of books on American immigration that has an eight page description of Lithuanian immigrants in a part titled, "New Immigrants: East European States." It is Francis J. Brown and Joseph A. Roucek, One America: the History, Contributions and Present Problems of Our Racial and National Minorities (1952).

Lithuanians, however, are not altogether unknown in the United States. On some occasions the American public has learned dramatically about them by means of the mass media. When Upton Sinclair's book, The Jungle, was published in 1906, Americans became aware of not only the evils of the meat packing industry but also of the hard life of Jurgis Rudkus, a peasant youth from Lithuania, who became a worker in the stockyards and lived in Chicago's oldest Lithuanian settlement, which adjoined the meat packing area. American newspapers in their sports pages in 1932 informed Americans that Jack Sharkey, whose real name was Juozas Zukauskas, had won the world's heavyweight boxing title from Max Schmeling. A year later, they reported that he had lost it to Primo Carnera. On February 23, 1948, Life magazine informed its millions of readers about the glamorous Eva Paul (Jievute Paulekiute), the daughter of a Lithuanian immigrant coal miner, and of her marriage to Winthrop Rockefeller, of the famous Rockefeller family. American newspapers circulated widely a news story about a Lithuanian, Simas Kudirka, when he jumped from a Soviet Russian ship into a United States Coast Guard cutter November 23, 1970, and was returned to the Soviets by the Coast Guard. Kudirka, who became a symbol of Lithuanian freedom from Communist rule, was returned to Russia and imprisoned for four years in a Siberian labor camp. He was released and permitted, with his family, to emigrate to the United States in 1974 after a baptismal certificate was found in a Brooklyn church, substantiating the claim of his mother, Maria Sulskiene, that she had been born in the United States. When Kudirka visited Chicago November 16, 1974, he was given a tumultuous welcome by thousands of weeping and cheering Lithuanian-Americans. The Chicago area has the largest Lithuanian population of any of the metropolitan areas in the United States - about 100,000. The Lithuanian communities in Chicago, swelled by thousands of refugees who fled their country at the end of World War II, have a bustling Lithuanian cultural life. The heart is Marquette Park, with its church, hospital, schools, stores, restaurants, a radio station, a Lithuanian daily newspaper, youth center, etc. Chicago, also, has the first Lithuanian cultural museum in the country, the Balzekas museum.

Extensive assimilation studies of Lithuanians in the United States are much needed. Heretofore, it has been assumed that the Lithuanians, as a new European immigrant group, would be expected to have a slow social and economic mobility rate. However, Harold J. Abrahamson, in his book, Ethnic Diversity in Catholic America (1973), based upon his review of data derived from the survey research conducted by the National Opinion Research Center at the University of Chicago, has found that Lithuanians show unusually high achievements in education for a predominantly second-generation ethnic group. Abrahamson is impressed, also, by the high rate of their movement from blue-collar to white-collar jobs, among the highest, as compared to all Catholic ethnic groups.

Various centers for immigrant studies are seeking to improve their collections of materials on ethnic groups, particularly those dealing with peoples from Eastern and Southern Europe. Among them is the Center for Immigration Studies and Immigrant Archives at the University of Minnesota, established in 1963. It includes in its larger collections materials (ethnic newspapers, various manuscript holdings and papers of ethnic leaders) pertaining to Finnish-Americans, Italian-Americans, Polish-Americans, Slovak-Americans and Ukrainian-Americans. It has recently become more interested in including in its collection materials on Lithuanians and Latvians. The most extensive university collection of materials dealing with Lithuania and Lithuanians in the United States is at the University of Pennsylvania, which has been collecting Lithuanian materials since 1948. It contains the Saulys collection, one of the most important collections on Lithuanian history available to scholars outside the Russian orbit. The University of Pennsylvania, under the leadership of Dr. Alfred Senn, has become the country's outstanding center for the study of the Baltic languages. Other libraries which are known for their Lithuanian materials are the Library of Congress and the Slavonic Division of the New York City Public Library.

The editor has been interested in the study of Lithuanian immigrants in the United States for many years. His father and mother were Lithuanian immigrants. As a member of the Social Studies Department at the State University of New York College at Fredonia for about 20 years he taught college courses on American racial and ethnic groups. He has visited the Library of Congress and various university libraries in search of studies, both published and unpublished, relating to Lithuanians and especially to Lithuanians in the United States.

There has been no publication of comprehensive studies, in a single book, dealing specifically with Lithuanians in the United States. The editor is pleased that he has been able to compile, in a single volume, significant published and unpublished studies of Lithuanians in the United States, a much neglected ethnic group.

This book is organized in three main parts: Part I - The Background of Lithuanian Immigrants; Part II - The Earlier Lithuanian Immigrants; and Part III - The Later Lithuanian Immigrants. Part I deals with the origins of the Lithuanians, a historical introduction to Lithuania, characteristics of the Lithuanian people and with the causes of Lithuanian immigration to the United States. Part II gives general characterizations of the Lithuanian immigrants, describes conditions in their life as immigrants in American communities, and analyzes their family, religion, press and their American politics. Part III describes the immigration of Lithuanian refugees to the United States after World War II and their various adjustments.

PART I. THE BACKGROUND OF LITHUANIAN IMMIGRANTS

Chapter 1. THE ORIGINS OF LITHUANIANS

Source - Dr. Jonas Puzinas, "In Search of the Origins of the Lithuanian People," Lituanus, No. 1 (10) March, 1957, 7-11.[1]

Overview

First, Dr. Puzinas has examined the theory of classical origins (Greek and Roman) of the Lithuanians and stated that such nationalistic theory was not discarded until a few decades ago when scholars began investigating the topic on a more scientific basis.

The science of linguistics has been a valuable aid in the research efforts to locate the original home of the Lithuanians. Linguistic investigations indicate that the Lithuanian, Lettic, Old Prussian, Curonian, Sengallian and the Selonian languages formed a single linguistic group, the Baltic, the name of the people who lived on the shores of the Baltic Sea.

Dr. Puzinas has analyzed the theories of Kazimieras Buga and other linguists and then turned his attention to the science of prehistory or archeology. He has cited the discovery of prehistoric remains in the Baltic area. Around 1000 B.C. the Balts began to split culturally and linguistically into the Western Balts, who included the Old Prussians and the Eastern Balts, who included the Lithuanians and the Latvians. There is a belief that the Western Balts lived at one time beyond the Vistula River, in Pomerania, and that the Eastern Balts, including Lithuanian tribes, once lived along the upper Protva River, west of Moscow, near the cities of Gzack and Mozhalsk, prior to their absorption in the Slavic westward expansion. The eastern part of the Baltic territory remains the least investigated, according to Dr. Puzinas.

The Lithuanians like all peoples conscious of their selfhood, began to explore the problem of their origins a long time ago. As early as the end of the 14th century or the beginning of the 15th, Lithuanians were theorizing that they were descended from the Romans. The Polish historian J. Dlugosz was the first to formulate such a theory in writing: In several places in his "History of Poland" he remarks that, to judge by similarities of language and religion, the Lithuanians must be descended from Romans--ones who escaped into Lithuania during the civil wars between Marius and Sulla and between Julius Caesar and Pompey. But this is really nothing more than an expression of the spirit of the times; during the period of humanism other nations, deeply impressed by the heroic histories and high culture of the ancients, put forth claims to Greek or Roman origins. Even in the early Middle Ages we find similar tendencies among the nobility. For example, the 12th century Polish chronicler Kadiubek searched for the ancestors of the Poles in classical antiquity; according to him, the first Polish duke, and later king, was Graccus, and he gave his name to the city of Cracow as his daughter Wanda gave hers to Vandalia. Even Alexander the Great is supposed to have received letters from Poland, and Julius Caesar to have married his sister to the Polish duke Leszko.

The desire of the Lithuanian nobility to prove their honorable ancestry to the Poles--"We are Roman noblemen!"--had much to do with the acceptance of the theory of classical origins in Lithuania. In the chronicle of the 16th century Lithuanian Grand Duchy we find mentioned a certain Roman prince Palemon or Pilemon, who is supposed to have fled Rome in the first century A.D. with his family and a retinue of 500 and to have founded the Lithuanian royal dynasty. This theory of Lithuania's Roman origins, which fortified the Lithuanian nobility in their rivalry with the Polish, was endlessly repeated, and was expanded and strengthened by new rationalizations. Many romantics of the early 19th century, and even the later Ausrininkai--followers of the newspaper "Ausra" (The Dawn), first published in 1883--accepted this theory. A castle-bill at Seredzius, near the Nemunas River, was named after this prince, and relatively recently a railroad station near Kaunas was named Palemonas.

During the course of centuries relationships were also claimed to exist between the Lithuanians and the Greeks, the Alans, the Heruli, the Slavs, the Tracs, the Phryglans and other peoples. These claims were unusually based on weak etymological speculation upon fortuitous resemblances between words in different languages or on correspondences in customs or religions. None of the theories was based on scientific evidence; they were created and promulgated in the main by amateurs who often try their hands at solving complex problems. These nationalistic theories were not discarded until a few decades ago, when many scholars began investigating the problem with scientific objectivity.

The science of linguistics has unquestionably made a very substantial contribution to the solution of this vexing problem of the original home of the Lithuanians and their relations with neighboring tribes. As the natural organ of man's spiritual, social and cultural communication, language is a primary source in the investigation of national origins and international intercourse. Language reflects a nation's antiquity and its spiritual and material culture. Words of native origin testify to a nation's creative powers; borrowings reveal the cultural influence of other nations, neighboring or far removed, and the ancient international relations. Peaceful relations with other nations include the exchange of ideas as well as the exchange of commodities; not only various articles but also their names reach other nations through the channels of trade. From the number and nature of these borrowings can be determined the creative powers of a particular nation and its role in cultural interchange. Finally, the study of proper names is of great importance. Place names, especially the names of rivers and lakes, often remain after a people has moved or disappeared. It is possible to determine from these names the homes of ancient peoples.

Comparative linguistics, based on the comparison of grammar and vocabulary, has reconstructed the over-all picture of many ancient languages and their old morphological forms, and has determined the ties and the degree of relationship among different languages along with answering and clarifying many problems of prehistory. Linguistics has shown that the Lithuanians, Slavs, Germans, Italics, Celts, Greeks, Armenians, Persians Hindus and other made up in the deep past a single people using the same language. Since the name of this prehistoric people has not been preserved scientists call it the Indo-European, after the eastern and western bounds of the present nations that share this origin. Linguistics has found that the Lithuanian, Lettic, Old Prussian, Curonian, Semigallian and Selonian languages are interrelated and form a single linguistic group, which is called the baltic or Aistian group. ("Baltic" from the Baltic Sea, "Aistian" from "Aestorium gentes," Tacitus' name for the people who lived on the shores of the Baltic). The Baltic languages have developed from a common root, and in ancient times all the Balts spoke the same language and made up one nation.

The distinguished linguist Kazimieras Buga made the greatest contribution to the scholarly investigation of this matter. While investigating place names in the territories of Minsk, Smolensk, Mogilev and Vitebsk, he established that in these regions, to the east of present-day Lithuania, lived the ancient Lithuanians and Latvians. In his opinion the ancient Lithuanians lived north of the Pripet River, along its left tributaries and along the Berezina and upper Dnieper almost to the middle of the Soze River basin. Buga counted in this area 121 river names of Baltic origin-- for instance the Lucesa (Laukesa), Volcesa (Vilkesa), Toluva, Dugna, Soze, etc. The neighbors of the Lithuanians to the north and east were the ancestors of the present-day Estonians and Finns and those to the south were the ancestors of the Slavs. Buga claims that the Balts did not always occupy these ancient territories. The first of the Balts to separate from the common nation were the Old Prussians, and they were the first to reach the shores of the Baltic. It would appear that even before the time of Christ the Old Prussians were living around the mouth of the Vistula. The Lithuanians and Latvians moved from their original territories much later; even in the sixth century they were still living in what is now Belorussia. At the end of the sixth century or the beginning of the seventh, when the Slavs began moving along the Dnieper and across the Pripet into the territory the Lithuanians were then occupying, the latter were forced to migrate to the west, to present-day Lithuania, where the ancestors of the Estonians Livonians and Finns had lived. The Slavist Max Vasmer came to the same conclusions when he investigated the eastern boundaries of the Lithuanian tribes, except that his further studies of place names led him to place those boundaries even farther to the east. He demonstrated that the Baltic tribes once lived in the territories of Smolensk and Kaluga, in the western part of the Moscow territories and in the southwestern part of the Tver and Pskov.

For a long time Buga's theories concerning Baltic as well as Lithuanian origins were the most widely credited. However, new archeological discoveries have led to a reinterpretation. A substantial part of his theory is incompatible with the latest results of prehistory studies. But the work of Buga, Vasmer and other linguistic scholars remains important, especially since they established that the boundaries of the Lithuanian and related tribes in prehistoric times are not limited by later ethnographic borders, but that Lithuanians lived far to the east in the lands of the Belorussians and the Russians. The linguists' conclusions are supported by the results of research into prehistory.

The origins of any nation are lodged in prehistory; therefore the science of prehistory, or archeology, is of immense importance. The essential sources of our knowledge of prehistory are the discoveries at ancient homesteads, castle-hills, burial grounds, and so forth. Such discoveries are direct witnesses to the life and culture of prehistoric times. It is now possible not only to investigate the development of material and spiritual culture but also to determine what people lived in a particular place at a particular time. Science has evolved a complex procedure to answer such ethnical questions. We know that any people that has retained primeval cultural traits and has not lost its identity through general cultural influences possesses its own unique material and spiritual culture, distinguishable from that of neighboring peoples. One can detect many differences even in different provinces of a single nation. In Lithuania, for example, the Žemaičiai (Lowlanders), the Rytieciai Aukstaiciai (Eastern Highlanders), the Dzukai and the Zanavykai differ not only in dialect but also in apparel, architecture, customs and even personality characteristics. These differences between various nations and tribes must have been even more noticeable in prehistoric times, when contacts among nations were limited. And indeed, when we examine prehistoric remains we find provinces and even groups with distinct cultures--differing in their ceramics, ornaments, household appliances, tools, weapons and burial customs--existing in various areas at the same time. Once these areas are clearly demarcated on a map, the areas and boundaries of cultural groups become apparent. Each such cultural group is assigned to the nation that is known to have inhabited that area in early historic times, and research is undertaken on whether or not there have been any changes in the course of cultural evolution. If this cultural evolution is continuous, it is often possible to trace a nation's primary origins. This continuity of cultural evolution is easily traceable in the case of Lithuania, as of other areas inhabited by the Balts. Let us, then, see what the science of prehistory has to say concerning Baltic, and at the same time Lithuanian, origins.

Lithuanian prehistory, like that of all nations, can be divided into three general periods: the Stone Age, the Bronze Age and the Iron Age. These periods receive their names for the substances on which the material culture of the time was based. During the Stone Age most tools and weapons were made of stone or bone; during the Bronze Age the first metal implements appeared and displaced those of stone; finally, in the Iron Age the bronze implements gave way to ones of iron. The first men appeared in Lithuania about 18,000 years ago, when the glacial period had ended and the country was free of ice. These first inhabitants were probably nomads. Few of their traces remain; it is impossible to determine the racial origins of these early inhabitants of Lithuania. It is clear only that they arrived from the south and east, following the retreating masses of ice. Around 3500 B.C. elements of Finnish cultural emerged. From these people evolved the present-day Estonians and Livonians, artifacts of whose ancestors are still found in Latvia. At the time the area was still thinly settled; the inhabitants were hunters, fishermen and gatherers of wild food plants.

The great migrations of the Indo-Europeans and other groups began around 2500 B.C. Various nations or groups of nations migrated from one region to another, attacking foreign territories, capturing the land and sometimes displacing the former inhabitants. The Baltic areas were not immune to these migrations. About 2300 B.C. people of an agricultural culture, farmers and shepherds, reached the southeastern shores of the Baltic. This was the Globular Amphora Culture, so called for their amphoras, or two-handled urns. Many modern students of prehistory link the spread of this new culture with the Indo-European advance. As for their center, there is a strong tendency to search for it in the Ukraine and the neighboring steppe regions to the east. New discoveries indicate that around 3500 B.C. the Indo-European tribes, already exhibiting some language differences, began to expand from these steppes in all directions. Some migrated to the north, reaching central Russia and southwestern Finland, and even Sweden; other tribes traveled northwest until they reached the shores of the Baltic Sea; still others found themselves in central Europe, etc. When the newly arrived inhabitants settled permanently in their new homes, the slow evolution of different Indo-European nations began. The process of cultural evolution was more rapid in those regions where the invaders found a more advanced culture, and the influence of the local culture is much more noticeable. And the evolution of language depended on the strength of the native element that influenced the Indo-European language. Consequently the Indo-European language began to break up, remaining closer to the original in places where few native inhabitants were encountered and taking on many foreign elements in places where large numbers of natives had to be assimilated. In Lithuania and the other Baltic lands the newly arrived Indo-Europeans met up with only a small number of native people; consequently, in this out-of-the-way place, far removed from all famous centers of culture, the language retained an astonishingly ancient character, and this had very important consequences for comparative linguistics. On the other hand, the Germanic tongues changed incomparably more, since the ancestors of the Germanic-speaking peoples found a much larger native element.

About 2000 years before Christ we find in the area from the Helos Peninsula to the Runa River an already-formed cultural group that can be considered to be proto-Baltic, the direct ancestors of the Lithuanians. The most substantial deposits of this new culture are found from the Bay of Danzig to the Nemunas River. Remains have also been found in West and East Prussia, Lithuania, Latvia up to the Duna River, and Belorussia. The Balts, as can be seen from the investigations of their homesteads, were sedentary people who remained in the more fertile regions, tilling the soil and raising domestic animals.

The continuing evolution of Baltic culture can easily be traced to the beginning of Historic times. The culture continued its development without interruption through the Bronze Age (1800-400 B.C.). The continuity of the culture can be observed not only in its material aspects but also chronologically and geographically. In the Bronze Age the Balts were completely formed, and lived very much where they live now: To the west they reached the Persanta River in Pomerania, to the North as far as the Duna and the Abava, to the east--as is shown by river names of Baltic origin--they reached Moscow, Tula and the Desna River, and to the south they reached the Pripet Marshes, the Bug and the Vistula.

At first the Baltic culture was more or less monolithic, but eventually, since it was spread over a large area, it began to differentiate, and this undoubtedly is connected with the division of the Balts. Around 1000 B.C. the Balts began to split, culturally and probably linguistically, into the Western and Eastern Balts. The Old Prussians gradually evolved from the Western Balts and the Lithuanians and Latvians from the Eastern Balts. Six centuries before Christ the Western Balts began to divide into tribes: Sembians and Notangians, Galindians and Suduvians; this substantiated by differences in handicrafts and somewhat different burial customs. The division of the Eastern Balts can be noticed just before the birth of Christ; lack of evidence prevents us from fixing the approximate date of its beginning. During the first centuries after Christ the division of the Eastern Balts into tribes becomes quite clear; one finds three distinct cultural groups: Lithuanians, Semigallians and Curonians. A high point in the cultural life of the Balts was reached 200 years after Christ. Even in what is now Estonia the Balts constituted a strong cultural influence. This development continued without interruption up to historic times. One can find more unifying elements than differentiating ones in all areas inhabited by the Balts. One must assume that linguistic differtiations accompanied new cultural patterns; as each new tribe emerged culturally, a new language began to emerge too, based on a dialect which gradually became a separate language under different conditions of life.

We find certain discrepancies between Buga's research and prehistoric data. As has been mentioned, Buga, basing his case on plaçe names, argues the necessity of looking north of the Pripet for the original Lithuanian homesteads, arguing that the present Lithuania was previously inhabited by the ancestors of the modern Livonians, Estonians and Finns, and that the Lithuanians did not migrate until the sixth or seventh century, in response to Slavic pressure. These theories of Buga's shared in part by other linguistics scholars, are incompatible with the results of modern prehistory studies. If, as Buga holds, the Lithuanians did not migrate until the sixth or seventh centuries, a new influence would be detectable in the Lithuanian material culture of the time. But no traces of such an influence have been found, the culture evolved without a break: consequently there can be no talk of migrations at this time. Almost all the Baltic tribes had been living on the shores of the Baltic Sea from 2000 B.C., when the proto-Balts settled there, to the beginning of historic times. This is where they originated; only the boundaries of their territories changed over the centuries. For example, in the Bronze Age the Western Balts lived even beyond the Vistula, in Pomerania; later they were forced out of this region by the Germans. The territory they inhabited in the south was also reduced when the decisive battles between the Jatvingians and the Poles took place. In the north, -he Balts were able to expand further and win new territories from the Livonians and the Estonians; here the boundaries were pushed from the Duma to present-day Estonia. The Balts suffered their worst losses in the east. The ancestors of the Lithuanians and Latvians, as studies of place names and archeological discoveries show, lived much farther to the east than their present ethnographical boundaries. Because of Slavic expansion, the area inhabited by the Balts in the east began to diminish in the sixth century A.D. It is possible that some Balts migrated westward, but prehistoric evidence indicates that most of them became absorbed into the Slavic culture. This Slavicizing of the Lithuanian and Latvian peoples took a long time; as late as the 11th and 12th centuries a remnant of the Lithuanian tribes--the Galindians--were living west of Moscow along the upper Protva River, near the present cities of Gzack and Mozhaisk. And the present southernmost Lithuanian islands, in Slonim and Lyda Districts, are probably remnants of territories that used to be inhabited entirely by the Lithuanians.

We see from this brief survey that the problem of Lithuanian origins has received substantial clarification recently, that the evolution of a Baltic culture can be traced from the first Indo-European settlements up to historic times. Many details still need clarification; the question of boundaries, especially, is in need of new evidence and study. Many problems are very difficult to solve because the eastern part of the Baltic territory remains the least investigated, and the material, ledged in Belorussian museums and Russian archeological collections, in inaccessible. It can only be hoped that these difficulties may be overcome in the future and the solution of the problem of Lithuania's origins may be formulated with precision.

BIBLIOGRAPHY

K. Buga, Die Vorgeschichte der aistischen (baltischen) Stamme im Lichte der Ortsnamenforschung, (Streitber-Festgabe, Leipzig 1924, 22-35.) Language and Antiquity 1. Kaunas 1922.

C. Engel, Die Baltische Besiedlung Weiss-und Mitteiruslands in vorges-schichtsicher Zeit (Literarum Societatis Esthonica 1838-1938. Tartu 1938, 904-910.)

M. Gimbutas, On the Origin of North Indo-European (American Anthropolo-gist, vol. 54, No. 4, 1952, 602-611).

L. Kilian, Haffustenkultur and Ursprung der Balten 1955;

J. Puzinas. The latest data of the prehistorical studies, Kaunas 1938. The theories of Lithuanian origin within the realm of ages, (The Literature Yearbook, Chicago, 1950, 193-244).

A. Salys. Baltic Languages (Encyclopedia Britannica, Vol. 3, 1955).

FOOTNOTE

[1] Reprinted by permission of the author and the publisher, Lituanus, Lithuanian Quarterly Journal of Arts and Sciences.

Chapter 2. AN INTRODUCTION TO THE HISTORY OF LITHUANIA

Source - Benedict V. Maciuika, Editor. Anton W. De Porte,
Benedict V. Maciuika and Luitgard Wundheiler,
Contributors. Lithuania in the Last 30 Years.
Prepared at the University of Chicago by a faculty
supervisory committee including Bert F. Hoselitz,
Chauncy D. Harris and George B. Carson. Printed
by Human Relations Area Files, Inc., New Haven,
Connecticut, 1955. The selection, "Historical
Introduction," is from pages 28-33 of this mono-
graph.[1]

Overview

Lithuanians are descendants of one of the eastern branches of the
Indo-European race. Their language is the oldest spoken European language
in its grammatical forms and is said to be closely related to Sanscrit,
Greek and Latin. The writers mention that the name of Lithuania first appeared in history in a German chronicle of 1009 A.D. They describe the
unification of the Lithuanians under their great rulers, Mindaugas and
Gediminas, the political union of Lithuania and Poland, and the development of the medieval Lithuanian empire.

During the 16th century, Lithuania lost a number of eastern provinces
as the power of Muscovy grew. In the final partition of 1795 Russia
seized all of Lithuania and then controlled both Poland and Lithuania. Beginning with Czar Nicholas I, a policy of Russification was applied to
Lithuania, resulting in the closing of Lithuanian schools and monasteries
and the banning of books in Latin characters. The Russification movement
backfired and a cultural renaissance developed, led by Roman Catholic
priests. Later, in the nineteenth century, Lithuanian peasants were able
to acquire increasing amounts of land while there was a decline of the
Polonized Lithuanian nobility. The priests and peasants helped to build
the foundations of a nationalist movement. Unsuccessful in the Revolution
of 1905, Lithuanian leaders were able to establish an independent republic
as a consequence of the collapse of the Russian Empire during World War I.

Lithuania initially set up a democratic republic, with a multi-party
system and a parliamentary government but in 1926 turned to an authoritarian regime under Antanas Smetona because of its external and internal problems. When Nazi Germany and the Soviet Union decided to carve Eastern
Europe in 1939, Lithuania was assigned to the Soviet Union. The U.S.S.R.
found it opportune with the Allied defeat in the West to annex Lithuania
forcibly in June, 1940. Since then, Lithuania has been a captive state
of the U.S.S.R., along with the other formerly independent Baltic countries
of Latvia and Estonia.

The Lithuanian people, like the Latvians, are descendants of one of
the eastern branches of the Indo-European race, and their language, which

is the oldest spoken tongue in Europe in terms of its grammatical forms, is closely related to Sanscrit, Greek and Latin. It is assumed that it was the ancestors of the present Lithuanians and Letts who are mentioned by ancient historians, as early as Herodotus, as inhabiting the eastern shores of the Baltic and engaging in trade, particularly in amber, with other peoples.

The name of Lithuania first appears in history in a German chronicle of 1009, but it was not until 1236 that the numerous principalities of Lithuanian peoples were united under the rule of King Mindaugas. The chief force promoting their unification was the external threat posed to the Lithuanian tribes by the incursion into their area of the German Knights of the Sword early in the 13th century. After victories had been won over the Knights at the battle of Siauliai (1236), and over Ruthenian princes and Tartar hordes, Mindaugas was baptized a Christian in 1251, and, two years later, he was crowned King of Lithuania by a papal emissary. His conversion, whose principle motive was to take from the Knights their claim to being the bearers of Christianity into a pagan region, did not bring the German invasions to a halt, and following the apostasy of the King the nation was not to become Christian for another century.

A period of disorder followed the assassination of Mindaugas in 1263, but Gediminas (1316--1341) succeeded in reuniting the state, and founded his capital of Vilnius at the confluence of the Neris and Vilnele rivers. Gediminas maintained a defensive policy against the Teutonic Knights, who continued their pressure from the west, while extending the Lithuanian state in the east to Kiev, Pskov and Novgorod. Under the joint rule of Kestutis and Algirdas, the latter defeated the Tartars in 1362, and secured Lithuanian control of Kiev and Podolia, although he failed to capture Moscow.

In 1386, Algirdas' son, Jogaila, was elected to the throne of Poland on condition that he marry the Polish Queen Jadwiga. Thus began the personal union of the two countries under the Jagellonian dynasty which lasted until 1572. At the same time, Lithuania finally adopted Roman Catholicism (1387). While Lithuania was under the direct rule of Jogaila's cousin, Vytautas the Great (1392-1430), a Lithuanian-Polish force crushed the Teutonic Order at the great battle of Tannenberg (1410), with the important result that Lithuania, in contrast to the territories to the north, was spared domination by the "German Barons" who were the descendants and heirs of the Knights. The medieval Lithuanian empire now reached its height, including the upper Volga and Oka rivers, and Smolensk, Vyazma, Mozhaisk and Kursk, with a population of some five million people. During this reign, Christianity became an integral part of the Western European cultural and religious community, but, at the same time, the diverse Lithuanian state was notable for its religious and linguistic freedom.

During the 16th century, however, Lithuania lost a number of her eastern provinces to the rising power of Muscovy, and this new danger impelled her to seek a closer association with Poland, with whom, to that time, she had been joined only in a personal union. By the Pact of Lublin (1569), Lithuania ceded her Ukrainian territories to Poland, and recognized Courland and Latgalia as being a condominium of the two states; each, however, retained its separate government, armed forces, treasuries and law courts. The Lithuanian state knew a considerable degree of prosperity in the 16th century, and the Pact of Lublin provided a short-lived security, but increasingly the Lithuanian nobility, imitating the example of their peers in Poland, tended to acquire more and more rights at the expense of the central authority of the state. Partly because of the internal weakness of the Lithuanian-Polish Commonwealth, it was defeated by the Russians in a long war which ended with the Peace of ANDRUSOVO (1667), by which Lithuania lost the province of Smolensk.

Despite the attempts of some Lithuanians to break the connection with Poland and form new relations with Sweden, the Lithuanian state tended increasingly to become the junior partner in the commonwealth, and the Lithuanian nobility became ever more polonized and divorced from their own nation. The weakness of the joint state became constantly more apparent during the 18th century, and, in the first partition of Poland (1772), important portions of eastern Lithuania were lost to Russia. Despite the last-minute efforts of the Commonwealth to reform itself, the second partition of Poland took place in 1793, costing Lithuania more eastern territory, including a small part of "ethnographic" Lithuania. By the final partition of 1795, Russia seized the whole of Lithuania, except for the territory south of the Nemunas River, the province of Suvalkai, which was taken by Prussia, but which, in 1815, was also assigned to Russia.

Five major revolts occurred in Poland and Lithuania in the succeeding 120 years, the most important being those of 1831 and 1863. Beginning with Nicholas I., an ever more drastic policy of russification was applied to Lithuania: schools and monasteries were closed; the Lithuanian system of law was replaced in 1840 with the Russian Code; in 1865 the printing of books in Latin characters was banned; the Catholic Church, some of whose clergy had been active in the rebellion of 1863, was attacked directly and indirectly. But these very attacks on the Lithuanian language and national character only impelled the population to cling to them more ardently, and, towards the middle of the century, there began a literary and cultural renaissance--based on books smuggled into Lithuania from across the German frontier. Then, as was so often the case in eastern and central Europe, cultural nationalism soon led to nationalist political manifestations.

From the beginning, the resistance of the peasantry--which formed the overwhelming mass of the population--was focussed and led by a number of Lithuanian Roman Catholic priests, who resisted both the russification of the country and the attempts of many priests and members of the ecclesiastical hierarchy--including both Poles and pro-Polish persons of Lithuanian origin--to polonize the Lithuanian church and people. In addition, as a result of the emancipation of the peasants in the Suvalkai area in 1807, and in the rest of the country in 1861 and 1863, a new type of national intellectual leader began to emerge from among them. Prior to 1865, the leaders of the rebellions had been largely polonized noblemen who joined with their associates in Poland proper in efforts to restore in some form the Polish-Lithuanian union--and their own privileges within it. The new leaders, however, were social reformers as well as nationalists, who aimed at agrarian reform, the democratization of Lithuanian society, and the defense of the Lithuanian national culture against both russification and polonization. Among this group were Dr. Jonas Basanavicius (1851-1927), whose magazine Ausra (Dawn) appeared in 1883 in Tilsit, Dr. Vincas Kudirka (1858-1899), and the Rev. Juozas Tumas (1869-1933).

It is therefore very important to note that as increasing amounts of the land in Lithuania passed into the hands of the peasantry during the nineteenth century, and as the Lithuanian nobility, fearful of reform, increasingly identified its cause and interests with the socially conservative nobles of Poland, the importance of the noble class in Lithuania dwindled, and the national movement developed apart from them. As will be seen below, when independence was at last established, the nobility in effect retired from Lithuania into Poland, allowing the establishment of the new Lithuanian state on the democratic and reformist bases envisioned by the nationalist leaders of the late nineteenth century.

To an even greater extent than elsewhere, it is significant that the national movement in Lithuania received important assistance and inspiration from Lithuanians living abroad, and particularly from the large number in America.

Political parties emerged in Lithuania at the end of the nineteenth century, and first manifested their desire for an autonomous, democratic, ethnographic Lithuania, within the Russian Em ire, during the Revolution of 1905. It was not until 1917, however, that this program was capable of realization, and then, in the midst of a most complex situation including war, revolution and counter-revolution, the Lithuanian leaders were able not only to win autonomy but actually to establish an independent republic. Their success, however, was due in large measure to the successive collapses of the Russian and German empires, and to the intervention of the Western allies, and it was limited from the first by the Polish seizure of Vilnius, which destroyed all hopes for cooperation between the two states, and by the occupation of Klaipeda (Memel) at the expense of Germany in 1923.

A democratic republic, however, was established after the war, on the political basis of a liberal constitution and a multi-party system, on which parliamentary government maintained itself for several years, and on the economic basis of an agrarian reform (1922) which, by partitioning the large estates--owned in many cases by polonized, often absent nobles--for the benefit of landless peasants, and those with small holdings, in effect provided that the country would be a nation of small farmers. In addition, the State assumed the responsibility of providing for the economic welfare of its citizens. In 1926, however, a military and conservative coup d'etat set aside the constitution in favor of an authoritarian regime, first under Professor Voldemaras, and later under President Antanas Smetona. These governments suppressed all other parties and established regimes which, at least in vocabulary, borrowed considerably from the contemporary German and Italian models. The increasingly dangerous international situation, which after 1936 involved the withdrawal of Great Britain and France from effective participation in the affairs of eastern and central Europe, left Lithuania and the other Baltic states--and eventually Poland herself--in the hands of Germany and the Soviet Union. When these two states divided eastern Europe between them in August and September, 1939, the fate of Lithuania, which was finally assigned to the Soviet zone, was sealed, though the U.S.S.R. did not actually seize and annex the country until the Allied defeat in the West in June, 1940, permitted her to do so without fear of retaliation or resistance from any quarter.

The year of the first Soviet occupation of Lithuania witnessed the establishment of a soviet republic, its admission to the U.S.S.R., and the replacement of the rather loose Nationalist authoritarian regime with a more thorough Communist dictatorship. Large industry was nationalized, and by limiting land holdings to 30 hectares land was seized from owners of large (1929 legal maximum of 150 ha.) and middlesized holdings, but it was only in the last days of the Soviet occupation that deportations and terrorism on a large scale were instituted.

In June, 1941, however, the Russians were replaced by the Germans in the occupation of Lithuania and, though many Lithuanians were inclined, in these circumstances, to accept the Germans as liberators, the latter com-

12

ported themselves in a manner which made their acceptance impossible. The country was harnessed to the German war machine, and little effort was made to restore the property of those who had been dispossessed by the Soviets. The German government, in fact, considered and proclaimed itself the legal heir of the expelled regime and on this basis took control of such land and industry as it chose. Thousands of Lithuanians were deported to Germany for labor duty; other thousands, and particularly very large numbers of Jews, were killed.

With the Russian restoration in 1944-45, the process of sovietization began in earnest. Russification of the government and the country was much increased; the administration and all strategic economic posts were in effective control of Russian personnel; and, in 1947, rural collectivization, long dreaded by the peasantry and long denied by the officials, was at last instituted, and, by 1953, substantially completed. Simultaneously, widespread deportations of suspect elements of the population took place, and, if these measures were mainly linked with specific events, such as collectivization, or were motivated by the desire to deprive the population of all possible articulate leadership, rather than actually to destroy the Lithuanian nation, nevertheless many hundreds of thousands of persons were involved, with serious results for a people of less than three million.

It is difficult to speak of the political history of such a state as the Lithuanian Soviet Socialist Republic, which is so closely dependent on the government at Moscow. It has exhibited, however, considerable continuity of personnel, at least at the upper levels, and the process of russification of the administration, which appeared so pronounced about 1950, seems to have decreased since 1953. All independent concentrations of power, such as the Church or the intellectual classes, have been thoroughly bridled, however, though some remnants of the underground resistance may remain, and, whatever the discontent of the population, effective and total Soviet control seems beyond question.

SOURCES: Thomas G. Chase, The Story of Lithuania, 1946, 343 pp.; Henry de Chambon, La Lithuanie Moderne, 19-3, 297 pp.; The Baltic States, prepared by the Information Department of the Royal Institute of International Affairs, 1938, 194 pp.; Owen J. C. Norem, Timeless Lithuania, 1943, 297 pp.; Third Interim Report of the Select Committee on Communist Aggression, House of Representatives (The "Kersten Committee"), 1954, 529 pp.; Malbone W. Graham, Jr., New Governments of Eastern Europe. 1927, pp. 250-408.

FOOTNOTE

[1] Reprinted by the permission of the editor and the printer, Human Relations Area Files, Inc., New Haven, Connecticut.

Chapter 3. LITHUANIAN NATIONAL CHARACTER TRAITS

Source - Juozas Lingis, "The National Character of
Lithuanian People," Baltic Review, Volume
1, No. 1, 1945, 3-13.[1]

Overview

An essential element in the development of national character is
language. Lingis has emphasized that the Lithuanian language is not Slavonic, although the Balts and Slavs have been neighbors for centuries and
there have been linguistic borrowings. Then, he has surveyed the ethnological structure of the Lithuanian people and identified the historical
areas of Lithuanian settlement in Europe.

Lithuanians have been agriculturists for centuries. They have a very
strong feeling of earth-mindedness. Their love of their soil has enabled
them to preserve their sense of national character inspite of long periods
of political control by a foreign power. He has also noted the distinc-
tive matriarchaic culture of the Lithuanians and how it has been reflected
in their popular art, folk-lore and legends.

The Lithuanian national character has been influenced greatly by contacts through the centuries with the Germans, on the West, and, on other
borders, with the Slavs, namely, the Poles and the Russians. Experiences
with the Germans have resulted in a hostile attitude toward them on the
part of the Lithuanians. Since the days of the invasion of the Teuton Order of the Knights of the Cross, they have regarded the Germans as intrud-
ers. As to the Poles, the Lithuanians accepted Christianity through them,
joined them in a political union, and later succeeded in cleansing themselves of Polish influence in creating their own national character. Their
experiences with the Russians, who undertook a subjugation policy against
them, both under Czarist and Communist Russia, have served to strengthen
their love for liberty and made them determined to fight for it.

In the following essay I shall endeavor to give a brief description
of the national character of the Lithuanian people. Before I do this, I
want to say a few words about the ethnological structure of the Lithuanians and their position among kindred people.

The Lithuanian people belong to a special, independent Indo-European
population group, the Aistii of the Baltic peoples[2],) as they have been
termed by philologists. From a philological point of view, the Lithuanian
language, as all the other Baltic languages, belongs to the East-Indo-
European group of Languages, the so-called Satem group, i.e. belonging to
the same group as Indo-Iranian or Aryan, as represented by the Vedic language, Sanscrit, Slavonic, Armenian and Albanian. In the professional literature it is often maintained that Lithuanian is a branch of the Slavonic
languages and that it has had a common primitive language besides the Indo-
European tongue. Yet, baltologists--specialists within this field--do not

14

find anything that points to the fact that there should have existed a common Baltic-Slavonic primitive language. If the Baltic language has anything in common with the Slavonic languages it only shows that the Balts and the Slavs have been neighbours from time immemorial, neighbouring languages, even if they are not related to one another, have often phonetic features in common as a result of having emanated from the same centre.

The Lithuanian language is the oldest living language in Europe. It has preserved many archaic features which are closely related to the common Indo-European primitive language. In comparative philology the Lithuanian language is of the same significance as old Gothic, old Gree, Latin, and Sanscrit.

The Baltic peoples are divided into the eastern group and the western group. The western group consist of the Borussii or the Prussians. » Prussians is another name for the Aistii whose dwellings Tacitus found about 97 B.C. along the river Vistula. During the 10th century the Aistii are longer to be found in the historical records, but instead one finds the name of the Prussians,» Pruzzorum fines » in Canaparii Vita St. Adalberti about 999 A.D. From that time onwards, all those Baltic tribes which inhabited and even crossed the borders of the present Eastern Prussia, were called Prussians.

The Prussians consisted of several tribes, yet, only eleven of them are known from historical records: I. the Pomesanians (between the Vistula, Nogat and Elbing), 2. the Pogesanians (the coast-line along Frisches Haff--or, as Wulfstam calls it in about 900 A.D., the Eistmere Sea or the Sea of the Aistii), 3. the Varmians (along Frisches Haff), 4. the Natangians (the north part of Frisches Haff), 5. the Sambians (between the rivers Deimena, Preglius and Kurisches Haff), 6. the Nadravians (to the east of Kurisches Haff), 7. the Shalanians (along the lower course of Nemunas), 8. the Sudanians (formerly gouv. Suvalkai and the adjacent part of Eastern Prussia; this tribe is also called the Jotvingians in other historical records, and their territory has been given the beautiful Lithuanian name of Dainava, the Land of Songs), 9. the Galindians (bordering on the Masurian Lakes to the south and the river Alna to the west), 10. the Bartians (to the east of the river Alna), 11. the Sasnians.

All these tribes were great and martial peoples, causing much trouble to the neighbouring Slavonic tribes. This state of affairs continued, until Conrad, Duke of the Masurians, appealed to the Order of the Knights of the Cross in 1228 to come to his assistance, as he found himself incapable of fighting against them. From that time onwards, an unceasing extermination of the gallant Prussian people begins, hand-in-hand with the colonization of their territory by the Germans.

After having crushed the Prussian people, the invaders adopted the name of the Prussians, as this name at that time was so deeply associated with fantastic hero legends.

Every knight in every country of Europe considered it a great honour to participate in the crusades against the pagan Prussians. This explains the disappearance of that honourable and gallant people. Only place-names, three translations of the Catechism and a small dictionary tell us now of their existence.

The eastern group of the Baltic people consisted of Lithuanians (Zemaitians or Samogitians and Aukstaitians), Latgalians, Zemgalians, Selon-

15

ians (living somewhere around the present Iluksta, Daugaupils [Dunaburg], Zarasai) and Kurians. The Goljadians mentioned in the Hipatii Chronicle about 1058, also belonged to the Balts in the east. This tribe was cut off from the neighbouring tribes by the Slavonic expansion to the west, and remained in their habitations, southwest of Moscow.

The habitations of the Balts in the east expanded rather far to the north. The most easterly boundary was, as far as their place-names tell us about it, the town of Tula, southwest of Moscow, and the most southernly boundary spread along the Pripet marshes as far to Tchernigov.

The Baltic tribes of the east were not subjected to the same destiny. But only the Lithuanians were politically organized and governmentally competent which enabled them to defend themselves against their ever aggressive enemies. This led also to the founding of a realm, expanding from the Baltic Sea to the Black Sea. The other Baltic tribes in the east, out of which the Latvian people emerged, were enslaved by the German Knights of the Sword. The Latvian people have preserved their national characteristics as regards language, customs and culture, in spite of outside influences and oppression.

All these tribes, those in the west as well as those in the east, formed ethnologically one people, but as they had no political organisation in common, they were considered as separate peoples by the foreigners with whom they came into contact. But in reality they were one people with the same religion, customs and culture. Notwithstanding the different dialects, they spoke a uniform language.

When and from where did the Baltic peoples come to their present habitations? It is difficult to give a precise answer to this question. In the dawn of the history of the Baltic people these tribes covered a much larger area than they do nowadays. In the north they bordered on the present-day southern boundary of Estonia, in the south they crossed the boundary of the present Eastern Prussia, in the west they expanded along the coast-line of the Baltic Sea all the way up to the Vistula, and in the east they reached the territory of Minsk. Even during the prehistoric aera, at the close of the earlier Stone Age, we find relics of antiquity, bearing witness to a culture which differs fundamentally from the rest of the neighbouring cultures. This is particulary the case during the Bronze Age. It is generally believed that the founders of this culture were ancient Balts. It should also be borne in mind that the neighbours of the Balts in the east ever since the beginning of the sixth century were not Russians as they are nowadays, but Mordvins, a Finno-Ugrian tribe, now driven away to the other side of the Volga. The major part of the present-day Russia was inhabited by Iranian tribes which were given several names by the ancient Classics, as for example, Askytians, Sakeians and Sarmatians. Further evidence of this fact is to be found in the names of the main rivers, such as Dniepr (Danapris), Dniestr (Danastrus), Danube (Danuvius) and Don (Tanais). These river-names are not of Slavonic origin. That they are of Iranian origin can easily be verified by the fact that they contain the word » danu » (in the Avesta), meaning river (in the Ossetic » don »).

*

After this brief survey of the ethnological structure of the Lithuanian people I will attempt to throw light on some psychological characteristics which have come from the mental structure of the Lithuanian people during the course of the centuries.

16

The national character of a people is formed by four factors: race, ethnological structure, landscape and historical destiny. I shall endeavour to give a brief description of two of these factors: the ethnological structure and the historical destiny.

The ethnological structure of the people, as shown in their psychological structure, exercises a powerful influence on the life and national character of the people. The ethnological structure is a much more important factor than is that of race. While the factor of race is a physical phenomenon, that of the ethnological structure is a mental one. And while race concerns itself about Man as a biological being, the ethnological structure concerns itself about him as a cultural being. The factor of race gives rise to certain physical peculiarities, the ethnological structure moulds him into a cultural being. That is why the ethnological structure is a much more important factor than that of race. A good deal of factual phenomena may best be explained, if one knows the ethnological structure of the people.

I shall not discuss the Culture Area Concept in the following. It may suffice to mention two ethnological types: the pastoral Nomad or the cattle-breeder and the Matriarchaist or the agriculturist.

Both of these types were, and still are, to be found among the Lithuanian people and the first type prevails more during the earlier phase of history, while the latter type comes to the foreground during the subsequent phase of history.

This fundamental element in the Nomadic culture characterizes all Indo-European peoples, more or less. This is the element which the Indo-Europeans brought with them to Europe, before they mingled with the original inhabitants. This explains why there is such a strong and obvious Nomadic element in the oldest of the Indo-European peoples, viz. the Lithuanian people. This element, however, is not quite pure, and the same thing applies to the rest of the Indo-European peoples.

But what are the characteristics of this ethnological type? Which of them are to be found in the Lithuanian people? I will mention a few of them.

Family life. Nomadic matrimony is brought about by capture of a girl or by purchase. The father-right is strongly emphasized, while the right given to the husband is of subordinate importance. The right of inheritance is handed down to the eldest son. Severe punishment is inflicted upon those who profane the chastity of the girls. All these characteristics may be found within the ancient Lithuanian family. The wedding ceremonies and the folk-songs are obvious reminiscences of that time.

Social life. The Nomadic element manifests itself in social life by war-mentality and desire for expansion. It also shows itself by the bias towards the vertical social structure. The Nomad is destined to rank high as the master and ruler over other peoples. In the wake of conquests followed also classdistinction. In studying the Lithuanian people, we are made aware of the fact that this stage of Lithuanian history is indisputable. The war-expeditions of Mindaugas and Gediminas to the Slavonic territories, as well as the war-expedition of Vytautas the Great from Tannenberg to the Black Sea, are good characteristics of the Nomadic war-exploits. Class-division and the appearance of the aristocracy are the phenomena by which the vertical culture finds expression within social life. The Lithuanian Statute, printed publicly as late as 1529, is the greatest monument of civilization from the first phase of the history of the Lithuanian people. This Statute can be regarded as the supreme manifestation of the Nomadic spirit, for the Nomad is a lawmaker, he has need for unshaken laws in order to establish his hierarchy. The Nomad is a keen promoter of laws and law-making. The Romans who were typical representatives of the Nomadic culture confirm this statement.

Religion. The religion of the Nomadic culture can be characterized by its belief in a divine being, frequently called God. This divine being is nothing else but a symbolization of the heavenly bodies. The religion of the Nomads is abstract. It is peculiar to this religion that it has no mythology and idols. This is clearly brought out, if we examine the religion of the ancient Lithuanians. Perkunas was at one time the greatest of Gods and the personification of the heavenly bodies.

On the whole, these characteristics must be regarded as the result of the Nomadic element.

It may be pointed out that there are many more characteristics of the Lithuanian national character than have been suggested above, but most of them are no longer in accordance with the Nomadic fundamental element. Another element comes also to the foreground, viz. that of the agriculturist or the Matriarchaist.

It is scientifically believed that Europe was inhabited by matriarchaic peoples before the Indo-European immigration to Europe. The European cultural progress was made possible by the fact that the Nomads had to settle down as agriculturists. It is evident that the growth and development of culture is only possible within a people who keep permanently to their habitations.

The chief features of Matriarchacy in the present-day Lithuanian culture are much more clearly shown than those of the Nomadic culture.

In the first place, the matriarchaic culture is analogous with agriculture. The Lithuanians have been agriculturists from time immemorial. As for Art, the matriarchaic culture is known for its conventionalization of geometrical figures, and her ornamentation is chiefly characterized by plant designs. The Lithuanian popular art is wholly matriarchaic. Conventionalization is the most conspicuous trait in Lithuanian ornamentation. The plant designs of Lithuanian popular art are so geometrical that the only evidences for their existence lie in the denominations of the patterns themselves.

Family Life. The family life is characterized by the superority of woman and strict monogamy. Primarily the Lithuanians are Nomads, secondly, they are matriarchaists. In the matriarchaic family stress is laid on the role of the brother. As far as the historical records go, this cannot be clearly distinguished with the Lithuanians, but we find many reminiscenses of it in Lithuanian folk-lore and legends. The protector of the girl in the matriarchaic family is not her lover, but her brother. There is a rich variety of Lithuanian folk-songs in which the girl seeks her brother's protection, instead of turning to her lover.

Religion. The religion of the matriarchaic culture is characterized by moon-worship, belief in reincarnation and ancestor-worship. These features are fully shown in the Lithuanian religion. In addition to these, there are two other features that combine the ancient Lithuanian religion with the matriarchaic culture: the presence of female divinities and the girls' participation in the religious cults.

As has been shown already, the ethnological structure of the Lithuanian people consists of two fundamental elements: the Nomadic element
which all Indo-Europeans have in common and the matriarchaic element which
originated among the ancient inhabitants of Europe.

One may easily raise objections to this statement, as these features
also occur in several other European peoples. I do not deny that this may
be the case. These features are not solely to be found with Lithuanians,
yet, it is necessary to bear in mind that they express themselves in different ways with different peoples, and this accounts for the fact that
these dissimilarities in a number of ways influence the national character
of the peoples.

In discussing the question of how the ethnological structure influences the national character, it is important to know in what ways the ethnological elements are related to one another. We might, for example,
look at the Russian people. It is obvious that the matriarchaic fundamental element is preponderant in the Russian national character. There has
never been intense Nomadic fundamental element with the Russians. The
Russian inclination to expansion and war did not originate from the Russian people themselves; it has, in point of fact, been influenced by alien
elements, for example, Scandinavians, Lithuanians, Mongols, Semites or
Caucasians. The Germanic people, on the other hand, have never been influenced by the matriarchaic element. This element is only slightly represented with them.

Which of these two elements dominate the Lithuanian people? It is
impossible to give a satisfactory answer. One might say that none of them
ranks higher than the other, as they are both vitally alive the Lithuanian
people. The Lithuanian historical records tell us about a profound expan-
sion- and war-mentality with a view to conquering, as well as ruling over
and making laws for every other people. The enormous stretches of land
through which the Lithuanians marched fascinated them much more than the
cultural institutions ever did. This was the case during the most intense
phase in the history of the Nomadic Lithuanians. Vytautas the Great, became the symbol and the end of their history. By the introduction of
Christianity, the Lithuanians were permeated with foreign cultural influences. The Lithuanians not only lost their territories, but also their
state and, subsequently, their liberty. The Lithuanian laws were no longer made use of, yet, the Lithuanians did not forget their language and
customs. And no one could ever take away their deep attachement to the
soil.

Each one of these fundamental elements in the national character expresses itself in outward behaviour. What are the characteristics of this
behaviour? In relation to other peoples, the Nomadic element has expressed
itself in endeavours at conciliation. Having conquered other peoples, the
gallant Nomad either exterminates them completely or he takes special care
to leave their culture intact, as he is well aware of the fact that it is
just as difficult to force a foreign people to submit to completely different ways of life, as it is to turn a goat into a cow. The first attitude
was taken by Attila and the Israelites. That is also the attitude of the
barbarians in modern times. The Romans chose another way, and the Lithuanians resemble them in this respect. The Lithuanians did not destroy the
culture and national peculiarities of the people they conquered; they rather adjusted themselves to their ways of life. The Lithuanians have done
no harm to the territories of the people they conquered; they have never

19

tried to subjugate foreign nationalities. Everybody has been given the same freedom and the same rights. The spirit of conciliation and tolerance was fully shown in 1939 when Lithuania, in spite of her own difficulties, received and did her best for about 60,000 Polish refugees and internces, notwithstanding the fact that the Poles were regarded as her bitterest enemies. There is not the slightest truth in the accusation that the Lithuanians joined the Germans during their occupation in murdering the Jewish population of Lithuania. The Lithuanians have never committed any outrage to their minorities, as long as they have been independent. And there was even less cause to do so on that occasion.

The matriarchaic fundamental element, explicitly expressed in the Lithuanian national character, has resulted in a strong feeling of earthboundness. The agriculturist is deeply rooted in the soil he tills. He loves his fields and meadows. His patriotism shows itself in the love of his native-place. This is a distinct feature in the Lithuanian national character. The Lithuanian loves his native soil; he is a mystic and an ethetician in his attitude to it.

The love for the land has, naturally, its bad points as well as its good ones. Earthbound human beings cannot be annihilated or stamped out. Their attachment to the soil makes them strong and vital. This explains why the Lithuanians have always preserved their national character, in spite of the long periods during which they have been under the political control of foreign sovereignty. Life means nothing to the Lithuanian, if he has to do without his soil. The attachment to the native soil has also its drawbacks. It may happen to exterminate such people. Needless to say, it is easy to enslave them.

These two characteristics--tolerance and the desire of conciliation with foreign people--are significant of the Lithuanian national character.

The ethnological structure of a people is the result of intensely dynamic forces. Affected by these forces, the people are gradually moulded into a natural unity, and the national character becomes more and more a part of Nature herself. And this has been brought about without their having made any efforts at all. These forces must be simultaneous with the historical development, otherwise they are likely to petrify the people. The historical destiny makes the people dynamic in a creative process of development.

The historical destiny of the Lithuanian people is significant from the very beginning. Their destiny has implied events which have been of decisive importance to the whole people. The most important are the following: Christianity, the relation to their neighbours, the loss and restoration of their state. It is obvious that the events which have recently taken place should deeply affect the Lithuanian national character. These events have taken place during a time when the Lithuanian people were about to create a synthesis out of the fundamental elements which were to reconstitute their national character. They have been deprived of that possibility through cunning and violence.

We shall consider one of these historical events: the relation to the neighbouring nations.

Those who do not sufficiently know the Lithuanian people are liable to say that Lithuanian culture and national character are the synthesis of Germanic and Slavonic cultural elements. They may also be expected to say that only common historical destiny can give rise to national culture. Let us examine the truth of that statement by looking at the Lithuanian people and their neighbours.

It is sheer nonsense to speak of a common destiny with the Germanic people. The history of Lithuania is an unceasing fight against the Germans and the German knights. We must not forget that one of the greatest battles of Lithuania was directed against the German Order of the Knights. It may suffice to mention the battle of Siauliai in 1236, the battle of Durbe in 1260, the most sanguinary one at that time, and the great battle of Tannenberg in 1410 when the German Order of the Knights was annihilated once and forever, saving the whole of Europe from the German expansion. The German was always the intruder and robber. There is a little episode from the history of the life of Vytautas the Great, the victor at the battle of Tannenberg, which shows his attitude to the Teutonic Orders of the Knights of the Cross. There was a controversy between Vytautas and the Order, concerning a part of the province of Zemaitija. (Samogitia) which the Order was anxious to get hold of. In order to settle the dispute, Sigismund the Emperor of Czecho-Slovakia, sent his negotiator Macra. Macra maintained that Klaipeda (Memel) and the other Samogitian fortresses ought to belong to Lithuania, as they had been built in Lithuania. During the course of the negotiations the marshal of the Order tried to convince Macra over and over again that the fortresses actually belonged to the Order. At this point Vytautas grew angry and said: You know very well that no one has ever won anything from me through cunning and falsehood. Those who do not show me any respect mean nothing to me. Even Prussia is my fatherland, and I desire to have it all the way up to Osa». He added, ironically:» And what kind of inheritance does the Order aspire to?» As the Emperor did not hand the Order over to the Samogitians, Vytautas wrote to him, saying:» If you have been willing to settle this dispute, you might have remembered that the Knights of the Cross are strangers who have come here from foreign German territories. You should also bear in mind that they have attacked the Prussians, and what they want to do now is to drive us out of our own country. Unless you alter this verdict, we shall always be enemies». This dispute was settled, as is well known, at the battle of Tannenberg in 1410.

The Lithuanian people have always been hostile to the Germans. We must not forget that the German in the mind of the Lithuanian people is the incarnation of the Devil. We find him under the name of Vokietukas in every tale and legend. The Lithuanians differ from the Germans, not only with regard to their mental structure, but also with regard to their historical destiny. They have never shared any cultural achievements with the Germans. This explains why they have always preserved their national character.

The contact with the Slavs dates back from time immemorial. The historical destiny of the Lithuanian people forced them to make up their quarters within Russian territory, not only because the Russians were their neighbours, but also because the Slavs attracted the Lithuanians as the magnet attracts iron. The Lithuanians and the Slavs tried to draw as much as possible out of each other. Yet, the Lithuanian relation to the Slavs is not the same in all cases.

The Lithuanians had, however, much better contact with the Russians than they had with the Germans. They ruled over large areas of Russia and they even went so far as to accept Russian as their official language. The reason for this was that the border-lands, lying around the Lithuanian realm, covered a much larger area than the country of Lithuania. But this is by no means a sufficient reason for the conception that these two peoples should have a historical destiny in common. These relations had only been established with a view to ensuring a political and strategical status; the Lithuanians were, as a matter of fact, rather loosely interwoven with their neighbours. In joining the Roman Catholic Church, they parted entirely with these people. They have never had any historical destiny in common with the Russians, neither during the time when the Lithuanians ruled over large areas of Russia, nor during the time when the Russians began to subjugate and exterminate the Lithuanian people.

The Lithuanian sway in Russia played an important role in forming the Lithuanian national character. The next phase, on the other hand, bred only hatred and distrust in the mind of the Lithuanian people against social and political institutions.

The contact with the Russians during the first phase took place about the time when the Nomadic element was at its height. As I have shown already, the Nomad is a state-founder. The Nomad is, above all, a law-maker and an organizer. The desire for vast stretches of land led the Lithuanian people to mingle with the Russians. Considering how the trend of the historical destiny of the Lithuanians in our days points towards the opposite direction, it is amazing to call to mind the Lithuanian parole during the 13th and 14th centuries: » The whole of Russia must be owned by Lithuania». This was the way in which the Lithuanian spirit expressed her vitality, and the expression for this vitality was made possible through the Russian people. The contact with the Russians strengthened the Nomadic spirit and transformed her into action. The historical warfares across the vast Russian territory heightened their interest in social and governmental affairs. They strengthened their capacity for organization, law-making and governing. Once in Russia, the Lithuanians reached the height of jurisprudence, governmental and social activity. We must not forget that the Lithuanians by no means acquired these qualities by taking them over from the Russians. The Russians had none of the qualities themselves. They were actually the very foreign element by which the political, legal and social consciousness of the Lithuanian people was called into being. It permeated the mind of the people so deeply that, although the Nomadic fundamental element weakened in the course of time, it could never be effaced.

The social consciousness of the Lithuanians in our own time is, therefore, a reminiscense of the aera of Vytautas the Great, during which time the Lithuanian culture reached its height. The Lithuanian will always derive inspiration from the legal, political and social spirit of the past; he will derive inspiration by remembering the fundamental Nomadic element which came to full realization during the grand historical epoch of Lithuania.

As far as the other Slavonic people, the Poles, were concerned, the contact became stronger. The fact that the Lithuanians accepted Christianity through the Poles brought these two peoples much more closely together. It should also be mentioned that the Polish cultural influences after the fortunate union were much more important than those of the Germans or the Russians. The two different national characters were never synthesized. There are two reasons for this: (1) the Polish influences reached Lithuania in the form of standardized cultural achievements and (2) the national character of the Poles is distinctly characterized by another fundamental element, viz. the so-called totemism.

As time progressed, the relationship between the Lithuanians and the Poles came to resemble the relationship which one finds between two cultures. The Lithuanians have never had any standardized culture. The Poles, on the contrary, came to Lithuania with a standardized religion. Although the Lithuanians adopted the standardized Polish culture, owing to the political union, it did not in any way affect the Lithuanian national character. The Lithuanians tried to discover the dynamic and vital forces of the Polish national character without ever being able to do so. What they actually did discover was a ready-made, petrified culture. The influx of vital forces stimulates culture, initiative and creative activity, while a petrified culture stifles such a creative activity. This is the reason for the division between Lithuanians and Poles. When the historical destiny of Lithuania took another trend later on, or about the time when the Lithuanians had broken with the Poles, the Lithuanians cleansed their culture of Polish influences. The Lithuanian culture of our time is free from every Polish influence.

As I have just pointed out, the Polish influences did not affect the Lithuanian national character. The Lithuanians avoided being Polonized both in respect of ideas and creative activity.

Yet, the contact with the Poles actually affected the Lithuanian national character in one particular respect. The fact that the Lithuanians did not receive any vital impulses from the Polish culture explains why they shut themselves up in a strong mental isolation.

The Lithuanian people found strength and comfort in their own self-esteem. The overweening Poles have never made the Lithuanians feel that they should be inferior to the Poles. On the contrary, the Lithuanians began to feel confident about themselves and to think the best about their future. The contact with the Poles was, therefore, of great use to the Lithuanians, as it meant the gathering up of their mental energies for the benefit of their nation. They learnt how to suffer, and they learnt how to win in the end. This was especially important to the Lithuanian people at the time when czarist Russia began its subjugation policy against them. Faced with the Russian threat, the Lithuanian people stood now strengthened and self-confident.

It must also be pointed out that the contact with the Poles provided the Lithuanians with the possibility of attaining prominent public positions, as this possibility was no longer open to them in their own country. The Lithuanians have provided the Poles with a large number of politicians, strategists and other eminent personalities. The Lithuanian contact with the Poles proved their capacity for resistance to foreigners. It also showed their power of ruling over other people.

To sum up: the characteristics of the national character, due to ethnological structure, as well as to historical destiny, are the following:

The Nomadic element gave rise to: (1) the desire for vast stretches of land and (2) endeavours at conciliation with conquered peoples and foreigners. The Matriarchaic elements gave rise to: (1) the attachment to the native soil and (2) the possibility of enslavement. The contact with the Russians during the first phase of Lithuanian history gave rise to: (1) the power of ruling over vast stretches of land and (2) social and political consciousness.

The historical destiny which the Lithuanians had in common with the Poles forced the Lithuanians to: (1) shut themselves up in a concentrated mental isolation and (2) infuse confidence about themselves. All these characteristics were positively Lithuanian.

The national character is made up of inner bonds, uniting one human being with another, resulting in a unity which we call a nation. A nation is by no means an outward gathering of individuals, coming together. It is, in point of fact, a body of individuals who live in close intimacy. They try to express themselves by taking a keen interest in organizing and creating a free and independent state. Furthermore, they express themselves by taking a keen interest in art, science and social activity. The national character can only come to full realization within a free state. If a nation has to live in a foreign state, it is, as a rule, incapable of attaining any high level of culture. The loss of liberty results, on the other hand, in a close intimacy. Unless the individual is given the opportunity of expressing himself in golden deeds, the will become divided and listless. The contradiction between his own way of life and public institutions will fill him and distrust and hatred against everything. The loss of independence not only stifles the creative power of the people, it also does great harm to the individual.

In spite of the fact that the Lithuanian people have once known a period of independence, their national character is still the same. The Lithuanians have always been passionately interested in the welfare of their state. They have always, even during the period of subjugation, fought and longed for liberty. It is not true that the Lithuanians were given a chance of establishing an autonomous state after the last World War. Everyone who has studied the history of Lithuania knows that the independence and restoration of Lithuania implied the last stage of a tenacious struggle. This independence was made possible because of the Nomadic element which has always been so vitally alive in the Lithuanian people.

The present war has been a terrible blow to Lithuania. It broke out about the time when the Lithuanians were recovering from the blows to their lost liberty. The tendency for the time being is to make the Lithuanians accept a way of life that differs radically from that of their own.

We shall never cease to fight for the right to independence and national integrity. The right to independence must not be determined by radical, economic, political or strategical factors, for it is far more important to make into consideration the factor of national character. And the right of independence must also be given to the very small nations, inspiring them in their creative activity. When that has been attained, the world will be a world of strong and united nations.

FOOTNOTES

[1] Reprinted by the permission of the author. The <u>Baltic Review</u> suspended publication August, 1971.

[2] The Estonian people, being a branch of the Ugro-Finnic family tree, do not belong to this group. The concept of "Balt", commonly used in regard to the inhabitants of Estonia, Latvia and Lithuania, is a modern invention and has been formed by the adjective "Baltic"; it was first used in the expression "Mare Balticum" by Adam of Bremen about 1075. The concept of Balt, Baltic peoples and Baltic states, such as is thought of at the present time by the daily press and in everyday life, indicates Estonians, Latvians and Lithuanians and their states, but in archaeological and phil-

ological terminology the word Baltic is always used to denote the Indo-European peoples around the Baltic Sea, as will be more closely described in the following article.

Chapter 4. THE PSYCHOSOCIAL TRAITS OF LITHUANIAN PEASANTS

Source - Peter Paul Jonitis, The Acculturation of the Lithuanians of Chester, Pennsylvania. Thesis in Sociology, the University of Pennsylvania, 1951. The
selection is from Chapter VIII, "Psychosocial Aspects of the Peasant Lithuanian Family," pages 202-
213.[1]

Overview

Lithuanian peasant society, unaffected by the industrial revolution,
had a very slow rate of change and was a stable and predictable system of
social control. Social organization, not disorganization, was the norm
for the Lithuanian peasant society. Lithuanian peasants who emigrated to
the United States found themselves confronted with difficult adjustments
in the changing, more urban and industrial American society.

In the peasant Lithuanian society social status was abscribed rather
than achieved. Most peasants remained in the status abscribed to them at
birth. Social control in the form of folkways, myths, mores and laws
strongly governed the behavior of the Lithuanian peasants and, for all of
their rigidity, gave them a certain security. They accepted readily the
authority of the family, the priest and civil officials.

Village life cultivated in the Lithuanian peasants a strong feeling
of mutual aid and strong primary group relationships. Prior to World War
I, a rural wedding would last a week with all of the neighbors of the village taking part in the festivities. Lithuanian peasants were deeply religious. Lithuanian legends pictured God as a good, old man who took care
of all those who sought his advice.

Lithuanian peasant society exhibited a very slow rate of social change.
Social controls were fixed and formalized. In the daily process of living,
the peasant faced very few new situations which required new forms of behavior and new ways of thought. The individual peasant adjusted successfully to his daily situations in the light of knowledge gained from his ancestors. Since there was little new experience the statis norms minimized
the possibility of personal or social disorganization. The industrial revolution had not made its impact upon old patterns of conduct. Hence, the
peasant social norms developed in relative tranquility. Lithuanian peasant
society was not dynamic. Out of the commonality of group experiences Lithuanian peasant society developed habits of thinking, feeling, and acting
which crystallized into its particular systems of social control. These
included the folkways, customs, mores, laws, and institutionalized patterns
which have come to characterize that society. Thus, the social life of the
peasant took on a comparative orderliness and predictability and produced
a routinization of life which the average peasant seldom seriously questioned. When minor changes in his routine life became necessary, the peasant generally met them by employing the conventional procedures which his

society had established. The traditional patterns proved adequate to successfully meet the recurrent problems of his everyday life. Thus, the old equilibrium was maintained. Social organization, not disorganization was the normal characteristic of Lithuanian peasant society.

Under Tsarist domination relatively few new elements were introduced into the Lithuanian culture pattern. It is a sociological truism that where the process of social accumulation is slow or non-existent, the society is usually comparatively stable. Since there was not an acceleration in the rate of social change, the stability of Lithuanian peasant society was not threatened. Living in the United States required increasingly difficult adjustments of newly-arrived immigrants. Failing to make these adjustments to American life satisfactorily, provided many an immigrant with the impetus to return to his native land. In Lithuanian peasant society change took place at a very slow rate not only in the material aspects of culture, but also in the ideas and ideologies which defined and gave meaning to the whole way of life. Lithuanian society was a stable equilibrim with a minimum of conflicting forces.

An adequate understanding of the social disorganization and acculturation of the Lithuanian peasant in Chester depends upon an understanding of peasant social organization. Since social disorganization and acculturation are the result of disturbed and re-established social relationships of the immigrant, the normative aspects of Lithuanian peasant society constitute a relevant subject for analysis in any discussion of such social processes. Therefore, before we can understand the nature of immigrant acculturation, we must understand the nature of peasant Lithuanian social organization. As Elliott and Merrill state, social organization is the opposite of social disorganization.[2] "Social organization," according to these sociologists, "is a state of being, a condition in which the various institutions in a society are functioning in accordance with their recognized or implied purposes. Social organization is characterized by the harmonious operation of the different elements in a society...Social organization depends upon common definitions of social goals and a commonly accepted program for their achievement."[3]

SOCIAL CHANGE AND SOCIAL ORGANIZATION

The organization of peasant Lithuanian society was dependent upon the type or social structure and the extent of consensus which characterized its members.[4] By social structure we mean the particular arrangement of the functionally interrelated institutions and social relationships, as well as the statuses and roles that each peasant Lithuanian assumed in the group. During the period under examination, the Tsarist Empire and the Roman Catholic Church dominated Lithuanian peasant society. Peasant Lithuanian society was characterized by a relatively large number of ascribed, as compared to achieved, statuses. Social mobility was comparatively rare and most peasants remained in the status ascribed to them by birth. In this relatively static society, status and role were more secure and the adjustment of the individual was less difficult than in a modern, urban, and industrial society. Hence, considerable conformity in status and role was a characteristic of such a society.

Social change in peasant Lithuania was slow. The productive techniques by which the society made a living did not undergo any significant change. Inventions from within the culture or by borrowing from without did not materially affect agricultural technology. The economic institutions and relationships, based on this simple peasant agriculturalism, were static under the Tsarist regime. The rural social class system was frozen. The social institutions of the family, the school, the church, and the state were largely unaffected by a more rapid change in the outside world. The agricultural way of life influenced the nature and tempo of the peasant social institutions. The non-material elements, that is, the folkways, myths, mores, and ideologies probably were the least affected by social change.

Social controls were relatively rigid. Russian occupation authorities were opposed to social change. The group-imposed controls resulted in consistency and stability to peasant society. Briefly stated, these controls took the form of folkways, mores, laws, and institutions. The presence of these rigid elements, in addition to the Russian controls, were responsible for the resistance to large-scale social change in peasant Lithuanian society.

As background for the foregoing observations, the analysis of the general characteristics of the Lithuanian peasant family, its size, the status and role system, the nature and meaning of the interpersonal relations, the marriage customs, birth and child care, the sex attitudes, and the attitudes toward divorce and separation should be kept in mind. When all these factors are taken into account, we can see that the Lithuanian peasant family fostered a sense of personal security in the individual. This particular type of family life provided a specific pattern of existence. Hence, there was a minimum of personal and social disorganization or demoralization. Recreation was obtained primarily within the confines of the family circle and in the local village church.

THE PSYCHOSOCIAL TRAITS OF LITHUANIAN PEASANTS

In order to understand the psychosocial traits of the Lithuanian peasant, the geopolitical position of Lithuania should be considered. For centuries Lithuania was located on the threshold which separated the Germanic from the Slavic world. Large nations have been her neighbors--the Russians, the Poles, and the Germans--all of whom exerted an influence on the development of her culture. Despite this influence Lithuanian culture has preserved its original character to a large degree. In fact, Lithuanian culture, is quite independent and in no way identical with either Germanic or Slavic culture. This is to be attributed to the historical evolution of Lithuania.

The psychosocial traits of the Lithuanian peasant may best be observed in their customs and manners in everyday life. The community of a Lithuanian village was like a big family, and all neighbors were like relatives. Lithuanian hospitality to guests was well known. When family festivities occurred, expenditures were of secondary importance. In the period before the first World War rural weddings used to last a week and all the neighbors took part in this festive occasion. To a saying like "Time is money," the typical peasant would have answered, "Your life won't last as long as that of the sun, and you can't take anything with you when you die!" The Lithuanian peasant did not evaluate everything from the monetary standpoint. He was not a utilitarian in this respect. The idea of mutual assistance was not only a sentimental affair, but was based on the concept of being prepared to help wherever help was needed. This idea extended to holidays as well as work days. In Lithuanian the word for this idea of mutual help was talkos. This word cannot be translated into West European languages since the custom is peculiar to Lithuania. A farmer, who for one reason or another, was unable to complete any urgent task by himself, his neighbors, without being called or asked, came to his assistance. Characteristically, this kind of assistance remained unpaid. Usually a festival when the work was completed and a heartfelt thanks was all the helpers received for their work. The proposal of any kind of reward was regarded as an insult to the helpers. This Lithuanian talkos cannot be compared with the so-called gemeinschaftshilfe in Germany because mutual help in the former country was not ordered by some superior authority. Such assistance was not granted for any pecuniary reward but was given on the basis of the feeling of moral obligation to offer help, a categorical imperative to act as a philanthropist.

This trait of the Lithuanian peasant was not the sociability of a mass-man. Down to his finger tips the Lithuanian was not a mass-man. He embodied many of the qualities of the so-called "rugged individualist." He did not like to demonstrate the content of his innermost feelings as though he were present at a confessional. Although the peasant was always open-hearted, he never forgot that the true quality of communicativeness always required a certain reserve. For this reason, to the outsider the Lithuanian appeared to be cold and suspicious. But these barriers broke down with increased time and intimate contacts.

The Lithuanian peasant was characterized by a disregard for political or power values. The Lithuanians were a peace loving nation. A militaristic worship of war was not a part of their value system. This characteristic was emphasized by the French anthropo-geographer Elisée Reclus. Although the Lithuanians have had a glorious past history--in the Middle Ages their empire extended from the Baltic Sea to the Black Sea--and although they might be proud of many heroic deeds of war, their folksongs do not mention these events. Rather, they portray their desire for love, of the happiness of youth, and of the natural beauty of their homeland. Neither was the Lithuanian peasant too deeply concerned with economics. He was industrious. He did not believe too much in the value of economic goods. Nor did he slavishly worship power or wealth. In his daily struggle for existence the peasant relied more upon hard work than luck. He placed great faith in complete independence in all spheres of life.

The Lithuanian peasant was deeply religious. To him the highest form of love was the Lord. Old Lithuanian legends, which were well-known in the period of 1900-1914, pictured God as a good, old man who walked among men and who gave advice when it was necessary. God was like an old husbandman who promenaded the fields. Animism abounded in rural regions. Lithuanian religiousness was characterized by a metaphysical longing which made the peasant's being melancholic. But this melancholy was not a futilitarian one. The Lithuanian deeply experienced the beauty of nature and the pleasures of this world. But at the same time he was aware of the transitoriness of all earthly pleasures and the imperfections of the real world. Therefore, he longed for a perfect world. This sense of longing never was quenched in the soul of the Lithuanian. Many emigrants came to America in order to find a more perfect life. He was and is a profound lover of freedom.

The psychosocial traits of Lithuanian peasants were expressed in primary group relationships. In Lithuania these relationships were characterized by relative endurance, their personal or gemeinschaft nature, lack of specialization, informality, and the bond of affection. These relationships were sentimental rather than rational or mental. People were ends in themselves rather than utilitarian or instrumental means to other personal aggrandizement. Personal contacts were face to face. Significant symbols dealt mainly with personal-social and common-human relations.

Interpersonal relations were concrete, immediate, and replete with personal, rich, deep, and individualized meaning. Folklore, tradition, stereotypes, and common sense prevailed in primary village group relationships.

The relations between the social classes of Lithuanian society were fixed and unchanging. The peasant expected very little, if any, change in the social structure. There was for him practically no vertical mobility during the period under review. This tendency to accept the status quo was characteristic of the attitude of the peasant. The peasant landowner usually felt that he was superior in some respects to the ordinary day-worker. Even though he owned but a little land and had migrated to America to labor in a factory, yet he was always proud of his social standing in the Old Country. Attitudes of superiority were more pronounced among the government officials, intellectuals, and the professional classes in Lithuania. The daughters of these latter groups, as contrasted with those from the landless peasantry classes, did not seek work in a factory in Lithuania. Another characteristic attitude of the Lithuania peasant, was the lack of envy of the people who occupied what constituted the upper-classes in Lithuania. The average peasant took everything for granted and moved along in his own groove. It was only after they learned of the economic potentialities of the United States that they became conscious of their own particular lot. Migration and improvement of one's economic position became synonomous.

Photographs meant much to peasant Lithuanians. About the likeness of a dear one rested a halo of sacredness. Even peasants who had very little to spend for food would sometimes "double up" and divide the cost of such pictures. This was particularly true in the case of photographs of weddings and funerals.

Among Lithuanian peasants there was a profound respect for authority. This respect extended not only to the leaders of the family group but to the civil officials as well. The relationship between the master and servant was one of superordination and subordination. The master's attitude toward the peasant servant's place in the community was decidedly paternalistic, and the peasant, especially the landless group, gathered about the landlord and accepted that relationship as a binding one. The leadership of the movement to overthrow the Russian occupation during this period (1900-1914) and earlier years was essentially spearheaded by the intellectual classes.

All Lithuanians were kindled with the fire of ardent nationalism. While living under the domination of the Tsars, they yearned for a free and independent country. This fire reached its zenith in the chauvinistic expressions and activities of the intellectual and more vocal groups. A high degree of patriotic feeling for the mother country existed during the early years after arrival in America. Letters between those in Lithuania and those in America frequently contained words of protest if the immigrant displayed any loss of interest in his native land. In general, allegiance to Lithuania gradually diminished with the length of residence and the degree of economic well-being achieved in the new country of adoption.

FOOTNOTES

[1] Reprinted by the permission of the author.

[2] _Social Disorganization_, New York, Harper and Bros., 1950, p. 4.

[3] Elliott and Merrill, _op. cit._, pp. 4-5. The theoretical formulations underlying this analysis of Lithuanian society are to be found in this text, Chapters I-III, pp. 3-49.

[4] Cf. Talcott Parsons, "The Position of Sociological Theory," _American Sociological Review_, Vol. 13, (April, 1948), pp. 156-164.

Chapter 5. CAUSES OF LITHUANIAN IMMIGRATION
TO THE UNITED STATES

Source - Peter Paul Jonitis, The Acculturation
of the Lithuanians of Chester, Pennsylvania. Ph.D. Thesis in Sociology,
the University of Pennsylvania, 1951.
The selection is from Chapter XI, "The
Background and Causes of Lithuanian Immigration," pages 236-264.[1]

Overview

Economic, political and social factors accounted for the Lithuanian
immigration to the United States. Lithuanians wanted to emigrate in order
to make a better living. The agricultural economy in their native land
offered little opportunity, especially for the non-landowning peasants,
who, in some districts, were one-third of the population. Also, Tsarist
government policies gave them no opportunity to buy land when the government did expropriate land and offered land at advantageous prices only to
Russian colonists.

Political conditions caused many Lithuanians to seek a new country.
The introduction of compulsory military service for all Lithuanian men,
married or unmarried, when they became 21 years of age, was an important
factor in the emigration. Draft-aged Lithuanians disliked the idea of
serving as soldiers for a foreign power that occupied their land and ran
their lives. European transportation companies encouraged emigration with
their promotion of travel through low rates. Secret travel agents not only sold travel tickets but procured passports and even smuggled Lithuanians
across the border, emigrants who, for military or other reasons, could not
secure passports.

Earlier Lithuanian immigrants to the United States became an important
reason for the immigration of other Lithuanians. Friends and relatives,
particularly by means of letter writing, informed Lithuanians who remained
in the old country about the advantages of laboring and living conditions
in the new country. Many of the letters contained remittances in the form
of prepaid travel tickets complete from a German port to a city in the
United States where a friend or relative was waiting to welcome his coun-
tryman. Returned immigrants on their visits more often than not encouraged
Lithuanian peasant youth to leave their villages to seek freedom and opportunity.

The major causes of Lithuanian immigration to the United States may
be classified as economic, political, social, and religious. The following analysis is concerned with the period of 1900-1914. The discussion
will begin with the economic causes.

The immigration of Lithuanian peasants to Chester, Pennsylvania, was, in the largest measure, due to economic causes. In the main, this migration resulted from a widespread desire for better economic conditions rather than from the necessity of escaping intolerable Russian occupation. In short, the Lithuanian peasant came to Chester not merely to make a living, but to make a better living than was possible in his native land. He came because of the allurements of promised wealth and material comfort. In this connection the words of Henry P. Fairchild are pertinent:

"The natural causes of immigration at the present time lie primarily in the superiority of the economic conditions in the United States over those in the countries from which the immigrants come. Modern immigration is essentially an economic phenomenon. Religious and political causes have played the leading part in the past, and still enter in as contributory factors in many cases. But the one prevailing reason why the immigrant of to-day leaves his native village is that he is dissatisfied with his economic lot, as compared with what it might be in the new world. The European peasant comes to America because he can-or believes he can-secure a greater return in material welfare for the amount of labor expended in this country than in his home land. This fact is recognized by practically all careful students of the subject, and is frequently emphasized in the report of the Immigration Commission."[2]

A period of good economic conditions in this country attracted large numbers of Lithuanian immigrants, while industrial depressions checked the incoming current. This relationship between the economic situation in the United States and the volume of immigration had been analyzed statistically by Commons, and is presented in graphic form in a table in his book, Race and Immigrants in America.[3] With comparatively few exceptions, the Lithuanian immigrant of that period was essentially a seller of labor seeking a more favorable market. To a considerable extent this incentive for emigration was accompanied by a certain spirit of unrest and adventure and a more or less definite ambition for socio-economic betterment, but primarily the movement was accounted for by the fact that the remuneration for labor was much greater in the United States than was possible in Lithuania.

The agricultural economy of Lithuania yielded small wages to the peasant. As has been stated above, in some districts one third of the peasants did not own land. The series of agrarian reforms, inaugurated by Tsar Alexander I, which aimed at the parceling of land among the peasantry, were of little benefit to this landless class. In its efforts to protect its own nationals, the Russians Government left the less productive land to the Lithuanians. Whenever the opportunity arose, the Russian Government expropriated all the land available and offered it for sale at advantageous prices to the Russian colonists. The less fertile land held by the Lithuanians produced smaller crops. To make a living the peasants worked on the more prosperous farms. During economic depressions, such as the one in 1867-1868, the family of the Lithuanian peasant was forced to borrow money and to mortgage the small land holdings. Interest payments were so heavy that many peasants were forced to sell their land and become hired laborers. Such family misfortunes were common among the Chester Lithuanians when they were living with their parents in the Old World. This economic position further influenced their social status by preventing them from attending school and thus forcing them to accept mential tasks in agriculture. Between the ages of 10 to 21, peasants were employed as shepherds and ordinary farm hands.

According to the Chester Lithuanians, the general economic condition of the Lithuanian peasant could be described in one word, namely, "difficult." In short, they had to work hard and live frugally in order to satisfy basic needs. Such a life was especially characteristic of the unskilled laboring class from which so large a proportion of the emigration to the United States in the period of 1900-1914 was drawn. Skilled labor, which was virtually non-existent in the migrating group, was poorly paid when compared with the wages for like service in the United States. It must also be remembered that an official governmental decree barred Lithuanians from employment in governmental positions. An important cause of the emigration from Lithuania was the inability of the landless peasantry to gain an adequate livelihood in agricultural pursuits. The Tsarist government did not allow the peasant to purchase land unless he demonstrated an unflinching loyalty to the Russian government. In the period before the first World War Lithuanians hated the Russians because of the occupation and also due to the fact that the Tsar and his local administration were anti-Catholic and anti-clerical. The Chester case histories reveal the fact that the Lithuanian peasants frequently did not receive any wages in the form of money but were rewarded with a share of the farm produce and a house for their families, which was on their landlord's property and close to the scene of their daily work. Since agricultural labor was seasonal in character, some of the peasants had to seek employment in lumber camps and in near-by towns. In the relatively few cases where peasant land ownership was possible, the holdings were so small, the methods of cultivation so rudimentary, and the taxes so high, that even in productive years the struggle for existence was a hard one. In addition, famines and crop failures, which were not uncommon in the peasant economy, meant poverty for both the small farmer and the farm laborer. Such agricultural conditions constituted the background economic factors which stimulated emigration.

The fragmentary nature of the available data relative to the wages in Lithuania during the period makes it impossible to present a satisfactory comparison with wages in the United States. The Dillingham Commission Report states in this connection:

> "It is well known, however, that even in England, Germany, France, and other countries of western Europe wages are below the United States standard, while in southern and eastern Europe the difference is very great. The Commission found this to be true in its investigations in parts of Italy, Austria-Hungary, Greece, Turkey, Russia, and the Balkan States. In fact, it may safely be said that in these countries the average wage of men engaged in common and agricultural labor is less than 50 cents per day, while in some sections it is much lower. It is true that in some countries agricultural laborers receive from employers certain concessions in the way of fuel, food, etc., but in cases of this nature which came to the attention of the Commission the value of the concession was insufficient to materially affect the low wage scales."[4]

Several of the informants in this study reported that they made only two dollars in cash per year.

The political situation of Lithuania in 1900-1914 also was a contributory background factor in Lithuanian emigration. The suppression of the Lithuanian Government, the colonization of Lithuania by the Russians, the ascendancy of Russian Orthodoxy, the control of the Lithuanian schools,

Catholic Church, and press by the Russian government were the more important political factors involved in the emigration from Lithuania.[5] After the Insurrection of 1863, Michael Muraviev inaugurated his two-year dictatorial rule (May, 1863-March, 1865), as Governor-General of the Russian-occupied Grand Duchy of Lithuania. He not only completely and ruthlessly suppressed the insurrectionists, but also laid down the foundation for the series of severe repressive measures for the following forty years. In short, Muraviev's policy had been the complete Russification of the so-called Northwestern Provinces (the name of Lithuania after the Third Partition of 1795). This policy was closely followed by the Russian authorities for four decades with varying intensity. It did succeed to a large degree in Russifying the White Ruthenian or eastern areas of the former Grand Duchy of Lithuania. Nevertheless, among the truly Lithuanian element of Lithuania Major it proved a total failure. This oppression deprived the Lithuanian nation of its already strongly Polonized gentry, who later definitely began to consider itself as part of the old Poland, both politically and culturally. At the same time, it merely created a reaction among the Lithuanian-speaking people, which in turn aroused a deep national consciousness, particularly among the Lithuanian intellectuals.

The desire to escape military service in the Russian Army was also an important factor in the emigration from Lithuania. In 1874, the Russian government introduced obligatory military service for all Lithuanian men when they had attained the age of twenty-one years. The young married men with children were hit particularly hard by this measure. In view of the fact that a considerable number of the peasant Lithuanians were not members of the landowning classes, were employed at low wages as farm hands for some landlord, it can be seen that the removal of the household head as a chief source of family support for the period of the military service provided a strong stimulus for emigration. In the great majority of the cases of the Chester Lithuanians, the economic condition in addition to this military service drove many young men out of their native homeland. Military service in the Tsar's Army was anything but utopian in character. Quite apart from the factor of the dissolution of family solidarity, these young Lithuanian men, in the prime of their productive years, possessed a negative attitude toward serving as soldiers for a foreign country which dominated their own native soil. The Chester informants stated that many youths did all in their power to somehow evade military service before they reached the age of twenty-one. The material conditions of military life were primitive, food was good but scarce, the remuneration was low (fifty cents a month), freedom to go into towns or cities was not granted too often, travel was rudimentary by means of box cars and locomotives powered by wood, and the manoeuvres involved crossing the vast stretches of sub-zero Siberia. The journey from the northwestern parts of Russia to Vladivostok via the Trans-Siberian railroad, according to Chester informants, took from two to three months. Under these conditions it becomes understandable why the Lithuanian youths sought by all possible subterfuges to avoid military service. In Chester there was only one case of a man who really liked Russian military life. This man was a cook for a Commandant of a Russian Army Medical Detachment, which spent most of its time traveling from town to town caring for sick soldiers. According to this informant, this particular unit had the best of food, quarters, travel conditions, and some freedom. But the rest of the Chester case histories reveal the incontrovertible fact that young Lithuanian men preferred emigration to military service in the Tsar's Army.

Most crimes committed by the Lithuanians during the period prior to emigration were perpetrated in the name of Lithuania's freedom and against the Tsar's determined oppressive policy to exterminate all evidences of

Lithuanian national life and culture. Such crimes were severely dealt with on the spot by the local Russian authorities. The penalty of death was frequently meted out to those who sought to resist the Russification program. Suffice it to say that the emigration of Lithuanian criminals, from the numerical point of view, was a neglible factor in the Lithuanian immigration to the United States.

The putative advantages of the economic life in the United States in some cases existed, not in hard fact, but in the mind of the prospective Lithuanian immigrant. Such a belief was equally potent in stimulating emigration, whether it was grounded in fact or fiction. This group of immigrants, whose venture was based on a tragic misconception of America, had been effectively propagandized by outside agencies. In short, a very considerable part of Lithuanian emigration was not of a spontaneous character and due to natural causes, but was artificial and stimulated.

Three principal sources stimulated or encouraged Lithuanian emigration --the transportation companies, the labor agents, and the previous emigrants. During the period the carrying of immigrants from Europe to America was a large and lucrative business. The cost and degree of hardship involved in coming to the United States was an important factor in determining the volume of Lithuanian immigration at any particular time. The great changes which affected the conditions of immigration in this regard have been well described by General Francis A. Walker as follows:

> "Fifty, even thirty, years ago, there was a rightful presumption regarding the average immigrant that he was among the most enterprising, thrifty, alert, adventurous, and courageous, of the community from which he came. It required no small energy, prudence, forethought, and pains to conduct the inquiries relating to his migration, to accumulate the necessary means, and to find his way across the Atlantic. To-day the presumption is completely reversed. So thoroughly has the Continent of Europe been crossed by railways, so effectively has the business of emigration there been exploited, so much have the rates of railroad fares and ocean passage been reduced, that it is now among the least thrifty and prosperous members of any European community that the emigration agent finds his best recruiting-ground. The care and pains required have been reduced to a minimum; while the agent of the Red Star Line or the White Star Line is everywhere at hand, to suggest migration to those who are not getting on well at home. The intending emigrants are looked after from the moment they are locked into the cars in their native village until they stretch themselves upon the floors of the buildings on Ellis Island in New York. Illustrations of the ease and facility with which this Pipe Line Immigration is now carried on might be given in profusion."[6]

In 1910, over $118,000,000 was invested in transatlantic steamship lines which were largely owned by foreigners.[7] The increased number of lines, the frequent number of sailings, and the larger ships, have made it easier and cheaper for the immigrant to come to this country. For example, in July, 1894, the Cunard, White Star, Hamburg-American, and American Lines charged $15 from South Liverpool or London to New York, and for the return trip $10. In the summer of 1904, a rate war resulted in the reduction of the steerage passage from Liverpool to New York to $8.75, and from London or Liverpool to Quebec to $10. The American Line for a short time carried passengers to Philadelphia for only $7.50. In 1901, the rate from Bremen to New York was $36.50 and from Antwerp $29.50.[8] From Hamburg and the latter two ports many Lithuanian immigrants embarked for the United States. Special railroad rates were usually made in connection with steamship steerage rates, both to interior points in this country and in Europe from the immigrant's home to the port of embarkation. In 1896, for example, the immigrant rate from New York to Chicago was only $13. Low transportation rates were important contributory factors in the volume of emigration.

According to the Dillingham Commission Report,[9] the propaganda conducted by the steamship firms and their ticket agents was undoubtedly the most important immediate cause of emigration from Europe to the United States. This propaganda flourished in all the important emigrant-furnishing countries of Europe, despite the fact that the promotion of emigration was prohibited by the laws of many such countries as well as by the United States.[10] It was difficult if not impossible to secure a really effective enforcement of this provision of the United States law, but undoubtedly it did supplement the emigration laws of various European countries in compelling steamship ticket agents to solicit emigration in a sub rosa manner rather than do it in the open. It does not appear that steamship companies as a rule openly or directly violated the United States law, but through local agents and subagents of such companies, who operated their business at the various ports of embarkation, it was violated persistently and continuously. Selling steerage tickets to America was the sole or chief occupation of large numbers of persons in southern and eastern Europe, and from the observations of the Immigration Commission, it is clear that these local agents solicited business by every possible means and consequently encouraged emigration.[11]

Data showing the total number of such agents and subagents engaged in the steerage ticket business are not available. Hall states, "The Red Star Line alone formerly had 1500 of them".[12] Many Chester Lithuanians reported the activities of such agents in Lithuania. The total number of such agents was without doubt very large, for the steerage business was vastly important to all the lines operating passenger ships, and all competed for a share in this traffic. The great majority of emigrants from southern and eastern European countries sailed under foreign flags. Italian emigrants, a large proportion of whom sailed under the flag of Italy, were the only conspicuous exception. Lithuania did not operate her own ships in this business. The larger part of the Lithuanian emigrants boarded German vessels which departed from German ports. There was at the time that the Commission issued its Report in 1911 an agreement among the larger steamship companies which in a measure regulated the distribution of this traffic and prevented unrestricted competition between the lines, but this agreement did not affect the vigorous and widespread hunt for steerage passengers which was carried on throughout the chief emigrant-furnishing countries.

The Dillingham Commission Report of 1911 reveals that the attempted promotion of emigration by steamship ticket agents was carried on to a larger extent in Austria, Hungary, Greece, and Russia than in other countries.[13] Lithuania at this time (1911) was under the domination of Tsarist Russia and therefore Lithuanian emigrants were subject to the Russian emigration laws of the period. About 1885, during the reign of Alexander III (1881-1894), when the majority of the Lithuanian emigrants first saw the light of day, the Russian government prohibited all out-migration except that of Poles and Hebrews. All European countries except Russia and Turkey recognized the right of their people to emigrate during this period. Under the Russian law, citizens of the Empire were in general forbidden to leave the country to take up permanent residence elsewhere, but the fact that Russia in 1907 was third among the emigrant-furnishing nations of Europe indicates that the law in this regard was practically obsolete. In the case of Russia there seems to have been a well-grounded and increasing objection to emigration in some sections because of the economic loss which resulted from the exodus of so many agricultural and other laborers. The Russian law did not recognize the right of the people to emigrate permanently, and while the large and continued movement of population, including the Lithuanians, from the Empire to over-seas countries was proof that this law was to a large degree inoperative, it nevertheless seemed to restrict somewhat the activities of steamship agents.

Emigration from Tsarist Russia, which included a considerable number of Lithuanians, was, or at least was made to appear to be, a difficult matter, and the work of the secret agents consisted not only in selling steamship transportation, but also in procuring passports, and in smuggling across the frontier emigrants who for military or other reasons could not secure passports, or who because of their excessive cost elected to leave Russia without them. In the Chester study, from what evidence is available, not more than one-third of the Lithuanians had such government passports issued to them by the Russian authorities. Many of those who did secure passports have since lost them. What few passports still exist contain items set down in Russian characters. It seems safe to conclude then, that a fairly large number of Lithuanians of Chester who emigrated from Russian Lithuania in the period of 1900-1914, did so without any passports and thus constituted illegal departures.

Some of the better informed persons in Chester stated that Jewish secret agents of British and German lines had been employed in Lithuania and Russia to induce Christians, instead of Jews, to emigrate to the United States. One informant, for example, stated that letters had been received by prospective emigrants which contained more information than the dates of sailing, terms, and similar facts.[14] Other informants revealed that on market days in some towns, agents of steamship firms mingled with the people and attempted to incite them to emigrate to the New World. These personal contacts and letters from the steamship agents, who carried on this type of activity surreptitiously, to prospective emigrants advised him how to leave Lithuania without the approval of the Tsarist government. As a result of this kind of activity, how many Lithuanians illegally crossed the German frontier and emigrated to the United States will never be known. Some of these letters contained crudely drawn maps indicating the location of all the known Russian control stations on the border regions. They also contained detailed information on the routes of travel by which such stations could be avoided. According to the Chester informants, the area of concentration of these secret agents was along the frontier regions between Germany and Lithuania. It cannot be stated with any degree of accuracy just how extensive or effective such ticket-agent agitation was relative to emigration from Lithuania. Even if such information could be procured, it would be difficult to correctly assess the significance of such activity because it took place some forty or fifty years ago. Nevertheless, it is fair to say that the solicitations of these secret agents coupled with the poor economic conditions of the Lithuanian peasants exerted considerable influence in the stimulation of emigration.

From the quantitative viewpoint it would be difficult to state the extent of such agitation of Lithuanian emigration. It must be remembered that Tsarist Russia at that time did not allow emigration. Therefore, it follows that such solicitation was forbidden by Tsarist law. Ten Chester Lithuanians recounted the propaganda activities of steamship ticket agents in Lithuania. In view of the particular situation of Lithuania, it would

be pertinent to state that such agents found fertile soil for their operations. So far as is known there is no mention made in the available literature on Lithuanian immigration of any reference to the nature, extent,
number, or efficacy of the solicitations of these steamship ticket agents
in Lithuania. The interpretations of this study are based solely upon the
statements of Lithuanians in Chester. It should be added that these statements showed a high degree of consistency and therefore conclusion drawn
from them possess some validity.

Another important source of Lithuanian emigration was the earlier immigrant himself. In this connection Fairchild writes:

"He is probably the greatest factor of all induced immigration,
and his influence is utilized in various ways by both emigration
agents and labor agents, and made to contribute to the success
of their efforts. Every stream of immigration must have its origin in some few individuals, who, the first of their region,
break the ties of home and fatherland, and to seek their fortune
in a new and far-away land. Upon their success depends the question of whether others from the same district shall follow in
their footsteps. If they fail in their venture, it serves as a
discouraging factor as respects further emigration from that region. But if they succeed, and win a position which makes them
envied in the eyes of their fellow-countrymen, it furnishes a
powerful stimulus to further emigration. Sooner or later, there
will be some who succeed from every region, and the example of a
few successful ones is likely to far outweigh numerous failures.
Something like this is going on in countless remote districts of
the south European countries, and has gone on for decades in
every country which has sent us numbers of immigrant."[15]

The advice and assistance of relatives or friends who had previously emigrated to the United States constituted an important contributory or immediate cause of emigration. Through the medium of letters from those already here and the visits of former emigrants, the emigrating classes of
Lithuania were kept constantly, if not always reliably, informed as to labor conditions in this country, and these agencies were by far the most
potent promoters of this movement of Lithuanian population which took place
in the two decades preceding the first World War.

Among Chester Lithuanians, letter-writing to relatives and friends in
Lithuania was a very common practice during the period 1900-1914. Not a
single person out of fifty who was questioned on this point stated that he
did not write such letters after he had arrived on these shores. Of the
two instrumentalities--letters and assistance--mentioned, however, letters
seem by far to have been the more important in stimulating emigration. In
fact, it may be ventured that letters to friends in Lithuania from persons
who had emigrated to the United States have been the immediate or exciting
cause of by far the greater part of the remarkable movement from the Old
Country during the years 1900-1914. There was hardly a village or community in Lithuania that did not contribute a portion of its population to
swell the tide of emigration to the various cities of the United States,
including Chester, Pennsylvania. A geographical determinant existed in
connection with this movement. The larger part of the Chester-Lithuanians
originated in those regions of the native land which were closest to the
German ports of embarkation. Most of these emigrants departed on German
ships from German ports, such as Bremenhaven and Hamburg. The case histories also revealed that the greater proportion of these emigrants began
their Atlantic Odyssey from the villages in southern and western Lithuania.

These areas were most proximal, either by rail or sea, to the German ports. The distance traveled between the village of origin and the port of embarkation seems to have been a direct function of the financial status of the emigrant. Lithuania peasant agriculturalism was characteristically sessile; poverty was common. Money was a very scarce commodity in the lives of the average peasant, many of whom did not own any land in their native village. Some emigrants went into considerable debt in order to finance the trip across the Atlantic, to say nothing of paying the transportation costs to the port of embarkation. Thus, only those more affluent individuals, and there were not many, could afford to initiate the journey from the more eastern regions of Lithuania. There were some persons who wanted to come to America but were unable to do so because of lack of financial resources. Some of these less fortunate Lithuanians negotiated loans from Jewish bankers and merchants in Lithuania. Some had to wait one or two years before a friend or relative in the United States had accumulated enough money and sent it to an emigrant. The majority of peasant Lithuanians had their passages paid for by relatives and friends who had come to the United States and had saved enough funds to send it back to those who desired to make the crossing to America.

Most of the Lithuanians who now live in Chester stated that during the years just before the first World War the desire to return to their native fatherland was uppermost in their minds. This attitude probably explains the active interest in the homeland and, in consequence, the large amount of correspondence which flowed back and forth across the ocean. For the student of immigration and acculturation these letters could well be an extremely pregnant source of information, but, unfortunately, these letters have not been preserved. Chester Lithuanians stated that these letters were passed from hand to hand until most of the emigrant's friends and relatives were thoroughly acquainted with the contents. Each newcomer to the United States wrote a letter to relatives or friends in their native village in Lithuania. These letters went the rounds, adding to the growing knowledge of life in America, and the general discontent with peasant Lithuanian life by comparison. Once it was started, this letter-writing movement emanating from the United States increased in geometrical proportion. Its effect may be enlikened to the dropping of a pebble in a pool of still water. In the course of time more and more distant villages heard about the United States "as the best of all possible worlds" and the first small trickling stream became a large tide of immigrants bound for the New World.

Students of immigration call this the chain-letter system. It developed into an irresistible network of communications which drew the peasants from Lithuanian villages to American cities, including Chester. Letter-writing is recognized by all authorities as probably the most powerful single causative factor in stimulating emigration from southern and eastern European countries. The Chester case histories also reveal its significance in stirring up emigration.

During periods of prosperous economic conditions, the letters so circulated in Lithuania contained optimistic references to good wages and ample opportunities for employment in the United States. When comparison was made between the home conditions and the economic possibilities of America, large segments of Lithuanian villages and towns became inoculated with a heightened desire for emigration. Just the opposite picture was portrayed abroad during periods of industrial depression in Chester and other cities here. When economic depression characterized the urban economy Lithuanians who were planning to migrate were informed by their friends in the United States with regard to the conditions of employment and the result was a falling off in the tide of emigration. In short, economic conditions in the United States acted as a barometer of the volume of Lithuanian emigration.

Pioneer Lithuanian emigrants who returned for a visit to their native village, after some years of prosperous life in America, were also important promoters of emigration. Among the returning emigrants were always some who had failed to achieve success in the United States, and some who through changed conditions of life and employment went back in broken health and spirits. In fact some desired to return to Lithuania as soon as they saw New York City. As one woman in Chester put it: "When we landed in New York and saw that the streets did not have electric lights, I felt a terrific letdown and wanted to get right back on the boat for my native land." It is but natural that this group who had failed to experience success in America acted as a deterrent influence on emigration. However, on the whole, this influence was relatively unimportant, for the returning immigrant was, as a rule, one who had amassed a considerable amount of cash before going back to Lithuania. Such persons became indeed the "observed of all observers" in Lithuania. There many interested people gathered around the emigrant and received a first-hand account of America. This pioneer was greatly admired for his worldly manners, his shining jewelry and fine gold watch, strange American clothes, and his wealth. In breathless awe peasants listened to his description of his American saga and the wonders of "that far-off land." When such a person returned to the United States it took no urging on his part to induce a group of peasant Lithuanians to make the journey in his company. Returning emigrants were a great source of inspiration to the youth of the village to follow in their path. Thus, the home visit and the returned immigrant added their influence to the stream of letters.

From the Chester colony the individuals who made the trip back to the homeland achieved their success in small business enterprises, such as grocery stores, taverns and restaurants. Six Lithuanians from the Chester area have visited Lithuania. One person financed the journey by means of factory work over many years. In general, the business and professional classes of Chester are the ones who have gone back to the Old Country for a visit on one or more occasions. In most of these cases return trips to Lithuania were made only after two or three decades of residence in Chester. The underlying reason for the visit was purely social and not one person wanted to remain permanently in Lithuania. However, as these Lithuanians approach the age of sixty or more there seems to be a strong desire to return to the place of their birth and to be interred with their ancestors. All such persons hasten to add, with mournful voices, that this will be impossible and undesirable so long as Lithuania is a part of the Soviet Union.

It must be pointed out that while the total Lithuanian population of Chester, that is, foreign-born, does not exceed one hundred, the number of persons who visited Lithuania was likewise small. However, the number of emigrants from other American cities was very much larger. It is to this total group of Lithuanians that reference is made in connection with returning emigrants as factors in stirring up departures for the United States. According to the Annual Report of the Commissioner-General of Immigration for the fiscal year ending June 30, 1910, there were 1812 Lithuanian emigrant aliens who departed for Lithuania.[16] In the same year there were 22,714 immigrant aliens admitted from Lithuania.[17] These figures afford some idea of the number of emigrants who returned to their native land.

41

The importance of the advice of friends as an immediate cause of emigration from Lithuania is also indicated by the fact that nearly all the Chester group, according to their own statements, came to join relatives or friends. Not a single person was found who did not have a specific relative or friend to whom he was destined in America. Upon disembarking from the ship in New York or Philadelphia, these emigrants went to Chester. Frequently the agent of a factory in the United States met the emigrant at the port of entry and supervised his journey to a particular mill town where already many Lithuanians had made their residence. The foregoing comments not only indicate a very general relationship between admitted immigrants and those who follow afterwards, but it suggests clearly that emigration from Lithuania proceeded according to well-defined individual plans rather than in a haphazard way.

Actual contracts involving promises of employment between employers in the United States and laborers in Lithuania were not responsible for any very significant part of the emigration movement. This last statement refers only to cases where actual bona fide contracts between employers and laborers existed rather than to so-called contract labor cases as defined in the sweeping terms of the United States Immigration Law, which classified as such all persons

"who have been induced or solicited to migrate to this country by offers or promises of employment or in consequence of agreements, oral, written, or printed, express or implied, to perform labor in this country of any kind, skilled or unskilled..."[18]

Under a strict interpretation of this law it would seem that in order to escape being classified as contract laborers, immigrants coming to the United States from Lithuania must be entirely without assurance that employment will be available here after arrival. Indeed, it is certain that Lithuanian immigrants, and particularly those coming from the peasant classes, were, under any literal construction of this law, for the most part contract laborers. In the Chester case histories the one thing that stands out is the fact that not one emigrant embarked for the United States without some previous knowledge of exactly where they were destined for and where they would work if admitted to the country. This is not to say that all emigrants immediately stepped right into a factory directly upon arrival. Some had to shop around for days and weeks before employment was secured. But most of them found work very soon after establishing domocile here. Most Chester Lithuanians came to the United States with definite promises of jobs awaiting them after arrival. The persistent pattern throughout the case histories was the situation in which the friends or relatives of the emigrant had obtained employment for the emigrant before he had arrived in this country. The emigrant who went to a previously-arranged job was by far the more common than the case where the man came without such assistance.

The Immigration Commission Report of 1911 did find many cases of bona fide labor contracts. In fact, they constituted one of the more serious problems which confronted the Commission. Actual and direct contract labor agreements played an important, but not the leading, role in causing Lithuanian emigration. As stated above, Lithuanian emigrants who were destined for the Philadelphia-Chester area had practical assurances of employment before they left their homes for ports of embarkation. Such pre-arrangements for work were the result of letter-writing across the Atlantic. There is no evidence to suggest a padrone system which characterized much of the Italian immigration. In the case of the Lithuanian emigrant, each one simply informed his closest friends in Lithuania that employment

42

could be obtained and advised them to come to America. It was these personal appeals which, more than all other agencies, promoted and regulated the tide of Lithuanian emigration to America.

Many of the letters from Lithuanians in America contained remittances from the immigrants to their friends and relatives in Lithuania. Frequently these remittances took the form of prepaid tickets, complete from some German port of embarkation to the city in America, where the friend or relative was waiting for his country-man. These prepaid tickets were commonly orders, which were exchanged by the emigrant, in Europe, for the actual certificate of transportation. When a peasant in Lithuania received such a ticket, the desire to emigrate became a reality. Steamship transportation was primarily a business enterprise and the physical comfort of immigrants was a secondary consideration. The railroad companies also cooperated by giving special immigrant rates in conjunction with these prepaid passage tickets. It was natural for the Lithuanian immigrant in Chester (or any other city) to have wished for his relatives and friends from the Old World to join him in the Lithuanian-American community. There was also the feeling that if the person in America could afford it, he should send money to Lithuania so that another could come to this country. This was a very common practice among the early immigrants who came here. It is manifestly impossible to estimate correctly the actual volume of remittances sent to Lithuania. The general suspicion of immigrants whose journey was financed for them, which characterized our immigration law during the period, induced many emigrants to practice misrepresentation in this matter when reporting such assistance to government officials. The case studies of Chester Lithuanians show that about one-half of them received this kind of assistance.

Even when these remittances were not in the form of prepaid tickets, nor were sent with the intention of paying passage to America, they exerted a potent influence in stimulating immigration, through the tangible evidence of the materialistic success in America. From the peasant Lithuanian point of view, there could be no stronger proof of the success of Lithuanian immigrants in the United States than the constant stream of money which was sent from this country.

For the sake of clarity, these different forms of stimulation of Lithuanian immigration have been treated separately. In actual practice, they overlap and combine in a variety of complex relations. As a result of this combination of motives and forces, America became a household word even in the remote corners of Lithuania. Thus, any form of immigration propaganda found fertile fields in which to work. Ignorant peasant Lithuanians knew a good deal about conditions in the United States. The economic situation was of major interest. But there was also a good amount of knowledge about American social and political subjects. There were, of course, many misconceptions and erroneous impressions, but it is evident that the network of lines of communication between America and Lithuania was well established. We may summarize by saying that the main causes of Lithuanian immigration, as revealed in the Chester case studies, were economic, political, religious, and the lack of desire to serve in the Russian army.

FOOTNOTES

[1] Reprinted by the permission of the author.

[2] _Immigration_, New York, The MacMillan Co., 1913, p. 148.

[3] New York, The MacMillan Co., 1907, opposite p. 64. Cf. also the testimony of Prescott F. Hall in _Report of the Industrial Commission_, House Documents, 57th Congress, No. 184, Vol. 15, Washington, D. C., pp. 49fr, and the chart annexed; Harry Jerone, _Migration and Business Cycles_, New York, National Bureau of Economic Research, Inc., 1926, pp. 89-122. A systematic treatment of the interrelations between migration and economics is Isaac Julius, _The Economics of Migration_, New York, Oxford University Press, 1947.

[4] Dillingham Commission Report, _op. cit._, p. 186.

[5] For more details on Lithuania under Russian occupation see A. Sapoka, _op. cit._, pp. 440-532, Thomas G. Chase, _op. cit._, pp. 199-257; and Owen J. C. Norem, _op. cit._, pp. 74-90; 248-270.

[6] From _Discussions in Economics and Statistics_, New York, Henry Holt and Co., 1899, Vol. 2, p. 446.

[7] Prescott F. Hall, _Immigration_, New York, Henry Holt and Co., 1906, p. 23.

[8] _op. cit._, p. 24.

[9] _op. cit._, Vol. I, p. 189.

[10] _op. cit._, Vol. II, p. 734.

[11] _Ibid._, Vol. I, p. 190.

[12] _op. cit._, p. 26.

[13] _op. cit._, p. 190.

[14] That is, contrary to Section 7 of the United States Immigration Act of 1907. See Dillingham Commission _Report_, _op. cit._, Vol. II, p. 734.

[15] Fairchild, _op. cit._, pp. 157-158.

[16] Cf. Immigration and Naturalization Service, Washington, D. C., Government Printing Office, pp. 22 and 23. Of this number 1361 were males and 451 females. 120 were under 14 years of age, 1504 were 14 to 44, and 188 were over 45 years. 1579 had not over 5 years of continuous residence in the U. S., and 200 from 5 to 10 years.

[17] _Ibid._, pp. 20 and 21.

[18] Cf. Dillingham Commission _Report_, _op. cit._, p. 188.

PART II. THE EARLIER LITHUANIAN IMMIGRANTS

Chapter 6.   GENERAL CHARACTERIZATIONS OF LITHUANIAN
             IMMIGRANTS

Source -   Joseph S. Roucek. American Lithuanians.
           Published by the Lithuanian Alliance of
           America, 307 West 30th Street, New York,
           N. Y., 1940. The selection is from pages
           5-34[1] and is a revised version of his ar-
           ticles on "Lithuanian Immigrants in Ameri-
           ca", in American Journal of Sociology,
           Vol. 41, January, 1936, pp. 447-453, and
           in The Baltic & Scandinavian Countries,
           Vol. IV, September, 1938, No. 3. Roucek
           also has had published a chapter on "Lith-
           uanian-Americans," pp. 190-198, in Francis
           J. Brown and Joseph S. Roucek, One America,
           Prentice-Hall, Englewood Cliffs, N. J.,
           3rd edition, 1952.

Overview

Roucek has described the immigration of the Lithuanians to the United
States in the early period between the end of the Civil War and the end of
the nineteenth century and in the next period from 1900 to World War I. In
the early period Lithuanian immigrants tended to come to the anthracite
coal regions of Pennsylvania, although some settled in New England communities. In the next period there was a greater geographical distribution of
Lithuanian immigrants, with a noticeable movement to middlewestern states
such as Illinois, Michigan and Ohio. Chicago, especially, attracted Lithuanians. Roucek has noted the difficulty of determining the exact number
of Lithuanian immigrants, who, because they carried Russian passports, were
listed as Russians. They were also misidentified as Poles and Germans.

Although farming was their way of life in their old country, only a
minority of Lithuanian immigrants in the United States turned to farming.
The majority of them became factory workers and coal miners. They belonged
to the working class. The second generation has experienced a general up-
ward occupational mobility. American Lithuanians have become prominent in
the arts, education, politics, as well as sports. Their names have included Anna Kaska, the opera singer, V. D. Brenner-Baranauskas, designer of the
American Lincoln cent, Dr. J. Raymond Rimavicius, Columbia University
scholar, and Casimir Kriauciunas, Superior Court judge in Seattle, Washington. Outstanding sports figures have included Jack Sharkey, the former
world's heavyweight boxing champion, Billie Burke, golf champion, Emma
Shemaitis, swimming star, Joe Bartulis, of the Chicago White Sox baseball
club, and Ed. Krause, of Notre Dame University football and basketball
fame.

In religion the majority of American Lithuanians are Roman Catholics.
They have organized many churches and schools. The Sisters of St. Casimir
not only operate schools but also a hospital, the Holy Cross Hospital, in
Chicago. Lithuanian newspapers reflect religious views, such as the Draugas, and also political views, such as the Naujienos and Vilnis. Lithuanian immigrants became inclined early to form fraternal organizations.

The largest, the Lithuanian Alliance of America, was organized in 1886.

EARLY IMMIGRATION

Detailed information concerning Lithuanian immigration to the United States is lacking until 1850, though it is recorded that the first Lithuanians landed at New Amsterdam (now New York) in 1688.

In 1850 the present territory of Lithuania was seized by famine, and a former priest, Petras Svotelis, headed a company of Lithuanian immigrants to America. The exodus became more marked after the second Polish-Lithuanian insurrection of 1863, which was followed by bitter persecution. The famines of 1867 and 1868 and poor economic conditions led to the migration of other groups. Some of the immigrants settled on New England farms, while many others were lured by the agents of the railway companies into Pennsylvania. In 1868, four Lithuanians settled in Shamokin, Pennsylvania, and were soon followed by others. The newcomers spread to Danville, Sunbury, Mount Carmel and other mining towns in Pennsylvania. While in 1871 and 1872 Danville had the largest Lithuanian colony in the United States, numbering about 200 persons, Lithuanians were shortly afterwards found scattered throughout the whole of the anthracite region, especially in Schuylkill, Luzerne and Lackawanna counties, and in all the towns of the Wyoming Valley.

In 1874 the Tsarist Government introduced compulsory military service and this had the effect of driving many young men to America; in addition, both the abolition of serfdom and the policy of bitter religious, political and national oppression pursued by the Russian authorities contributed to swell the stream of immigrants. Their influx into America increased after the early nineties and was strengthened by the fact that during this period Lithuanian rye, wheat and flax could find no markets abroad. Books and newspapers published by Lithuanians in America and smuggled across the German border were passed from hand to hand in the Lithuanian towns and villages and attracted considerable attention. The revolution of 1905 and renewed Russian oppression gave a further stimulus to immigration, and many Lithuanian socialists and revolutionaries sought refuge in the New World.

Reviewing this influx of Lithuanian immigrants, we find that the first wave was composed of the so called "Zanavykai" and "Kapsai" elements, nicknames for the population living to the south of the Niemen and adjoining the German frontier. They were followed by the "Dzukai", whose homeland was to the south-east on both sides of the river on the Lithuanian-Polish border. As the early immigrants made their way chiefly to the anthracite coal regions of Pennsylvania, the "Zanavykai", "Kapsai" and "Dzukai" elements predominated there.

By 1880 the stream of Lithuanian immigrants was composed largely of "Zemaičiai", or "Lowlanders" from the western part of the former government district of Kaunas, north of the river Niemen, and was directed chiefly to the cities of Chicago, Philadelphia and Boston, and to the bitumen fields of West Virginia. Riga, Liepaja (Libau) and St. Petersburg were the main points of departure, where in many cases the immigrants had first to earn the money for their journey. Jews began to emigrate to America about 1885. Those from Kaunas went chiefly to the great cities, whence they soon scattered over several States. Lithuanians first arrived in New York, Chicago and Cleveland in 1870; in Boston, Waterbury, Connecticut and Pittsburgh in 1871; in Scranton in 1878; in Baltimore in 1881 and in Saint Louis in 1886. At the end of the nineteenth century many Lithuanians settled in the coal regions of Illinois (Springfield, Spring Valley, Taylorville, Oglesby, etc.) but they subsequently left these districts when the mines were closed down.

PRE-WAR ESTIMATES

Lithuanian writers estimate that before 1899, 275,000 Lithuanian immigrants had arrived in the United States. In that year a separate classification was established by the American government. Between 1896 and 1914, 252,294 more Lithuanians entered the country.

The practice was long pursued in America of grouping Lithuanians and Letts together under the "Slavic Division", and as the figures then drawn up do not distinguish between Lithuanian and Letts, they are useless. Many Lithuanians were listed as Poles, Russians or Germans. Before the World War most of the immigrants carried Russian passports, and as they usually went through Hamburg and Rotterdam on Russian passports, they were registered as Russians. On the other hand, many declared themselves Roman Catholics and were therefore classified as Poles.

The Rev. A. Kaupas estimates that in 1904 about 50,000 Lithuanians were living in the anthracite region of Pennsylvania; 25,000 in West Pennsylvania and West Virginia (Pittsburgh, its vicinity and near the soft coal mines); 10,000 in Philadelphia and Baltimore; 15,000 in Greater New York (almost exclusively in Brooklyn and Long Island City) and its environs (Yonkers, New York and Jersey City, Elizabeth, Newark, Paterson, New Jersey); 25,000 in New England (Boston, Brockton, Lawrence, Worcester, Waterbury, Union City, Hartford and Bridgeport); 10,000 in Ohio and Michigan (Cleveland, Detroit and Grand Rapids); 50,000 in Illinois and Wisconsin (Chicago 25,000-30,000, Spring Valley, Westville, Collinsville, East St. Louis, Waukegan, Ashland, Sheboygan and Milwaukee); while several thousand were scattered over the States of Missouri, Kansas, Oklahoma, Montana, Colorado and Washington. The southern States were practically untouched by Lithuanian immigration.

At the outset the Lithuanians lived in close relations with their co-religionists and nearest European neighbours, the Poles. In many districts such as Shamokin, Mount Carmel, and Shenandoah in Pennsylvania, they united with the Poles to form parishes and societies and joined the same benevolent societies. But a trend towards separation became apparent in 1885; the differences came to a head in 1889 when the Poles refused to acknowledge Father Alexander Burba as the priest of the local church in Plymouth, Pennsylvania [2]. In 1892 the Lithuanians of Shamokin separated from the Poles and established own parishes at Mount Carmel and elsewhere in Pennsylvania.

RELATIONS WITH THE HOMELAND

Before the War the Lithuanians were active supporters of the nationalist movement in their native country. In 1864 the Tsarist government prohibited the publication of Lithuanian literature printed in Latin characters, and the use of the Lithuanian language was proscribed in schools and in all government offices. Prohibited in Russia and suppressed in

Prussia, Lithuanian cultural and patriotic activities were transferred to the United States. They were given their first impetus when Dr. Jonas Šliupas[3], who had been associated with the first journal of the Lithuanian national renascence movement. "Aušra" (The Dawn), published at Tilsit, came to America. In 1886 he edited and published the first Lithuanian newspaper in the United States, "Lietuviškas Balsas", and was instrumental in inducing a number of American Lithuanians to organize their own social and religious institutions independently of Polish organizations. As a result of his initiative numerous Lithuanian parishes and other organizations began to flourish in America. In 1886 the Lithuanian National Alliance of America was formed. Certain educated Lithuanians began to publish newspapers and books, and a book publishing society, the "Tėvynės Mylėtoju Draugija"> (Lovers of the Fatherland), was founded. Šliupas himself wrote several books, mostly on Lithuanian history, such as "Lietuviu Proteviai" (The Ancestors of the Lithuanians), "Lietuviu Tauta" (The Lithuanian Nation) and "Lietuvos Raštai ir Raštininkai" (Lithuanian Literature and Writers). The poet Jonas Žilius devoted his talents to lyrical descriptions of Lithuanian peasant and immigrant life in the New World. Other writers and publicists prominent in the liberal and national movement in the United States were the Rev. A. Burba, V. Dembskis, J. Šernas (Adomaitis), Kalėdu Kaukė (K. Jurgelionis), Karolis Vairas (V. K. Račkauskas), J. Širvydas and others. In all, several hundred Lithuanian books were printed in America and smuggled into Lithuania, together with Lithuanian newspapers. Beyond doubt the contact between those who had remained at home and those who had emigrated was a major factor in arousing the national aspirations of the Lithuanians under the reactionary Russian rule[4].

At the outbreak of the World War the Lithuanian Social Democrats and the Lithuanian National Democrats, who were patriotic and very liberal in religious matters, most of them being Free Thinkers, met in Brooklyn on October 1-2, 1914. Owing to certain differences of policy, the delegates of the National Democrats held another convention of their own after the adjournment of the Brooklyn meeting, and founded the Lithuanian National League of America, commonly known as "Sandara" (Concord). The Social Democrats, on the other hand, organized the Lithuanian Fund ("Lietuvos Šelpimo Fondas"). The Lithuanian National League created the Autonomy Fund which was later converted into the Lithuanian Independence Fund. In addition, the Lithuanian Roman Catholic organizations founded their own National Fund ("Tautos Fondas") controlled by the American Lithuanian Roman Catholic Federation, and eventually collected several million dollars. The money raised by these various Funds was used to aid Lithuanian Information Bureau in Washington and in Lausanne (Switzerland), and to support the Lithuanian Council of America, Press propaganda, the Lithuanian delegation to the Versailles Conference, war refugees, and war prisoners in Germany. The publication in Switzerland of books in French and German was financed from the same source, and after the War the money was turned to educational purposes, enabling many Lithuanian students to pursue advanced studies at European and American universities.

The primary purpose of the Lithuanian organizations founded in America during the War was to aid Lithuanian war sufferers and to assist Lithuania to secure autonomy and independence. As early as 1916 the organizations appealed to Congress to help the Lithuanian war sufferers. Congress thereupon authorized the President to set aside a day for the collection of funds for this purpose. November 1, 1916, was named Lithuania Day and about 200,000 dollars were raised and turned over to the American Red Cross on condition that the money should be spent in Lithuania. The American Red Cross also collected considerable sums and under the direction of the Lithuanian Council of America sent food, clothes, ambulances and money to

Lithuania. On June 8-11, 1919, a Lithuanian convention was held in Chicago, where the Lithuanian Liberty Bell, now in the War Museum in Kaunas, was rung for the first time.

When the independence of Lithuania was finally proclaimed on February 16, 1918, a group of over two hundred ex-service men from the American army went to Lithuania to join the Lithuanian military and air forces. At the head of this group was Captain Stephen Darius, who with Lieutenant Stanley Girenas made the ill fated Transatlantic flight in July 1933. In February 1920 the Lithuanian Financial Mission came to America to raise a loan for the needs of the new State--the Lithuanian Liberty Loan. Over a million and a half dollars were subscribed by American Lithuanians. America formally recognized the new State on May 31, 1921.

POST-WAR IMMIGRATION

With the foundation of a free Lithuania, some thirty or forty thousand Lithuanians elected to return to their native country. But when the rouble and the mark fell, only about 10,000 remained in their native land and the rest sailed back to America.

We learn from the official United States statistics that in 1920 there were 135,068 foreign-born Lithuanians in America and in 1930 193,666. In addition there were in this country in 1930 245,589 native born persons of Lithuanian stock ("native white of foreign or mixed parentage"). But these figures are open to certain objections. Lithuanian critics claim that many persons listed as Poles, Russians and German were really Lithuanians. The Lithuanian convention held in New York in March 1918 adopted 750,000 as the minimum estimate. But these figures made no allowance either for those who had returned to their country (about 10 per cent) or for those who had died, and the figure is therefore too high. Dr. Kemešis estimated in 1924 that a total of 455,000 American Lithuanians were distributed as follows:

TABLE 1

Distribution of American Lithuanians

Pennsylvania anthracite region	200,000
Pittsburgh district	25,000
Philadelphia district	20,000
Baltimore	10,000
New York & New Jersey States (Atlantic coast)	4,000
Western section of New York State	6,000
Connecticut	5,000
Massachusetts, New Hampshire & Rhode Island	40,000
Detroit and Michigan	13,000
Cleveland and Ohio	13,000
Chicago and suburbs	90,000
Wisconsin	9,000
To the south and west of Chicago (Illinois, Indiana, Kansas, Iowa, West Virginia, Oklahoma, Louisiana and California	20,000
	455,000

The discrepancies between the American and Lithuanian estimates are more evident when we discover that only 156,152 persons registered Lithuanian as their mother-tongue in the census of 1930. There is some connection between this fact and the proportion of Lithuanian News, who numbered 25,886, or 2.1 per cent of the Lithuanian immigrants.

With regard to the distribution of American foreign-born Lithuanians, the United States statistics show that largest group lives in the Middle Atlantic and the next largest in the East North Central and New England States. The figures are as follows:

TABLE 2

Distribution of American Foreign-born Lithuanians

Illinois 44,733
Pennsylvania 37,079
Massachusetts 25,219
New York 22,933
Connecticut 13,247
New Jersey 9,870
Michigan 9,430
Ohio 7,581
Wisconsin 4,109
Maryland 3,422
Indiana 2,109
California 1,776
Minnesota 1,283

TABLE 3

Distribution of Foreign-born Lithuanians according
to Mother-tongue in Cities of over 25,000
Inhabitants

Massachusetts:
    Boston 4,512
    Brockton 1,587
    Cambridge 1,112
    Lawrence 1,294
    Worcester 3,921

New Jersey:
    Elizabeth 1,584
    Newark 1,194

Ohio:
    Cleveland 3,666

Michigan:
    Detroit 3,666
    Grand Rapids 1,340

Connecticut:
    Hartford 1,361
    New Britain 1,233
    Waterbury 2,840

TABLE 3 Continued

New York:
New York 9,146

Pennsylvania:
Philadelphia 5,471
Pittsburgh 2,623
Scranton 2,424
Wilkes Barre 1,236

Maryland:
Baltimore 2,236

Altogether 86.8 per cent of the foreign-born Lithuanians live in urban districts. Their distribution, according to mother-tongue, in cities of over 25,000 inhabitants is shown in Table 3.

The largest Lithuanian colony is in Chicago--about 100,000[5]. In Pennsylvania there are large groups of Lithuanians in Scranton, Wilkes Barre, Shenandoah, Shamokin, Mahanoy City and Mount Carmel. In Spring Valley and Westville, Illinois, Lithuanians hold most of the public offices. In Shenandoah and New Philadelphia (Pennsylvania) and certain other towns the municipal officers are nearly all Lithuanians, from the Mayor down to the secretaries.

OCCUPATIONS

Several attempts to start Lithuanian farming colonies have ended in failure. "Buffalo Bill" Cody attempted without success to persuade a number of Lithuanians to colonize his land in Wyoming. About 1895 a Lithuanian settlement was started in Prairie City, Arkansas, but after years it was abandoned. In Pennsylvania, Michigan, Illinois and Wisconsin the Lithuanians are engaged in general farming, in Massachusetts and New Jersey in dairy farming, in Connecticut in tobacco farming. There are Lithuanian farmers in Northern Wisconsin around Rhinelander. The largest agricultural colony of Lithuanians exists in Mason, Lake, and Oceana counties in Western Michigan.

But only a minority of American Lithuanians are farmers. Most of them associate farming with the ruinous taxes and unprofitable drudgery it was their lot to experience in the home country, and they have turned to industrial pursuits instead. They are found as foundry men in Western Pennsylvania; as weavers in the cotton mills of New England and the silkmills of Paterson, New Jersey; as tanners in Philadelphia, hatmakers in New York, dockworkers in Cleveland, tailors in Brooklyn, Baltimore and Chicago. Many are employed in the packing houses in Chicago, in the oil and sugar refineries around New York, and in the shoe factories in Binghampton, New York, and Brockton, Massachusetts.

In general they belong to the lower working class. The second generation, however, tends to enter the professional class.

RELIGIOUS DIVISIONS

The majority of American Lithuanians are Roman Catholics, but there are a number of Lutherans, Calvinists and Free Thinkers. The Roman Catholic Church bulks large in the life of the members of every Lithuanian parish, as most of their social organizations are connected with it. In 1871 the Lithuanians of Shenandoah at the request of the Archbishop of Philadelphia, invited the Rev. Andrew Strupinskas, M. I. C. to take care of the Lithuanians in that community and its vicinity. A year later, the Rev. Juškevičius organized a Lithuanian and Polish parish in Shamokin, Pennsylvania. In 1892 the split with the Poles led to the formation of an independent Lithuanian parish in that city. In 1886 Lithuanian parishes had been established in Brooklyn, Mahanoy City and Hazelton, Pennsylvania and in 1887 in Baltimore. In 1913 the Lithuanians supported about 80 churches of their own and 22 elementary schools, mostly administered by the Order of the Sisters of St. Casimir. In all, 118 parishes were organized between 1886 and 1929. Today there are about 120 Lithuanian parishes in the United States.

The first Lithuanian National Catholic church was founded in 1914 by the Lithuanians of Scranton, Pennsylvania, with the help of Bishop Hodur, head of the Polish National Catholic Church of America. S. B. Mickievicz was appointed its pastor, being succeeded by J. Gritenas. Mickievicz subsequently organized several Lithuanian congregations in Chicago under the jurisdiction of Archbishop Carfora of the Old Roman Catholic Church. At a synod held by the Polish National Church in 1924. Gritenas was elected Bishop of the Lithuanian Churches. But the group seceded from the Poles and today is headed by Archbishop Geniotis. These Lithuanian Churches accept the first four general councils of the Roman Catholic Church and use the Niceno-Constantinopolitan creed. The liturgy is Lithuanian. The supreme authority is vested in a Synod. There are parishes in Lawrence, Massachusetts, Scranton, Pittsburgh, Philadelphia and Chicago.

SOCIAL DIVISIONS

The religious background is also intimately connected with the factions among the American Lithuanians, which are based on religious ideas rather than on economic, class or intellectual tendencies[6].

Before the World War the three largest Lithuanian associations in America were the "Tevynes Myletoju Draugystė" (Society of Lithuanian Patriots), the "Susivienijimas Lietuviu Amerikoje: (The Lithuanian Alliance of America), and the "Susivienijimas Lietuviu Rymo Kataliku" (The Union of Roman Catholic Lithuanians). Each body published at its own expense books for gratuitous distribution in Lithuania. For the rest, the Lithuanian immigrants were split into three distinct groups. The Social Democrats comprised the "radical" fraction, and many eventually drifted into Communism. The Clerical group voiced its policies through the medium of four weekly publications, especially the "Draugas". The National Party represented the Lithuanian patriots; they were less interested in Catholicism but were enthusiastic nationalists.

The majority of the Lithuanians are Catholic and their views are represented by the Chicago daily "Draugas" (Friend) and the weekly "Garsas" (Sound). The Lithuanian Nationalists, on the other hand, are represented by the Brooklyn daily "Vienybė" (Unity), the Cleveland weekly "Dirva" (Field), and the Worcester weekly "Amerikos Lietuvis" (American Lithuanian). All of them heartily support the Lithuanian national government. The Socialists maintain the Chicago daily "Naujienos" (News) and the Boston weekly "Keleivis" (Traveller) and weekly "Naujoji Gadyně" (New Era). The Communists also publish newspapers, the Brooklyn daily "Laisvě" (Freedom) and the Chicago "Vilnis" (Wave).

ORGANIZATIONS

The tendency of the Lithuanians to form compact settlements enables them to organize their social life through social, literary, religious, benevolent and cooperative societies, imitating as far as possible their social institutions at home. These activities were suppressed in pre-War Russia, with the result that they have found strong expression in America. There is an organization for almost every purpose, and sometimes several of them.

It has been estimated that there are over two thousand Lithuanian charitable and mutual aid organizations in America. The largest fraternal organizations are the Lithuanian Alliance of America, 307 West 30-th Street, New York, founded in 1886[7], and the Lithuanian Roman Catholic Alliance, 73 East South Street, Wilkes Barre, founded in 1901 when it separated from its parent organization, the Lithuanian Alliance of America. It has a membership of 11,942 (and 789 juveniles) and assets of 1,217,522 dollars.

All these groups are sub-divided into thousands of local societies. The American Lithuanian Roman Catholic Women's Alliance for instance has 1,016 members and assets of 64,832 dollars. The Knights of Lithuania ("Lietuvos Vyčiai"), founded in 1912, number over three thousand.

Formerly there was hardly a Lithuanian colony without one or more cooperative societies, clubs and stores--a situation which reflected the conditions in Lithuania where cooperative stores formerly existed in almost every town, city and village. The first cooperative store was opened in Waterbury, Connecticut, in 1885. Unfortunately the Lithuanians are inclined to bring over to America their religious and political differences and these have tended to disrupt the cooperative movement. Originally fourteen cooperative societies were organized in Massachusetts, but none have survived. The peak of the movement was reached in 1919--20[8].

There are over one thousand mutual benefit societies, providing in most cases only sick and death benefits. The tendency has been to amalgamate smaller societies with one of the two central bodies of Lithuanian alliance. There are twenty building and loan associations in Illinois, four in Pennsylvania, three in Maryland, three in New Jersey, one in Ohio and one in Massachusetts, with "predepression" combined assets of about ten million dollars. But there are few large Lithuanian companies and corporations in America. The Universal State Bank of Chicago, the Kazemekas Bank of Waterbury, Connecticut, and others disappeared during the depression. The Metropolitan State Bank of Chicago, the Polithania State Bank of Pittsburgh and the Savings and Loan Bank of Cleveland successfully weathered the pre-Roosevelt banking difficulties.

The Lithuanians have had to fight a particularly hard and long battle for their national independence, and this may explain in part the fact that Lithuanian immigrants do not quickly become assimilated. Even though so many Lithuanians were driven from their homes and forced to shift for themselves as best they could, their country has retained its spell over them. The American Lithuanian is proud of the tenacity with which he has preserved his language and his traditions. The national spirit is strengthened by frequent contacts with the home country and by numerous cultural activities. In every colony a marked interest is taken in Lithuanian literature, drama, painting and other forms of art. Lithuanian parishes frequently organize dramatic performances, where they sing their old "dainos" and dance their traditional dances. About fifty Lithuanian radio programmes are broadcast in most of the larger Lithuanian colonies.

NATURALIZATION AND LITERACY

The tendency to assimilate less rapidly than other immigrant groups is reflected in the low rate of naturalization--47.5 per cent in 1930, one of the lowest among European immigrants, the Yugoslavs, Bulgarians, Turks, Greeks, Albanians, Spanish and Portuguese alone showing lower rates. The position, however, appears more favourable when we view the percentage of naturalization among foreign-born Lithuanians aged 21 years or over for 1920 and 1930: while the 1920 percentage was 26 per cent, in 1930 the rate reached 47.7 per cent. Even so, the rate is lower than that of most of the other immigrant groups.

Originally higher education was practically unknown among the Lithuanian immigrants, but the situation in this respect is rapidly improving and there are now a considerable number of Lithuanian physicians, priests, surgeons, lawyers, actors, professors, etc. Yet in 1930, it is estimated that 24.5 per cent of foreign-born Lithuanians (10 years old and over) were illiterate, a very high rate surpassed only by the immigrants from Italy, Portugal, Syria and the Azores. But it should be remembered that before the War there were no Lithuanian schools in the home country and private teaching of the native tongue was strictly forbidden by the Russian government.

The first Catholic Lithuanian school in America dates from about 1895[9]. It was founded in Chicago and instruction was in the hands of non-Lithuanians, usually sisters of the Polish congregation of the Nazarene Sisters. The first purely Lithuanian educational establishment was founded at the Parish School at Mount Carmel, Pennsylvania, in 1907, under the control of the Sisters of St. Casimir. In 1933 the Sisters of St. Casimir managed 22 schools with a staff of 170 teachers and a total attendance of 5,527 Lithuanian children, of whom all but ten per cent were native born. In 1936, the Catholic parishes conducted 48 parochial schools, attended by over 10,000 pupils.

The Lithuanian Catholics also support a number of other educational institutions. The Marianopolis College and High School, Thompson, Connecticut, was founded in 1931 by the Marian Fathers, though the origins of this foundation date back to 1926. The student body is composed of 80 Lithuanians and 14 teachers.[10] Its Lithuanian-American Students and Professional Association ("Amerikos Lietuviu Kataliku Studentu ir Profesionalu Sajunga") publishes a well-edited monthly, "Studentu Žodis" (Students' World) in Lithuanian. There are a number of other Lithuanian educational foundations.

Dr. J. Raymond-Rimavičius, Lecturer on the Lithuanian Language and Literature at Marianopolis College, offers a similar course at Columbia University. Courses in Lithuanian are also given by Professor Carl Darling Buck at the University of Chicago (Lithuanian and Church Slavic). Professor Samuel H. Cross at Harvard University ("Balto-Slavic Philology"), Professor Roland G. Kent at the University of Pennsylvania ("Lithuanian"),

Professor Harold H. Bender at Princeton University ("Lithuanian"), Dr. Edward Prokosch at Yale University ("Lithuanian"), and Professor H. Senn at University of Pennsylvania.

THE PRESS

An important role in the life of the American-Lithuanians is played by the Press. In 1879 Tvarauskas issued the first American-Lithuanian publication, a Lithuanian-English dictionary, but it was not finished. In the same year he started to publish in New York City a Lithuanian newspaper, "Lietuviszka Gazieta" (Lithuanian Gazette). The first Lithuanian newspaper in pure text was the "Vienybē Lietuvininku" (Lithuanian Unity), which appeared in Plymouth, Pennsylvania, in 1884. It was later transferred to Brooklyn, and is now published as the "Vienybē" (Unity). In 1885 Dr. John Sliupas inaugurated publication in New York of the nationalist "Lietuvos Balsas" (Lithuanian Voice). Today Lithuanian-American publications are printed in pure Lithuanian.

According to Professor Park, 38 Lithuanian newspapers were founded between 1884 and 1920, but only 16 were still in existence in the latter year. In all 31 Lithuanian periodicals are now being published in America.

OUTSTANDING AMERICAN LITHUANIANS

The American Lithuanians are not far behind other nationalities in providing leaders in the arts, education, business and sports.[11]

AMERICAN-LITHUANIAN MUSICIANS, ACTORS, ARTISTS

Mikas Petrauskas, composer of a very large number of popular Lithuanian songs, about 20 Lithuanian operettas and a Lithuanian opera, was the first musically trained Lithuanian to work among his people in America[12]. In addition to writing music, he did much to popularize Lithuanian folk dances, and was an able organizer of Lithuanian singing choirs. He maintained at different times three conservatories of music, in Brooklyn, in Chicago and in Boston. With the exception of his opera, Eglē-Žalčiu Karalienē, presented in Boston in 1924, his compositions were of a light, popular character, utilizing extensively motives from the numerous Lithuanian folksongs. His exceptionally pleasant personality, unlimited energy, and remarkable teaching talents, together with his musical works have endeared him to American Lithuanian. He is universally considered to be the most popular Lithuanian composer and the foremost worker in the field of Lithuanian folk song music.

There are other well-known musical leaders, Anna Kaska, contralto, was one of the first singers to be chosen for stardom with the Metropolitan Opera Company from radio auditions; she was born of Lithuanian parents in Hartford, Connecticut, and after studying two years at the Hartford Conservatory of Music went to Lithuania and later to Italy for further study. Joseph Babravičius has returned from New York to his native land and joined the National Opera there. Emilija Mickunas of Philadelphia and the Misses Marijona Rakauskaitē and Margareta Česnavičiutē are well known as singers. Professor Joseph Žilevičius, former director of the Conservatory of Music at Klaipēda, and composer, now lives in America. Among other prominent Lithuanian musicians in the United States are Alexander Aleksis, formerly of the Conservatory of Warsaw; the violinist, Professor J. Židanavičius; Anthony Pocius, Director of the Beethoven Conservatory of Music of Chicago; Peter Sarpalius, composer; John Čižauskas and his brother, Reverend Joseph Čižauskas. Helen Mickunas and F. Jakavičius are connected with the Chicago Civic Opera, Ralph Zuska with the Philadelphia Civic Opera and S. Paskewicz with the Hippodrome Opera Company.

In the field of acting, Ivan Lebedeff is a featured player in Hollywood, where Shirley White also plays in motion pictures. June Barron, Betty Dumbris and Helen Brown were members of the Ziegfield Follies, while M. Taparauskas is a member of the Globe Theatre.

The late V. D. Brenner-Baranauskas was the designer of the American Lincoln cent. Louis Rosenthal is a well-known sculptor. M. J. Šileikis is connected with the Chicago Art Institute. In the field of painting, Ignas Ylekis of Chicago stands out and Jonas Szileika was awarded a first prize by the Chicago Art Institute while he lived in America.

AMERICAN LITHUANIAN MEN OF LETTERS

The American Lithuanian group is very rich in talented literary men: K. Jurgelionis and J. Jokubaitis, poets; Vitaitis, editor of the daily "Vienybē"; J. Tysliava, poet and editor of the monthly "Lietuva"; Rev. Casimir Urbonavičius (Jonas Kmitas), poet and editor-in-chief of the "Darbininkas"; Rev. Joseph Židanavičius (Sherijų Juozas), writer and dramatist; Rev. Anthony Milukas, editor, publisher, writer; Pius Grigaitis, editor of the socialist daily "Naujienos" and writer; Nahurnauskas of Baltimore, author of several successful dramas; Leonard Šimutis (Šilelis), editor-in-chief of "Draugas", publicits, writer and poet; Rev. J. Navickas, publicist, writer, historian; Karpius, editor of the "Dirva", publicist and writer of many novels; Rev. John Balkunas, editor of the "Amerika" and publicist. Among other prominent literary men are Rev. Francis Vaitukaitis, St. Jasiulonis, P. Bajoras, Ant. Tulis, Jonas Šliburis, and R. Mizara. Dr. M. J. Vinikas, secretary of the Lithuanian Alliance of America is the author of "Economic Relations of Lithuania" and "Diplomatic Relations of Lithuania" (theses, American University, Washington, D. C., 1933, 1934).

In the field of education we hear of Rev. Joseph Vaitkevičius, formerly Professor of the Seminaries of Vloclavek and Vilna and the University of Lithuania, at present Professor of Theology at Marian Hills Seminary, Hinsdale, Illinois; Dr. J. Navickas, Rector of the Marianopolis College, Thompson, Connecticut; Rev. Michael Civulskis, Director of the La Salette College, Hartford, Connecticut. Dr. J. Raymond-Rimavičius lectures on Lithuanian at Columbia University; E. Žiurys is connected with Yale University; Lieut. P. Moncius, a graduate of Annapolis Academy, is now with Harvard University.

AMERICAN LITHUANIAN IN PUBLIC OFFICE

In civic and political affairs, Casimir Kriaučiunas (Kay) was Judge of the Superior Court of Seattle, Washington, William Laukaitis occupies a judicial bench in Baltimore. J. Žuris is a Chicago judge and Frank Mast, formerly Counselor of the Lithuanian Legation, was Assistant District Attorney of Chicago. Dr. A. Velybus and A. Janušaitis (Janushat) are members of the Pennsylvania, and J. De Righter-Deraitis of the Ohio State legislature. Bolic A. Degasis is Police Court Judge at Nashua, New Hampshire; W. J. Wimbiscus, Judge of the Cook County Circuit Court of Chicago, and J. P. Uvick, Judge of the City of Grosse Point, Michigan. J. Kairis, Mayor of Seatonville, Illinois, Anna C. Lakawitz, Mayor of Linndale, Ohio, and J. Vansavage, Mayor of New Philadelphia, Pennsylvania, are others who have achieved prominence in civic affairs.

AMERICAN LITHUANIAN ATHLETES

In the field of athletics, Jack Sharkey (Juozas Žukauskas), the former World's heavyweight champion; Billie Burke (Vincas Burkauskas), golfer, Jack Goodman, golf champion; Albina Osipavitch, member of the United States Olympic swimming team; John Macionis, member of the Yale University swimming team and record holder; Emma Shemaitis, swimming star; George Chip, former boxing champion; Yustin Sirutis, former national amateur boxing champion; Joe Bartulis, member of the White Sox baseball team; V. Tamulis, member of the New York Yankees and Newark Bears baseball teams; J. Broaca, member of the New York Yankees baseball team; B. Boken, member of the Washington Senators baseball team; Willie Scrill, an outstanding basketball professional; J. Grebauskas, captain of Princeton's basketball team; F. Lubin, captain of the United States Olympic basketball team are a few of the outstanding American Lithuanian athletes. In the field of wrestling, Carl Pojello is holder of British and European championships; Andy Kandrat and Joe Komar are strong men of the old school; Dr. Sarpolis and Jack Ganson have also made their reputation in this field.

Many American Lithuanians are active on college and university football teams. In the fall of 1935, the majority of players on the football team of the Catholic University of Washington were Lithuanians. Others who are famous are Ed. Krause, Plansky, Adomavicius, Dranginis, Miciuta, Jablonsky and Karpovich.

* * *

No description of the life of the Lithuanians in America would be complete without reference to their love of the "dainos", or national songs. As soon as Lithuanian immigration to America set in, the newcomers organized and supported choirs. Many prominent Lithuanian singers received their early training in these choirs and singing groups. Numerous Lithuanian orchestras and bands supply music for the Lithuanian colonies.

One must admire also the willingness of the American Lithuanian to support his cultural institutions financially. The Holy Cross Hospital of Chicago, under the supervision of the Sisters of St. Casimir, employs a staff the majority of which are Lithuanians. The Darius-Girėnas Monument of Chicago was built with the funds collected from American Lithuanians and erected to perpetuate the memory of Captain S. Darius and Lieutenant S. Girėnas who lost their lives during their flight from New York to Kaunas. This monument has been erected in a beautiful corner of Marquette Park in the centre of a large Lithuanian colony in Chicago.

The Lithuanian Cultural Garden, Cleveland, built entirely with funds collected from American Lithuanians, houses busts of prominent Lithuanians and numerous other items imported from Lithuania. The Lithuanian Room at the Cathedral of Learning of the University of Pittsburgh was also furnished in traditional Lithuanian style by funds raised among these immigrants and their descendants.

In spite of the strong efforts of the American Lithuanians to preserve their original culture within the framework of American influences, the process of Americanization is making more and more ground among the Lithuanians, particularly among the American-born generation. Yet Lithuania has a tenacious hold on her sons in America. How to integrate this cultural allegiance of the American Lithuanians to their native country with the allegiance they owe to their country of adoption is the central problem of this cultural group in America.

FOOTNOTES

[1] Reprinted by permission of the author and the publisher, the Lithuanian Alliance of America.

[2] A. Kaupas, "L'Eglise et les Lituaniens aux Etats-Unis", Annales des nationalites, Vol. XI, pp. 232-234.

[3] Dr. Šliupas was a colleague of Dr. Jonas Basanavičius, known as the Patriarch of Lithuanian Renascence. His newspaper "Aušra", founded in 1883 at Tilsit, opened a new era in the Lithuanian national movement.

[4] For a list of the pre-war American Lithuanian periodicals, see Kemešis, "Cooperation among the Lithuanians in the U.S.A.", p. 12, note 10.

[5] Foreign born Lithuanians and their American born children.

[6] See V. M. Palmer, "Field Studies in Sociology" (Chicago, University of Chicago Press, 1928) pp. 257-265, an account of the Lithuanian colony at Canalport, Chicago. Also R. E. Park, "The Immigrant Press and its Control" (New York, Harper's 1922) pp. 52-54; concerning the nationalizing and denationalizing influences of the church among Lithuanians.

[7] According to its Secretary, the Lithuanian Alliance of America in December 1937 had 375 lodges with a membership of from 15,000 to 25,000. Its assets as of that date exceeded $2,100.000.

[8] See P. Šalčius, "Cooperative Movement in Lithuania"; E. J. Harrison, "Lithuania, 1928" (London, Hazell, Watson and Viney, 1928) and "Lithuanian Cooperation in the United States" in Cooperation, October 1924, vol. X, p. 175.

[9] J. J. Simonaitis, "The Lithuanian School and its Service for Good Citizenship", an unpublished thesis, Fordham University, 1933.

[10] According to a letter from the Director of Marianapolis College, dated 2/17/36.

[11] The best work in this field is: Susivienijimo Lietuvių Amerikoje, Auksinio Jubiliejaus Albumas 1886-1936 (New York, Lithuanian Alliance of America, 1936). Although the principal aim of the Album is to record pictorially the 50 years' activities of the Alliance, it nevertheless represents a fair picture of Lithuanian workers in cultural and political activ-

ities of America. The work contains portraits of many outstanding American Lithuanians and of some prominent leaders in the re-establishment of the independent State of Lithuania.

[12]Petrauskas was born on September 29, 1873 and died in Lithuania on March 3, 1937. He first came to the United States on June 13, 1907, but after a concert tour of Lithuanian settlements, returned to Italy for further studies. He came back to America again in 1909.

Chapter 7.   THE LITHUANIAN IMMIGRANTS IN THE CITY

Source - Vivien M. Palmer.   Field Studies in Sociology.   A Student's Manual.   The University
of Chicago Press, Chicago, Illinois, 1928.
The selections are from "Type Study No. 1,"
pages 213-217 and from "Appendixes - Type
Study 3," pages 256-265.[1]

Overview

The leading American city in the number of Lithuanian immigrants is
Chicago. Lithuanians in Chicago have been studied over the past fifty
years in a few research investigations conducted under the direction of
the faculty of the University of Chicago, a pioneer institution of higher
learning in American urban ecological studies.

In this study of Canalport, one of the oldest sections of the city,
Vivien M. Palmer has pointed out that Lithuanians began to appear in Canalport as early as 1885 and by 1891 they had organized a parish. By 1920
Lithuanians outnumbered all foreign-born groups in Canalport except the
Polish, who lived in the neighborhood to the east of them. Old hard feeling between these two ethnic groups continued after World War I because of
the Vilna boundary dispute and local politicians exploited these ethnic
tensions.

In the Lithuanian neighborhood of Canalport there was a mixture of
laborers, skilled mechanics, professional people, businessmen, artists,
church people, nationalists and socialists. There was a noticeable struggle for power between the socialists, clericals and the nationalists, who,
in their own ways, sought to control the thinking and behavior of Lithuanian immigrants.

Palmer has provided case studies which reflect the variety of cultural problems experienced by Lithuanians in Chicago. One case study recalled the frustrations of a Lithuanian socialist. Another case study described the determination of a Lithuanian immigrant to revive Lithuanian
culture, especially music and dances, in Chicago. A third case study
brought out the many problems faced by a child of Lithuanian immigrants.

TYPE STUDY NO. 1

STUDY OF A TERRITORIAL GROUP: CANALPORT

Canalport, one of the oldest sections of the city, originated at the
junction of the Illinois-Michigan Canal with the Chicago River. In the
forties it was an important transfer point between the Great Lakes boats
and the Mississippi River barges. Industries flourished along the water-
ways in the port town. Railroads coming in the fifties superseded the
water travel, and though Canalport became surrounded with railroad lines

and industries, it was no longer the dominant industrial and transportation center. Successive waves of immigration have poured their quota into Canalport, with the result that it has had many cultures implanted upon its soil. The existing literature which was found at the outset of the study of Canalport may be summarized as follows: (1) Literature dealing with the Illinois-Michigan Canal and its successor, the Ship and Drainage Canal. Describes origin of Canalport and the economic forces which affected the community. A few concrete references to the community itself. (2) The usual sources of city, county, state, and church histories scanned for the occasional meager references to this area which they contained. (3) This community has been recognized as one of the "problem spots" of the city, and reports of civic and social agencies contain occasional references to it. Also, one or two limited social studies have been made at different times. (4) Occasional references to the community have been made by investigators who were studying surrounding areas. (5) The series of maps showing the spotting of social phenomena over the city as a whole give social statistics with respect to Canalport. The census data for 1910 and 1920 were also available for the small areas of the city. (6) Since Canalport contains the outstanding Lithuanian settlement in Chicago and the dominant Lithuanian settlement for the entire country, all available literature on the Lithuanians in America and Chicago was also digested.

Bibliographies were made and excerpts copies. The material was filed chronologically and by subtopics. Much of this background work was done by members of the research staff and placed at the disposal of students. Some of the work was also done by students who preferred library study and who worked along with field investigators engaged on the same community.

A working digest of the material secured from existing documents was prepared and is presented. References to sources are omitted from the digest, for the investigator familiar with the material can readily find these in the file of excerpts.

DIGEST OF DATA

I. PERIOD PREVIOUS TO ORIGIN OF CANALPORT

1673.   Joliet mentions possibility of canal across this section of the country to connect the Lake of Illinois (Lake Michigan) with the St. Louis River (the Des Plaines and Illinois) and complete the waterway to the Gulf, and hence to Florida.

1808-36.   National agitation for the canal.--1808, Secretary of Treasury recommends the waterway; 1810, Congress passes resolution in its favor; 1812, secures strip of land along canal way from Indians; 1817, first canal survey made. State promotion of canal.--1822, newly created state of Illinois petitions Congress for right to build waterway and receives grant of land; 1825, state incorporates company to build canal--is unsuccessful; 1827, Congress donated additional land to be sold to finance canal and new Commission created; 1830, plats Chicago and Ottawa at either end of the canal route; 1833, Commission abolished because it could not raise funds; 1835, another Commission appointed.

2. PLATTING OF CANALPORT TO FIRE (1836-71)

1836.   Canal commissioners plat town of Canalport on the river about three miles from its mouth in the center of city. Construction work on canal began. Scarcity of labor, floods, epidemics, and panic of 1837 retard work.

1842.   State bank failed and Illinois faced bankruptcy. Work on canal stopped. Men working on construction of canal receive canal scrip in payment; this becomes unnegotiable; exchange it for canal land. Thus some settlers come into land in and about Canalport. They farm.

1843.   Loan floated, board of trustees created, and work began again. Shallow-cut channel substituted for larger scheme.

1847.   St. Patrick's parish organized in Canalport; "Irish immigrants settling here in ever increasing numbers."

1848.   First boat passed through the locks at Canalport.

1854.   Railroad built and canal is doomed. Rail travel begins to supercede water travel. Same year passenger packets on canal sold.

1856.   "Feud that has been brewing between Irish and Germans resulted in open fight. Irish have won and Germans are withdrawing north across the river, leaving Canalport to the Irish" (political fight).

1863.   Township in which Canalport is located is annexed to the city. Description by newspaper man: "There are clusters of low constructions along A--Road. These are either slaughter or packing houses with a glue factory and some rendering establishments. It is an area with a reputation. Here crowded boats and long lines of wagons meet." German Protestant church founded.

1865.   Packing plants move to new area two miles south.

1869.   Swedish Evangelical church built; 200 members; a mission church.

3.   FIRE TO 1900--PERIOD OF NEW POPULATION INFLUX

1871.   Distribution and realignment of population following the great fire brought influx of a number of new families into Canalport.

1872.   First Polish family entered Canalport.

1875.   Omnibus line opened extending from center of city to Canalport.

1880.   Beginning of influx of Russian Poles into Canalport.

1882.   Peak of tonnage reached on Canal.

1885.   Lithuanians begin to appear in Canalport. Movement of some of the old German and Irish families out of the community begins to be marked.

1889.   First Polish Catholic church built at 32d and F--; this marked the center of their neighborhood with T-- Street as the business thoroughfare.

1891.   Lithuanians organize parish; thirty families.

1895.   Italians begin to enter southeastern corner of Canalport.

1900.   Canal abandoned as waterway.

4. 1900 TO PRESENT[2]

1902.   Ship canal construction began.

1908.   The first large manufacturing district in the city opened. It extends into the southeastern part of Canalport.

1919-20.   Maps showing the distribution of social phenomena over the city for one year during 1918, 1919, or 1920 give facts concerning Canalport as shown in Table I.

TABLE I

	Total Cases	Rate per 1,000 of Population	Rank among Other Communities*
Poverty	195	3.23	14
Delinquent girls	16	.26	18
Delinquent boys	31	.49	28
Suicides	3	.05	45
Gangs	61**		
Divorce and desertion	56	.93	42

*The eighty local communities of the city are ranked in order of their rate per thousand, that community with the highest rate being ranked first.
**Ranks fourth among other communities with respect to the number of gangs.

1920.   Population of Canalport (compiled from United States Census tract figures for 1920):

	Number
Total population	78,755
Native white of native parents	11,464
Native white of foreign parents	32,075
Native white of mixed parents	5,598
Foreign-born white	28,252
Native-born colored	962
Other colored	404

The major foreign-born groups were represented as follows in the 1920 census figures.

Polish	6,789
Lithuanian	5,057
Italians	4,397
Germans	2,827
Irish	2,267

A study of these statistics raises many questions which only further research in the area can answer.

In making this digest of existing material, spaces were left between each date so that additional material could be added as it was secured in the field. This insured an up-to-the-minute summary. The task was to fill out this skeleton into a realistic picture of life in Canalport as it had evolved. The remainder of the outline for Type Study No. I suggests the kind of material that is sought. The summary puts the investigator into touch with all the concrete facts that bear upon each particular phase of his study as he undertakes it.

STUDENT'S CASE INTERPRETATION[3]

(a) People have a <u>categorical</u> conception of a group which is foreign to them; they have a <u>general attitude</u> toward the group as a whole, and treat each member of it as a member of the <u>class</u>, not as an individual. This is because they have had few primary, intimate, face-to-face contacts with individuals in the group, and have gained their knowledge of it indirectly. There is, however, considerable <u>stratification</u> and <u>variation</u> among individuals belonging to any group.

(b) This <u>pattern of leadership</u> was transplanted from the Old World and maintained during the early days on this soil while the Lithuanians were beginning to make their adjustments to American life. Gradually, however, a new leadership is emerging; local politicians, real estate and other business men who have made the adjustment to American life are leaders in bridging the gap between the Lithuanian colony and the rest of the city. These men still get their backing within the Lithuanian colony, are still regarded as Lithuanians by the American group, but their culture is a mixture of the old and new. Their life-histories would throw light on the processes of assimilation and accommodation.

(c) With their eyes fixated on the problems of the Old World, the radical leaders have proved themselves <u>conservative forces</u> in many ways. They have, with few exceptions, paid little attention to the problems of the new life, and spend their time in a mental world of foreign culture. Probably some of their <u>eccentricities</u> may be traceable to this <u>isolation</u> from the current life and their absentee relationship to a life with which they no longer have first-hand contact.

(d) People's religious loyalties seem to change slowly. Habits, traditions, customs, early associations, unrational and emotional "pulls" can be carried over in the church when in many other phases of life radical changes are necessary.

(e) The policy of the nationalists is manifestly one of <u>accommodation</u>. They desire the hyphenated American, the man who retains many of the essential cultural traits of his native land. They center their attention especially upon the second and third generation, children reared in this country, because these constitute the group which is rapidly becoming <u>assimilated</u> and losing the cultural heritage of its parents.

(f) The agitator's role may become so fixed that it is habitual. A negativistic attitude toward the social order may become so much a habit that it is an end in itself. As in this case, there is no longer an immediate issue (see case 7 also).

(g) Two types of conflicts are illustrated here: (1) the conflicts among factions within the same nationality, (2) the conflicts between people of two nationalities. The first type of conflict is among people who are close together, who speak the same language, have the same customs, share in the same traditions, and are conscious of belonging to the same nationality group. Their conflicts are bitter, but there is always an underlying sense of <u>security</u>, a feeling that nothing can break them asunder and that they will go on disputing continually. This leads to <u>organized conflict</u>, to the planning of attacks and counter-attacks and to <u>rationalizations</u>. The second type of contact is between two groups who are distinct in many ways but have been next door neighbors for years, have had numerous contacts, have suffered under a common enemy, and have had frequent disputes. The conflict is more <u>categorical</u>, the <u>social distance</u> between the groups being greater than in the first case, and there is less discussion and more emotional, unrationalized expression of the discord.

The attitude of the child <u>categorically</u> labeling the worst deed he could think of as being performed by the conflict group is a kind with stories of atrocities always current during a war. It also illustrates a <u>social heritage</u> unreflectively taken over by the child.

All these conclusions are suggested tentatively from the rather meager data presented here. More specific studies are necessary to establish them with more certainty and exactitude.

TYPE STUDY NO. 3[4]

DESCRIPTION OF THE COLONY

Most people in the city think of this section as a place where people of the same type live--all Lithuanians. But to one who really knows it, great variations are apparent. The people are really all Lithuanians, but there are professional people, laborers, business men, skilled mechanics, artists, musicians, nationalists, church people, and socialists. It is a mixture that almost makes the neighborhood a small town in itself (see <u>a</u>, "Student's Case Interpretation").

What we think of as the Lithuanian neighborhood is contiguous to the manufacturing district, in an area bounded by----, though of course the boundaries are not rigid and many families live without them. It is frequently stated that there are one-hundred thousand Lithuanians in the city, and that one-third of these live in Canalport.

The dynamic forces in the community are the leaders of the three groups, the socialists, the clericals, and the nationalists. Lithuania has always been a peasant nation, and the priests and intellectuals have fought over the direction of affairs for many years. They are still the powers to be recognized in this colony in the new world (see <u>b</u>, "Student's Case Interpretation").

The socialists are the most extreme group, and they contain a wide variety of radicals. For the most part their leaders were exiled, or practically exiled for their participation in Lithuanian uprisings against Russia, and they continued their interest over here, printing tracts, pamphlets, etc., to send into Lithuania, helping to finance new uprisings, affording homes for political refugees, and in general doing whatever they could to further their cause. They change their "isms" every once in a while and seem to have the habit of always standing on the opposite side of any established order. They are bitterly opposed to the clergy, whom they consider their arch-enemies (see c, "Student's Case Interpretation").

The clerical group, headed by the priests, still maintains considerable influence, especially over the average person. They have built up the largest Lithuanian parish in this country, and their handsome new church edifice is one of the largest buildings in the community (see d, "Student's Case Interpretation").

The nationalist group mediates, and sometimes cuts across, the other two. Its members are interested in keeping alive Lithuanian customs, folklore, music, dances, and language in this country, though they also want the Lithuanians to learn the American tongue and to adapt themselves to American ways. They give concerts, plays, and dances for the benefit of Lithuanian war orphans, the establishment of schools in Lithuania, and for other relief purposes. It is this group that has raised most of the funds that have been sent across the water. Many of them have been clericals and socialists in turn, and their connection with the nationalist group is a recoil from the others (see e, "Student's Case Interpretation").

Each group publishes its own newspaper, using it to set forth its opinions and launch its attacks on the others; there are long-drawn-out controversies in which they answer each other back and forth over some issue. Each group has its own forum where discussions and lectures are held. My father says that these people have gotten so into the habit of fighting for causes, of getting out propaganda, that they will always find something to fight for. I remember seeing a group of socialists carry the body of one of their deceased comrades to the door of the church and hold mock rites over it, and the controversies sometimes go beyond the verbal bantage (see f, "Student's Case Interpretation").

The old hard feeling between the Poles and the Lithuanians has been especially noticeable lately because of the Vilna controversy and because of the fact that the Poles in the neighborhood to the east of the Lithuanians have been spreading westward, crowding in upon the Lithuanians. The antagonism between the Poles and Lithuanians has been played upon so long by politicians that it seems to be ingrained in the mass of people. Two illustrations will show what I mean. I was in the C--- (a community house) the other day and saw a little Lithuanian boy looking at a book and muttering and gesticulating angrily to himself. He was looking at a colored picture of the Crucifixion and saying, "Dirty Pollacks, dirty Pollacks; hanging God." I was told by one of the people connected with the institution that for a time both nationality groups used the place, and then the Lithuanians began to come in greater numbers. Polish women began to shake their fists as they passed the house, shouting, "Lugans, Lugans, Lugans," their derisive name for the Lithuanians. This type of feeling is quite widespread between the two groups (see g, "Student's Case Interpretation").

The Lithuanians still preserve some of their native customs, and even where families have become Americanized in many ways they usually revert to them in connection with celebrations. One can still find families who spread clean hay over the table on Christmas Eve (though now they cover the hay with a cloth), eat fish and vegetables with no meat or milk, and invite in less fortunate people as their guests. Some of the old peasant dishes are revived at that time and seem a delicacy, though if they constituted part of the everyday diet, as they did in the Old Country, they would lose that glamor. One still sees funerals wending their way to the church with friends carrying the casket and mourners walking beside. An old woman sometimes accompanies the procession, crying forth the good deeds of the deceased. This procession is a revival of the old life when the church was usually located at one end of the village and the burying ground at the other.

Lithanians began coming into this neighborhood in large numbers about twenty years ago. One used to see them coming in on wagons with their trunks behind them, the women with their peasant blouses, cow-skin coats, and fur caps. Now they come in one or two at a time, dressed in the current fashion, and are "taxied" to the homes of their friends.

My father arrived before there were many Lithuanians in the city, and he became adjusted to the American life more quickly as a result. We have lived away from the colony for years, but we still have many friends in it whom we visit frequently.

The student's position is that of a detached observer who yet has intimate contacts with the group. As a member of the second generation he is not vitally touched by many of the issues that concern the older generation born in the homeland.

TYPE STUDY NO. 3

BASED ON ASSIGNMENT 6: LIFE-HISTORIES
OF IMMIGRANTS

Document 7

Confidential files
Lithuanian colony,
 Canalport
Socialist

This case study is made of a man with whom I am slightly acquainted. The data was obtained from (1) casual conversations with the man, (2) listening to him at forum meetings, and (3) comments which other people have made concerning him. Documented May, 1927.

Mr. A is one of the leaders of the socialist group, educated, and a brilliant writer and speaker. He is one of the most bitterly hated enemies of the clerical party because of his satire and ridicule.

I gained the story of his coming to America from conversations with him:

I was a member of the student group of revolutionists at the University of ---- and took part in the uprisings of 1905 and 1906. I was sent out into the country before the revolution was called to distribute literature and arouse the peasants to take a stand for their rights. I tacked tracts on the trees and held secret meetings, sometimes by candle light in the densest part of the woods, and sometimes in underground dugs. We failed in the revolution and I was sentenced to Siberia. I escaped through the winter snows of Germany into France. At Paris I met more of my comrades and we set to work at once, for though we were interested in Lithuania, our cause is universal. But the French government became suspicious and when we got word that we were to be arrested we fled to England. I was there for two years when the Lithuanian ---- sent me money to come to America, as they needed me in the fight over here. Here we would work unhampered and we printed many tracts and pamphlets and flooded Lithuania with them.

For a long time after his arrival Mr. A refused to learn English, and at the present time he speaks it only brokenly. Commenting upon this, he said: "The fools, don't they know that in a hundred years or so there will be a different language in this country which an American of today will not be able to understand, a language made up of all the different speeches? Why should all that is different be crushed out of the foreigners of the country?"

He has expressed himself several times with regard to the present trend of Socialism in the community. "The Socialists have lost their ideals for the dollar. In the old country they were idealists. When they first come here they are socialists; when they take out their first papers they become Democrats; and by the time they have their second papers they are sure to be Republicans. There is not much thrill now in being a Socialist. People's opinions have changed and are charged with a certain freedom of thought. There was more thrill in the early days in this country when conditions were so bad for us, and there was even more thrill back in Russia."

Mr. A's name has been connected with a recent difficulty in the colony. He has been accused of receiving more than his share of funds in a given enterprise. "He's become materialistic with success and has forgotten his Socialist principles," was the statement made by another leading member of the party.

Document 12

Confidential files
Canalport Lithuanian
    neighborhood
Nationalist

Mr. K is an old friend of our family, and my information concerning him has come through many contacts.

Upon his graduation from high school at the age of seventeen, Mr. K left Lithuania for America. The Z boys had come back from the New Country on a trip and had spoken eloquently of the opportunities over here. So Mr. K decided to come. He was on his way, via England, when his meager fund was stolen, so he had to remain in that country two years in order to get enough to complete his journey. "I didn't like England. There were so few of my countrymen there, and it was so hard to mix in or feel that you belonged."

Upon his arrival in the city he got a night job shoveling coal and attended a technical school in the daytime. While nearing his degree there he became interested in a profession, and his better command of language and his versatility made it possible for him to put himself through a professional school with ease after he finished his technical course.

Since about 1910 he has taken an active part in the revival of Lithuanian music and dances. Since Lithuania is primarily a peasant nation, she has had practically no literature of her own, and Mr. K has assisted in translating several of the classics of English literature into his native tongue. He was closely associated with Mr. X, who has done more than anyone else to revive Lithuanian culture and who has returned to Lithuania to an important government post.

The nationalist leaders have started many singing societies in the colony and support several girls whom they have sent back to Lithuania to collect folk music.

Just after the war Mr. K returned to his country for a visit. Since then it has been his ambition to "make his pile" and then return to Lithuania to live. "I want to spend my days in peace and happiness, to enjoy culture in a land where it and beauty are emphasized instead of the almighty dollar." His professional work keeps him in the colony and he has little opportunity to mix with his equals; he is shut off from the corresponding group in American society, and he finds few people interested in the things he likes. In Lithuania it is different; there he is free to come and go in the cultured group. I think that explains his attitude and his wish to go back to the Old Country to live.

Document 14

Confidential file
Canalport
Lithuanians

Source: Written by a student who was raised in the Lithuanian community of Canalport.

An immigrant child faces many problems, the existence of which the American is never conscious. My own experiences, I know, have been less severe than those which many of my friends have gone through, but still they have left their mark.

My parents brought me to America when I was eight years old. We came directly to this city, where several distant relatives and a number of home friends had come before us. My family settled just on the outskirts of the colony in Canalport, and, alas for me, the two blocks away meant that I had to attend a school where there were no other Lithuanian children.

I was large and awkward for my age, wore clothes that must have seemed outlandish to the other children, spoke practically no English, and was put into a class with smaller and younger children. They ridiculed me and called me "Dino." The teacher was no better than the children. She had no patience with my blunders, and joined in the laughter of the children. It was torture. I begged my parents to take me out of school or to move over into the colony where I could be with children of my own nationality. But they were anxious to have me become "Americanized," and thought that the chance to be with Americans was a help.

As I look back upon it now I can see that this school experience did a great deal toward making me stay always a Lithuanian. I considered my home more and more of a refuge to return to as quickly as possible from the taunting of the children, and the contrast between their cruel treatment of me and the kindness and sympathy of my parents made me stand up for my own nationality. Their ridicule did not make me ashamed of the fact that my parents and I were immigrants, and I have not changed my attitude.

During the time I spent at home I did a great deal of reading, and more and more I got used to being alone and shunning the other children. Whenever I sat down at home my mother would place a book in my hands; she wanted me to be a scholar. She had a better education than my father, and has always been hungry for more. When she finished the common school in Lithuania she won first prize in the government examinations and was awarded tuition and part of her expenses in a girls' school in a town close by. Her parents were too poor to send her, and she was needed for work on the farm. The prize she won, a book, is always on our parlor table, almost a family altar, a symbol of my mother's hopes, to be realized in me.

When I go to the library downtown to study mother likes to go with me. She just sits and watches. She is always eager to go because she likes the feel of so many books around her. The first time I asked her to come with me she went for her shawl. I felt embarrassed and explained that people did not wear shawls to the library. She understood quickly and waited until the next day, when she came with an American hat, the first she had purchased. That is the way I always explain American ways to my people; I never make fun of them, and they always try to change to please me. All through my high school days, and now that I am in college, my mother makes these occasional trips to the library with me.

I have never been in a real American home, and the few friends I do have belong to my own nationality. Yet I am almost a double personality. When at school I speak the American language and try to be as nearly like the others as possible. I am not always dressed as well as I would like to be, but my parents are giving me all they can afford and I never let them know how I feel. At home I am an entirely different person. I speak Lithuanian entirely, use respectful addresses toward my parents, and obey them as a son should. It is always a pleasure to be at home. In the homes of many of our Lithuanian friends the children sass their parents and act superior to them, so there is constant fighting; but in our home it is always peaceful. We three understand each other so well, and treatment of my parents is based on a genuine respect for them.

My father and mother rely on me for many things. "You know the ways of America; you look out for this," is frequently spoken as they ask me to take care of some business matter. I have done this for years. I always tell them what courses I am going to take at the University. They listen and always say, "You know best: we trust you to decide."

I tremble and am scared when I think of how much they rely on me. I am the only one in our group of Lithuanian friends who is being sent to college. The other families have all advised against it and tell my parents that they are wasting money and that I am wasting my time. It is mother who usually answers them, saying that I will make good, wait and see. They all think a lot of the professions and of someone with learning, but it is money that is the test of success with them. To a certain extent this is also true of my parents; they think that an educated person will be a success financially. It seems to me, though, that I would make more money in business.

At school I am handicapped in competition with American students. They have so much background in their homes, and most of them have had so many more opportunities than I have. They know how to fit in in a way I do not. I feel this difference keenly. And yet so much more seems to be expected of me than is expected of these students. I have never won a prize, like my mother, but she still has faith in me. I suppose I shall hang out my shingle among my own people and find my solution there.

Source - Upton Sinclair. The Jungle. Robert Bentley, Inc., Cambridge, Massachusetts, 1971. The selection is from Chapter 2, pages 21-30.[5]

Overview

Upton Sinclair's book, The Jungle, was one of the most widely read books written by the "Muckrakers," those writers who uncovered economic and political corruption in the American society and agitated for reform in what historians have called the "Progressive Era." On $500 given to him by a Socialist periodical, Sinclair lived for seven weeks in the Chicago district adjoining the stock yards. He observed first hand how the new immigrants struggled to adjust to their new land. Then he proceeded to write the tragic story of how a Lithuanian family became economically and socially disorganized as the result of their shocking experiences in their urban environment in the early twentieth century.

Sinclair began Chapter 2 by describing Jurgis Rudkus as an eager, strong and unbeaten young man, the kind the meat packing plant bosses wanted to get hold of. He was, obviously, in appearance and personality some one from the country. He knew nothing about city ways.

Vividly, Sinclair sketched the rural milieu of Lithuania which had influenced the earlier lives of Jurgis and his bride, Ona. In the remainder of the chapter Sinclair unfolded the details about the filthy and cruel "back of the yards" environment into which Jurgis and Ona were thrust soon after their arrival in Chicago.

Jurgis talked lightly about work, because he was young. They told him stories about the breaking down of men, there in the stockyards of Chicago, and of what had happened to them afterward--stories to make your flesh creep, but Jurgis would only laugh. He had only been there four months, and he was young, and a giant besides. There was too much health in him. He could not even imagine how it would feel to be beaten. "That is well enough for men like you," he would say, "silpnas, puny fellows-- but my back is broad."

Jurgis was like a boy, a boy from the country. He was the sort of man the bosses like to get hold of, the sort they make it a grievance they cannot get hold of. When he was told to go to a certain place, he would go there on the run. When he had nothing to do for the moment, he would stand round fidgeting, dancing, with the overflow of energy that was in him. If he were working in a line of men, the line always moved too slowly for him, and you could pick him out by his impatience and restlessness. That was why he had been picked out on one important occasion; for Jurgis had stood outside of Brown and Company's "Central Time Station" not more than half an hour, the second day of his arrival in Chicago, before he had been beckoned by one of the bosses. Of this he was very proud, and it made him more disposed than ever to laugh at the pessimists. In vain would they all tell him that there were men in that crowd from which he had been chosen who had stood there a month--yes, many months--and not been chosen yet. "Yes," he would say, "but what sort of men? Broken-down tramps and good-for-nothings, fellows who have spent all their money drinking, and want to get more for it. Do you want me to believe that with these arms"--and he would clench his fists and hold them up in the air, so that you might see the rolling muscles--"that with these arms people will ever let me starve?"

"It is plain," they would answer to this, "that you have come from the country, and from very far in the country." And this was the fact, for Jurgis had never seen a city, and scarcely even a fair-sized town, until he had set out to make his fortune in the world and earn his right to Ona. His father, and his father's father before him, and as many ancestors back as legend could go, had lived in that part of Lithuania known as Bre-lovicz, the Imperial Forest. This is a great tract of a hundred thousand acres, which from time immemorial has been a hunting preserve of the nobility. There are a very few peasants settled in it, holding title from ancient times; and one of these was Antanas Rudkus, who had been reared himself, and had reared his children in turn, upon half a dozen acres of cleared land in the midst of a wilderness. There had been one son besides Jurgis, and one sister. The former had been drafted into the army; that had been over ten years ago, but since that day nothing had ever been heard of him. The sister was married, and her husband had bought the place when old Antanas had decided to go with his son.

It was nearly a year and a half ago that Jurgis had met Ona, at a horsefair a hundred miles from home. Jurgis had never expected to get married--he had laughed at it as a foolish trap for a man to walk into; but here, without ever having spoken a word to her, with no more than the exchange of half a dozen smiles, he found himself, purple in the face with embarrassment and terror, asking her parents to sell her to him for his wife--and offering his father's two horses he had been sent to the fair to sell. But Ona's father proved as a rock--the girl was yet a child, and he was a rich man, and his daughter was not to be had in that way. So Jurgis went home with a heavy heart, and that spring and summer toiled and tried hard to forget. In the fall, after the harvest was over, he saw that it would not do, and tramped the full fortnight's journey that lay between him and Ona.

He found an unexpected state of affairs--for the girl's father had died, and his estate was tied up with creditors; Jurgis' heart leaped as he realized that now the prize was within his reach. There was Elzbieta Lukoszaite, Teta, or Aunt, as they called her, Ona's stepmother, and there were her six children, of all ages. There was also her brother Jonas, a dried-up little man who had worked upon the farm. They were people of great consequence, as it seemed to Jurgis, fresh out of the woods, Ona knew how to read, and knew many other things that he did not know; and now the farm had been sold, and the whole family was adrift--all they owned in the world being about seven hundred rubles, which is half as many dollars. They would have had three times that, but it had gone to court, and the judge had decided against them, and it had cost the balance to get him to change his decision.

Ona might have married and left them, but she would not, for she loved Teta Elzbieta. It was Jonas who suggested that they all go to America, where a friend of his had gotten rich. He would work, for his part, and the women would work, and some of the children, doubtless--they would live somehow. Jurgis, too, had heard of America. That was a country where, they said, a man might earn three rubles a day; and Jurgis figured what three rubles a day would mean, with prices as they were where he lived, and decided forthwith that he would go to America and marry, and be a rich man in the bargain. In that country, rich or poor, a man was free, it was said; he did not have to go into the army, he did not have to pay out his money to rascally officials--he might do as he pleased, and count himself as good as any other man. So America was a place of which lovers and young people dreamed. If one could only manage to get the price of a passage, he could count his troubles at an end.

It was arranged that they should leave the following spring, and meantime Jurgis sold himself to a contractor for a certain time, and tramped nearly four hundred miles from home with a gang of men to work upon a railroad in Smolensk. This was a fearful experience, with filth and bad food and cruelty and overwork; but Jurgis stood it and came out in fine trim, and with eighty rubles sewed up in his coat. He did not drink or fight, because he was thinking all the time of Ona; and for the rest, he was a quiet, steady man, who did what he was told to, did not lose his temper often, and when he did lose it made the offender anxious that he should not lose it again. When they paid him off he dodged the company gamblers and dramshops, and so they tried to kill him; but he escaped, and tramped it home, working at odd jobs, and sleeping always with one eye open.

So in the summertime they had all set out for America. At the last moment there joined them Marija Berczynskas, who was a cousin of Ona's. Marija was an orphan, and had worked since childhood for a rich farmer of Vilna, who beat her regularly. It was only at the age of twenty that it had occurred to Marija to try her strength, when she had risen up and nearly murdered the man, and then come away.

There were twelve in all in the party, five adults and six children --and Ona, who was a little of both. They had a hard time on the passage; there was an agent who helped them, but he proved a scoundrel, and got them into a trap with some officials, and cost them a good deal of their precious money, which they clung to with such horrible fear. This happened to them again in New York--for, of course, they knew nothing about the country, and had no one to tell them, and it was easy for a man in a blue uniform to lead them away, and to take them to a hotel and keep them there, and make them pay enormous charges to get away. The law says that the rate card shall be on the door of a hotel, but it does not say that it shall be in Lithuanian.

It was in the stockyards that Jonas' friend had gotten rich, and so to Chicago the party was bound. They knew that one word, Chicago--and that was all they needed to know, at least, until they reached the city. Then, tumbled out of the cars without ceremony, they were no better off than before; they stood staring down the vista of Dearborn Street, with its big black buildings towering in the distance, unable to realize that they had arrived, and why, when they said "Chicago," people no longer pointed in some direction, but instead looked perplexed, or laughed, or went on without paying any attention. They were pitiable in their helplessness; above all things they stood in deadly terror of any sort of person in official uniform, and so whenever they saw a policeman they would cross the street and hurry by. For the whole of the first day they wandered about in the midst of deafening confusion, utterly lost; and it was only at night that, cowering in the doorway of a house, they were finally discovered and taken by a policeman to the station. In the morning an interpreter was found, and they were taken and put upon a car, and taught a new word--"stockyards." Their delight at discovering that they were to get out of this adventure without losing another share of their possessions it would not be possible to describe.

They sat and stared out of the window. They were on a street which seemed to run on forever, mile after mile--thirty-four of them, if they had known it--and each side of it one uninterrupted row of wretched little two-story frame buildings. Down every side street they could see, it was the same--never a hill and never a hollow, but always the same endless vista of ugly and dirty little wooden buildings. Here and there would be a bridge crossing a filthy creek, with hard-baked mud shores and dingy sheds and docks along it; here and there would be a railroad crossing, with a tangle of switches, and locomotives puffing, and rattling freight cars filing by; here and there would be a great factory, a dingy building with innumerable windows in it, and immense volumes of smoke pouring from the chimneys, darkening the air above and making filthy the earth beneath. But after each of these interruptions, the desolate procession would begin again--the procession of dreary little buildings.

A full hour before the party reached the city they had begun to note the perplexing changes in the atmosphere. It grew darker all the time, and upon the earth the grass seemed to grow less green. Every minute, as the train sped on, the colors of things became dingier; the fields were grown parched and yellow, the landscape hideous and bare. And along with the thickening smoke they began to notice another circumstance, a strange, pungent odor. They were not sure that it was unpleasant, this odor; some might have called it sickening, but their taste in odors was not developed, and they were only sure that it was curious. Now, sitting in the trolley car, they realized that they were on their way to the home of it--that they had traveled all the way from Lithuania to it. It was now no longer something far off and faint, that you caught in whiffs; you could literally taste it, as well as smell it--you could take hold of it, almost, and examine it at your leisure. They were divided in their opinions about it. It was an elemental odor, raw and crude; it was rich, almost rancid, sensual, and strong. There were some who drank it in as if it were an intoxicant; there were others who put their handerchiefs to their faces. The new emigrants were still tasting it, lost in wonder, when suddenly the car came to a halt, and the door was flung open, and a voice shouted--"Stockyards!"

They were left standing upon the corner, staring; down a side street there were two rows of brick houses, and between them a vista: half a dozen chimneys, tall as the tallest of buildings, touching the very sky-- and leaping from them half a dozen columns of smoke, thick, oily, and black as night. It might have come from the center of the world, this smoke, where the fires of the ages still smolder. It came as if self-impelled, driving all before it, a perpetual explosion. It was inexhaustible; one stared, waiting to see it stop, but still the great streams rolled out. They spread in vast clouds overhead, writhing, curling; then, uniting in one giant river, they streamed away down the sky, stretching a black pall as far as the eye could reach.

Then the party became aware of another strange thing. This, too, like the odor, was a thing elemental; it was a sound, a sound made up of ten thousand little sounds. You scarcely noticed it at first--it sunk into your consciousness, a vague disturbance, a trouble. It was like the murmuring of the bees in the spring, the whisperings of the forest; it suggested endless activity, the rumblings of a world in motion. It was only by an effort that one could realize that it was made by animals, that it was the distant lowing of ten thousand cattle, the distant grunting of ten thousand swine.

They would have liked to follow it up, but, alas, they had no time for adventures just then. The policeman on the corner was beginning to watch them; and so, as usual, they started up the street. Scarcely had they gone a block, however, before Jonas was heard to give a cry, and began pointing excitedly across the street. Before they could gather the meaning of his breathless ejaculations he had bounded away, and they saw him enter a shop, over which was a sign: "J. Szedvilas, Delicatessen." When he came out again it was in company with a very stout gentleman in shirt sleeves and an apron, clasping Jonas by both hands and laughing hilariously. Then Teta Elzbieta recollected suddenly that Szedvilas had been the name of the mythical friend who had made his fortune in America. To find that he had been making it in the delicatessen business was an extraordinary piece of good fortune at this juncture; though it was well on in the morning, they had not breakfasted, and the children were beginning to whimper.

Thus was the happy ending of a woeful voyage. The two families literally fell upon each other's necks--for it had been years since Jokubas Szedvilas had met a man from his part of Lithuania. Before half the day they were lifelong friends. Jokubas understood all the pitfalls of this new world, and could explain all of its mysteries; he could tell them the things they ought to have done in the different emergencies--and what was still more to the point, he could tell them what to do now. He would take them to poni Aniele, who kept a boardinghouse the other side of the yards; old Mrs. Jukniene, he explained, had not what one would call choice accommodations, but they might do for the moment. To this Teta Elzbieta hastened to respond that nothing could be too cheap to suit them just then; for they were quite terrified over the sums they had had to expend. A very few days of practical experience in this land of high wages had been sufficient to make clear to them the cruel fact that it was also a land of high prices, and that in it the poor man was almost as poor as in any other corner of the earth; and so there vanished in a night all the wonderful dreams of wealth that had been haunting Jurgis. What had made the discovery all the more painful was that they were spending, at American prices, money which they had earned at home rates of wages--and so were really being cheated by the world! The last two days they had all but starved themselves--it made them quite sick to pay the prices that the railroad people asked them for food.

Yet, when they saw the home of the Widow Jukniene they could not but recoil, even so. In all their journey they had seen nothing so bad as this. Poni Aniele had a four-room flat in one of that wilderness of two-story frame tenements that lie "back of the yards." There were four such flats in each building, and each of the four was a "boardinghouse" for the occupancy of foreigners--Lithuanians, Poles, Slovaks, or Bohemians. Some of these places were kept by private persons, some were co-operative. There would be an average of half a dozen boarders to each room--sometimes there were thirteen or fourteen to one room, fifty or sixty to a flat. Each one of the occupants furnished his own accommodations--that is, a mattress and some bedding. The mattresses would be spread upon the floor in rows--and there would be nothing else in the place except a stove. It was by no means unusual for two men to own the same mattress in common, one working by day and using it by night, and the other working at night and using it in the daytime. Very frequently a lodginghouse keeper would rent the same beds to double shifts of men.

Mrs. Jukniene was a wizened-up little woman, with a wrinkled face. Her home was unthinkably filthy; you could not enter by the front door at all, owing to the mattresses, and when you tried to go up the backstairs you found that she had walled up most of the porch with old boards to make a place to keep her chickens. It was a standing jest of the boarders that Aniele cleaned house by letting the chickens loose in the rooms. Undoubtedly this did keep down the vermin, but it seemed probable, in view of all the circumstances, that the old lady regarded it rather as feeding the chickens than as cleaning the rooms. The truth was that she had definitely given up the idea of cleaning anything, under pressure of an attack of rheumatism, which had kept her doubled up in one corner of her room for over a week; during which time eleven of her boarders, heavily in her debt, had concluded to try their chances of employment in Kansas City. This was July, and the fields were green. One never saw the fields, nor any green thing whatever, in Packingtown; but one could go out on the road and "hobo it," as the men phrased it, and see the country, and have a long rest, and an easy time riding on the freight cars.

Such was the home to which the new arrivals were welcomed. There was nothing better to be had--they might not do so well by looking further, for Mrs. Jukniene had at least kept one room for herself and her three little children, and now offered to share this with the women and the girls of the party. They could get bedding at a secondhand store, she explained; and they would not need any, while the weather was so hot--doubtless they would all sleep on the sidewalk such nights as this, as did nearly all her guests. "Tomorrow," Jugis said, when they were left alone, "tomorrow I will get a job, and perhaps Jonas will get one also; and then we can get a place of our own."

Later that afternoon he and Ona went out to take a walk and look about them, to see more of this district which was to be their home. In back of the yards the dreary two-story frame houses were scattered farther apart, and there were great spaces bare--that seemingly had been overlooked by the great sore of a city as it spread itself over the surface of the prairie. These bare places were grown up with dingy, yellow weeds, hiding innumerable tomato cans; innumerable children played upon them, chasing one another here and there, screaming and fighting. The most uncanny thing about this neighborhood was the number of the children; you thought there must be a school just out, and it was only after long acquaintance that you were able to realize that there was no school, but that these were the children of the neighborhood--that there were so many children to the block in Packingtown that nowhere on its streets could a horse and buggy move faster than a walk!

It could not move faster anyhow, on account of the state of the streets. Those through which Jurgis and Ona were walking resembled streets less than they did a miniature topographical map. The roadway was commonly several feet lower than the level of the houses, which were sometimes joined by high board walks; there were no pavements--there were mountains and valleys and rivers, gullies and ditches, and great hollows full of stinking green water. In these pools the children played, and rolled about in the mud of the streets; here and there one noticed them digging in it, after trophies which they had stumbled on. One wondered about this, as also about the swarms of flies which hung about the scene, literally blackening the air, and the strange, fetid odor which assailed one's nostrils, a ghastly odor, of all the dead things in the universe. It impelled the visitor to questions--and then the residents would explain, quietly, that all this was "made" land, and that it had been "made" by using it as a dumping ground for the city garbage. After a few years the unpleasant effect of this would pass away, it was said; but meantime, in hot weather--and especially when it rained--the flies were apt to be annoying. Was it not unhealthful? the stranger would ask, and the residents would answer, "Perhaps; but there is no telling."

A little way farther on, and Jurgis and Ona, staring open-eyed and wondering, came to the place where this "made" ground was in process of making. Here was a great hole, perhaps two city blocks square, and with long files of garbage wagons creeping into it. The place had an odor for which there are no polite words; and it was sprinkled over with children, who raked in it from dawn till dark. Sometimes visitors from the packing houses would wander out to see this "dump," and they would stand by and debate as to whether the children were eating the food they got, or merely collecting it for the chickens at home. Apparently none of them ever went down to find out.

Beyond this dump there stood a great brickyard, with smoking chimneys. First they took out the soil to make bricks, and then they filled it up again with garbage, which seemed to Jurgis and Ona a felicitous arrangement, characteristic of an enterprising country like America. A little way beyond was another great hole, which they had emptied and not yet filled up. This held water, and all summer it stood there, with the near-by soil draining into it, festering and stewing in the sun; and then, when winter came, somebody cut the ice on it, and sold it to the people of the city. This, too, seemed to the newcomers an economical arrangement; for they did not read the newspapers, and their heads were not full of troublesome thoughts about "germs."

They stood there while the sun went down upon this scene, and the sky in the west turned blood-red, and the tops of the houses shone like fire. Jurgis and Ona were not thinking of the sunset, however--their backs were turned to it, and all their thoughts were of Packingtown, which they could see so plainly in the distance. The line of the buildings stood clear-cut and black against the sky; here and there out of the mass rose the great chimneys, with the river of smoke streaming away to the end of the world. It was a study in colors now, this smoke; in the sunset light it was black and brown and gray and purple. All the sordid suggestions of the place were gone--in the twilight it was a vision of power. To the two who stood watching while the darkness swallowed it up, it seemed a dream of wonder, with its tale of human energy, of things being done, of employment for thousands upon thousands of men, of opportunity and freedom, of life and love and joy. When they came away, arm in arm, Jurgis was saying, "Tomorrow I shall go there and get a job!"

FOOTNOTES

[1]Reprinted by the permission of the author and the publisher, the University of Chicago Press.

[2]This period is lumped because of the scarcity of data. As more material was collected it was divided into appropriate stages.

[3]This represents another technique of case analysis. Students find it a clear, facile way of handling data. In the Judge Baker Foundation Studies extensive use is made of this parallel system.

[4]This illustrates an alternative study substituted for the "First Impressions" (p. 137) by a student who is already familiar with the colony to be studied. This particular document was prepared by a Lithuanian student who had lived in the colony a number of years and who is still in close

contact with the life of the area.

[5]Reprinted by the permission of the publisher, Robert Bentley, Inc.

Chapter 8.   THE LITHUANIAN IMMIGRANT FAMILY

Source - Peter Paul Jonitis, The Acculturation
of the Lithuanians of Chester, Pennsylvania, Ph.D. Thesis in Sociology,
the University of Pennsylvania, 1951.
The selection is from Chapter XIII,
"General Characteristics of the Lithuanian-American Family," pages 274-321.[1]

Overview

First generation Lithuanians were inured to poverty and land tenancy
in the Old World. They practiced frugality and, because of their strong
determination, succeeded to a large degree in owning their homes in American communities in which they settled. They sought to transplant their
traditional folk-peasant family life habits to their American environment.
They tried to recreate their Old World models in their Church and Social
Club, conducting their services and activities in their native tongue.

However, their family values and life styles were severely tested in
the heterogeneous, urbanized and industrialized American culture. They
were saddened further by what they found happening to their American born
children, who could not achieve a sense of solidarity around anything
Lithuanian. The social distance between the European born parents and
their children became widened increasingly and conflict was evident in numerous ways, such as attitudes about language usage, celebrations of
feasts and holidays, food habits, etc.

The second generation experienced increasingly secularization and a
personal individualization that confused the older generation. In Europe
the Lithuanian family was responsible for economic maintenance, recreational outlets, religious life, social affairs and other matters but in
the second generation these functions became reduced in number and in meaning. In the large rural Lithuanian family children were distinctly an
economic asset and there was an expectation of care for aged parents. The
second generation lived more for themselves, exiting as soon as possible
from their parental control by means of education, marriage, occupational
selection, and changes in residence. The old Lithuanian family, patriar-
chial in structure, was not in favor with the American born children who
thought they wanted a democratic family form.

HOME AND LAND OWNERSHIP

Home and land ownership in peasant Lithuania was a Russian controlled
prerogative. About one third of the peasant class did not own any land.
Home ownership and having a small plot of land were ideals. Among the
first-generation Lithuanians in Chester, home ownership was the rule rather than the exception. After coming to Chester these immigrants practiced great frugality. This quality of saving was one of the cardinal

virtues which foreign-born parents with considerable perseverance attempted to inculcate into their native-born children. Lithuanians became inured to poverty and cultural suppression under the Tsarist Empire. In the early years after arrival in Chester these hard-working immigrants adjusted themselves to a low standard of living. After forty or fifty years of such hard work and saving most of these Lithuanians now boast of clear title to their property. About three-quarters of these people own their homes. Most of them have fulfilled their long-cherished dreams of having their own homes and back yards where they can work in small gardens. The majority of these homes are constructed of clapboard and follow the architectural pattern of the row house. A great many of them are of the two-story type which house the parents and frequently also provide quarters for their children during the first year or two after marriage until they achieve some degree of economic independence. Typically, among the second-generation Lithuanians, home ownership remains an ideal for which they strive for many years. The majority of them, however, until they can save the necessary finances, are content to live in apartments or flats close to their aging parents.

SOCIAL MOBILITY

We mentioned that a second general characteristic of the peasant Lithuanian family was that it was a relatively stationary unit. In contrast, the first-generation family in Chester has experienced a far greater amount of the various types of mobility outlined on page 84. Primary group contacts are the greatest influence in the acculturation process. This process has been fostered by contacts on the job, on the transportation systems, while shopping, in Americanization classes, and in other types of urban contacts. American-born youth of Lithuanian parents have had even more contacts with American goods, services, persons, and ideas. The marked differential in the amount and kind of acculturation in the second-generation youth vis-à-vis their parents, who were born and raised in a comparatively sessile, agricultural society, can undoubtedly be explained in terms of the different amounts of mobility and exposure to American culture and reactions to it in the personality structure. In general men experience more mobility than women who stay at home. Men usually know more of the English language and, therefore they know more of the American culture. Nevertheless, most immigrants spend most of their leisure time within the confines of the ethnic community. Language handicaps prevent many of the foreign-born from making and keeping meaningful friendships with members of the native-American groups in or outside the Lithuanian neighborhood. Living in the Lithuanian cultural cocoon probably has been the greatest impediment to a faster rate of acculturation.

URBANISM AND THE FAMILY

The third characteristic of peasant Lithuanian family life was its folk-peasant nature. At this point we may sum up the important, relatively constant, and causally connected qualitative and quantitative characteristics of urban Chester as compared with those of rural Lithuania as follows:

1. Physical environment: the important factors in the rural world were the predominence of nature over anthropo-social environment. Rural Lithuanians had a direct relationship with nature.

Urban Lithuanians experience a greater isolation from nature. In this type of society there is a predominance of man-made environment over the natural. Other important factors are poorer air, more noise, soot, etc.

2. Size of community: in rural life open farms and small village communities were characteristic. Agriculturalism and size of the community were negatively correlated.

   In urban life the size of the community is much larger than the rural community. In short, urbanism and size of community are positively correlated.

3. Density of population: rural density was lower than urban density. In general, density and rurality were negatively correlated.

   Urbanism and density show a positive correlation.

4. Heterogeneity and homogenity of population: rural Lithuanian communities were more homogeneous than urban communities with regard to racial and psychosocial traits. Rural communities display a negative correlation with heterogeneity.

   Urban communities are more heterogeneous than rural ones. Urbanism and heterogeneity reveal a positive correlation.

5. Social differentiation and stratification: rural differentiation and stratification less than urban.

   Social differentiation and stratification show a positive correlation with urbanity.

6. Mobility: territorial, occupational, ideological, and other forms of social mobility were comparatively less intensive in rural areas. Country-to-city migration in Lithuania was neglible during the period.

   These different forms of mobility are more intensive in urban, industrial Chester. Urbanity and mobility show a positive correlation. Migration of Lithuanians from city to country, even in times of economic depression, was insignificant.

7. System of interaction: in the rural community there were less numerous contacts per man. There was a narrower area of social interaction of its members with the whole aggregate. In Lithuania a more prominent part was played by gemeinschaft contacts. There was a predominance of personal and relatively durable relations. Relations were comparatively simple and sincere. "Man was interacted as a human person."

   In the urban life of Chester there are more numerous contacts. There is a wider area of interaction per man and with the whole. Secondary or gesellschaft contacts predominate. Social relations are characteristically impersonal, casual, and ephemeral. There is greater complexity, manifoldness, superficiality, and standardized formality in social relations. Man is interacted as "number" and "address."

8. Occupation: rural life consisted of the totality of cultivators

and their families. In the community there were usually few representatives of several non-agricultural occupations.

In urban Chester, the totality of people are engaged principally in manufacturing, mechanical pursuits, trade, commerce, professions, governing, and other essentially non-agricultural occupations.[2]

Lithuanian family life in Chester, as described in the present material, underwent a profound disintegration along certain lines. In addition to the factors enumerated above, the main causes of this breakdown of the traditional folk-peasant family have been the industrialization of Chester, its concomitant secularization, personal individualization, social isolation of the marriage group despite physical propinquity in the Chester community, and the gradual process of Americanization. The traditional Lithuanian peasant family evidently can persist only in an agricultural community which has been settled for at least four or five generations, in the same local region and which permitted no significant changes of class, nationality, religion or occupation. As has been pointed out, the Chester physical and social environments produced many changes in the traditional peasant family. As soon as these changes appeared disintegration became imminent. Personal and social disorganization follow the initial-contact stage when the foreign culture comes into continued and over-increasing contact with the new culture. Folk-peasant culture then goes through a conflict stage, namely, that of acculturation. Therefore, the first-generation Lithuanian family in Chester may now be characterized as possessing a quasi-urban culture or way of life. The second-generation Lithuanian family is considerably more urban and modern than that of its European-born parents.

FAMILY INTEGRATION

A fourth characteristic of the peasant Lithuanian family was that it was a well integrated family system and culture. The first-generation family in Chester was and still is in a state of culture conflict and disorganization. The main causes of family disintegration are analyzed in another section of this study.[3] A more detailed examination of the causes, nature, and significance of parent-youth conflict is given in the section on "Interpersonal Relations."[4]

With regard to the matter of the degree of integration, disorganization, and conflict in the second-generation family, we can say in a general way that it is pretty much a direct function of the particular family situation. In short, the amount and significance of these factors is rather variable, depending on the situation of the particular family in question. Much conscious effort is devoted to sloughing off any semblance of Lithuanian culture. Name changes, such as Davidonis to Davis, are frequent occurrences.

FAMILY ORGANIZATION AND AMERICAN CULTURE

In our analysis of the peasant Lithuanian family we pointed out that the family system was strong and that the community culture was also strong and well integrated. Due to the difference in attitudes and values of the Old World family and that of the second-generation members, the former family experienced culture conflict in America. This conflict occurred in the second stage of acculturation. In a later section we shall attempt to analyze the causes and nature of this family culture conflict in more detail with particular reference to the parents and their offspring.

With respect to the second-generation family in Chester we should add that the weakened family culture was a reflection of the vague American situation. The concept of "the marginal man" clearly applies to the members of this generation. Robert E. Park used the fitting phrase of "the marginal man" for the person who must live in two cultural worlds at the same time.[5] The marginal man may be defined as the individual who occupies an in-between position--a kind of no-man's land--between two cultural groups. He lives on the precarious margin between two cultures or societies that are in a state of deep-seated conflict and never completely fuse or interpenetrate into one. In the words of Park, such a person is

"...a cultural hybrid, a man living and sharing intimately in the culture life and traditions of two distinct peoples; never quite willing to break, even if he were permitted to do so, with his past and his traditions, and not quite accepted...in the new society in which he now sought to find a place."[6]

Louis Wirth puts it thus:

"He stands on the map of two Worlds, not at home in either. His self is divided between the world that he has deserted and the world that will have none of him."[7]

The marginal man is defined by Everett V. Stonequist as

"...one who is poised in psychological uncertainty between two (or more) social worlds; reflecting in his soul the discords and harmonies, repulsions and attractions of these worlds, one of which is often "dominant" over the other; within which membership is implicitly if not explicitly based upon birth or ancestry (race or nationality); and where exclusion removes the individual from a system of group relations."[8]

"He is called on by the situation," states Kimball Young concerning the marginal man, "to participate in two divergent sets of ideas, attitudes, and habits."[9]

Culture conflict between the parent and American-born youth, especially the educated group, is incessant and bitter. Examples of it are numerous. Only one case which symbolizes this conflict will be presented here. It vividly illustrates the insurmountable hiatus between the two cultural worlds of the immigrant and his offspring.

"This happened when I was a junior in college. It was the occasion of the Junior Prom. Despite the fact that most of my friends were poor and came from immigrant homes, we very much wanted to attend this important annual social event. Most social functions we had to miss because we couldn't afford them. I had two friends in college whose fathers allowed them to have the family car on many evenings. These boys never had any difficulty in procuring the car for such affairs as a Prom. So, two weeks before the night of the Prom, I went to my father and asked him if I might have the car for the night of dance. When you plan to ask father for the car you wait until you find him in a conciliatory mood. Whenever I ask for the car he freezes and conversation proceeds with the utmost difficulty. Very patiently I explained why I wanted the car for that evening. His stock reply always is that I put too

many miles on the car and do not pay for the gas. He always
checks the number of miles I make in an evening by going to the
garage so that he can harass me at breakfast. He never fails to
accuse me of having the car "full of college bums, drinking and
speeding on the road." None of these accusations are true. I
always lose my temper when so accused. Then my father becomes
less and less cooperative about the car. His argument is that I
can take the trolley and it will cost me only forty cents to get
to the Prom and home again. Trying to explain to him that my
girl friend will wear an evening gown and corsage makes absolutely
no impression. He doesn't understand what a Prom involves. Besides, I just could not have anybody see me in a trolley with a
nice date. Nor would any girl accept a second date with me if I
made her ride in a trolley to a Prom. The net result was that I
left my father cursing him and his car. And he has no kind words
for me. All he talks about is what great sacrifices they are
making for my education. I paid my own way through college by
working. So I wound up riding with a friend whose father let him
have the car for the evening. All my friends who have immigrant
parents have the same kind of fight. We just don't understand
each other and never will."[10]

COMMUNITY LIFE

We come now to the sixth characteristic of the peasant Lithuanian
family. That is the nature of the community. It was pointed out in some
detail that the peasant Lithuanian led quite an active life in his village. After settling down in the Chester community, there was a long
period during which the immigrant was relatively inactive in the American
community. Such inactivity naturally retarded the processes of acculturation. The most important point of contact between these two different
cultures was in the work situation. For this reason the male underwent
Americanization at a more rapid rate than the female housewife who usually
kept house and took care of the children. It is to be recalled that many
of these immigrant couples had their increments to their families from two
to five years after coming to America, and, consequently, the mothers had
most of their social life limited to the home and other mothers in the
neighborhood.

Social institutions, such as the Church and the Club, patterned in
some respects after Old World models, were recreated in Chester. This is
the typical institution-building behavior of most immigrants who have
come to the United States. But Lithuanian institution-building energies
were directed mainly and almost exclusively to organizing such social institutions as the Church and the Social Club, where the "birds of a feath-
er flocked together." In the early days after immigration, the Chester
Lithuanians were very active in supporting these institutions which in
large measure perpetuated the Old World traditions and customs. Church
services were conducted by a foreign-born priest in Lithuanian. The Old
World atmosphere of the Church in time caused the younger generation to
seek religious outlets in other Catholic Churches, such as the nearby
Irish Church. Despite the constitutional objectives of the Social Club,
which stressed the importance of becoming a naturalized citizen, the members always spoke Lithuanian while attending the various functions in the
Club, including the business meetings. All the activities which took
place in the Club, whether it was a wedding reception, a shower, choral
singing concerts, or business meetings, were done in the native tongue.
Thus, the Church and the Club impeded the rate of acculturation.

In the case of the second-generation youth and family life, they were, on the whole, practically inactive in the Lithuanian community and in the social institutions founded by their parents. The causative factors involved in this smaller degree of social participation may be traced to marked differences in interest, values, and attitudes. Consequently, the second-generation youth are and will be more active in the American community and social institutions.

IN-GROUP SOLIDARITY

In peasant Lithuanian society, there was manifested much strong in-group solidarity. Among the first-generation Lithuanians in Chester there is weakened in-group esprit de corps. Social cleavages form on the basis of religious affiliation, political loyalties, occupational pursuits, and interest in the fatherland. During the recent World War group loyalty and cohesiveness to Lithuanians qua Lithuanians was heightened. Support of the cause for Lithuanian independence during the post-war period cuts across these clique lines and produces a degree of solidarity.

In the second-generation members it is very difficult to achieve any semblance of solidarity around anything Lithuanian. A large number of this highly acculturated group attend the Irish Roman Catholic Church in preference to the Church of their parents, which is located in the neighborhood. This preference is caused by the fact that many of these American-born persons are not able to speak or understand enough of the Lithuanian language which is used by the Lithuanian priest. In fact, it is quite rare to find a member of this generation who speaks the parental language well and ever rarer to come across one who is proud of such ability. Most of these generation members feel ashamed to admit they are Lithuanian in descent. In order to overcome this loss of Lithuanian youth, the Lithuanian clergyman has attempted, with mediocre success, to conduct a part of the Mass both in his native tongue and in English. Despite this effort, even those young Lithuanians who understand the language prefer to go to a church where their friends attend and where the entire service is conducted in English.

In cases where the children live some distance from the parents, familial solidarity is difficult to maintain. Only Christmas and perhaps Easter and Thanksgiving Day provide the occasion for the intermingling of family members. In a few instances the wide hiatus between the two generations in the amounts of education precludes the possibility of building bridges of understanding. Still other factors which militate against family solidarity are different occupational activities and intermarriage with non-Lithuanians. Thus, there are two sets of influences which work against the formation of in-group solidarity between these two groups in the Lithuanian population: (1) the differential experience with rapid rate of social change in a dynamic society, and (2) the differential amounts and meanings attached to the acculturation of parents as compared with their children.

FAMILY COOPERATION

A ninth characteristic of the peasant Lithuanian family which we now want to contrast with the Chester Lithuanian family is the matter of sharing of common work and goals. In the analysis of the European peasant family the factors which made such cooperation necessary were presented. It is exceedingly difficult to state with any degree of accuracy just how much sharing was practiced in the Chester first-generation family. However, one conclusion is certain, namely, that the transition from ruralism to urbanism radically changed the economic base of family life in Chester. In the latter environment children did not have the same responsibilities as siblings had in rural peasant Lithuania. The degree of sharing of common work and goals in Chester was primarily a function of the economic status of the family. If the family was at the poverty level (and the vast majority were in the early years after arrival in Chester), then the children were expected and did make some contribution to the support of the family unit. Family chores were distributed on a sex basis. Girls assisted their mothers in the numerous tasks about the household, such as preparing meals, housecleaning, and caring for the younger children. Boys were delegated the responsibility of keeping the cellar full of wood, coke, and coal during the winter months, running errands for their mothers, and holding part-time jobs in local stores, or peddling newspapers.

Very little sharing of common goals and work occurred in the second-generation family. Just about the only occasions when this happened was when the parental generation experienced some crippling crisis, such as death, protracted illness, or some other emergency.

CHILDREN: AN ECONOMIC LIABILITY

The matter of large numbers of children being an economic asset in rural Lithuania has been discussed. In the first-generation family in Chester, children were an economic asset for a few working years only and then they married and moved away from the parental home. Most native-born children of Chester parents did not go to college. It was something of a rarity to have a daughter receive such an education. Most Chester families simply could not afford an education beyond high school. In fact, immediately following the years after the arrival of these families in Chester, only one or two boys were able to obtain an education beyond that level. According to the statements of several parents and school-teachers who taught such children in the Lithuanian community, parents insisted that their children conform to the legal requirements for education and that remunerative work be started as early as possible.

In the second-generation family, children were, as in the native-American families, an economic liability. In general, the amount of education received by this generation has considerably exceeded that given to the parental generation.

In our discussion of the peasant Lithuanian family we stated that the children lived for the parents. In rural society a large family system was distinctly an economic asset. Also, in the Old World family system children were cherished as an emotional prop for aged parents. The socialization process of children in Lithuania inculcated in them a strong sense of moral obligation to take care of their aged parents. In Chester children live for themselves, especially after puberty. When these American-born children make their exit from the parental family by means of marriage, education, change of residence, occupation, or conscious choice, it is conducive to a role reversal in the first-generation family. The factor which engenders considerable parent-youth conflict is the absence of any explicit steps in the institutionalization of parental authority in this exit from the parental family. As a matter of fact, this breaking away of children from the parental controls can and does initiate deep-seated tensions between the two generations. In some cases this conflict does not subside even after the second-generation children have married and have begun to raise families of their own. The moral concern for supporting aged parents manifests itself with far less potency in Chester than it did in the Old World. Most children are eager to set up their own independent households after marriage. The more education the second-generation member has the more this seems to be the case. The same operates for choice of neighborhood. When the American-born member belongs to one of the professional classes he prefers to live in a middle-class American community. A few children contribute regularly toward the support of their aged parents. Some seem to have guilt feelings on the subject of parental sacrifice for them and attempt to salve their consciences by hectic campaigns of gift-giving on Christmas, Easter, and Mother's and Father's Days. But with increasing acculturation of the second generation the geographical and social distance between European-born parent and American-born child is ever widening.

CHANGING FAMILY FUNCTIONS

The eleventh characteristic of the peasant Lithuanian family which we analyzed was the functions performed by the Old World family. In the European setting the family was responsible for the economic maintenance, the recreational outlets, the religious life, the social affairs, provided the affectional element, and acted as the protective mechanism for the family members. In Chester, among the first-generation family members the functions are narrowed down to the economic and affectional in the main. The functions in the second-generation family have been reduced to the affectional and economic, with the latter waning in importance. This reduction in number and significance of family functions has been the resultant of the complex web of factors associated with the transition from agriculturalism to urban industrialism.[11]

TRANSMISSION OF AMERICAN CULTURE

In peasant Lithuania culture was transmitted mainly by the family and the church. Education played a minor role in this process since the Lithuanian schools were controlled by the Russians who staffed these institutions with Russian personnel. Most of the education was given at home. Among the first-generation family members in Chester, Lithuanian culture is passed on by the parents to the younger American-born siblings. The Lithuanian language is spoken in the home until the children are well along in grammar school. As these children go through high school more and more English is used with the parents at home. In some homes the parents speak Lithuanian exclusively, while their children always answer them in English. This situation has fostered the development of the bilingual personality.[12] Since the children were educated in the American school system (there being no parochial school at the local church), they became important transmitters of American culture to their parents. The American way of life was also brought to the parents by American institutions, such as the economic system, political life in the community, the church, and by contacts on a personal basis with other Americans in the community. From the standpoint of acculturation it is important to emphasize the fact that there is a differential internalization of American culture between the parental and American-born generation.

FAMILY CELEBRATIONS

A thirteenth characteristic which we presented was the fact that in rural Lithuania there were many family celebrations, special religious feasts and fasts, holidays of religious and national importance, and name days. Among the first-generation Chester Lithuanians there are distinctly fewer family celebrations of feast and holidays. Urbanism, industrialism, and the forces of secularism have made considerable inroads into the continuation of these customs and practices. When twelve family heads were asked to explain the reasons for the weakening of religious and cultural traditions, they stated that after working twelve to fourteen hours in the factory (before 1920), they just did not have any energy left to comply with all the requirements of the church and the Old World culture.

The significance and the frequency with which the first-generation members observe the various religious and nationalistic feasts and holidays seems to be associated to some extent with the degree of religiosity of the family. In general, these observances were taken far more seriously by those families which were known as "good Catholics" in the neighborhood. According to the priest, a good Catholic is one who attends church every Sunday, goes to confession and Holy Communion as often as prescribed by the Church, adheres closely to Church law and ritual, such as during the Lenten season, and supports the Church and its objectives either by offering his personal services or by making donations of money. These constitute the criteria of a good Catholic and Church member. The priest stated that, according to these criteria, about one-half of his parishioners are good Catholics and had "good standing" in the Church. The other one-half observed only such holidays as Christmas, Easter, and the more important patron saint days, such as Svente Kazimieras, Lietuvos Globejas (St. Casimir's Day), which came on March 4th. Religious holidays assume more importance than nationalistic holidays among these people. The last World War caused a slight recrudescence in sentiment for the fatherland.

About one-fourth of the first-generation Lithuanian families in Chester observed the Christmas traditions and customs in 1948. In Lithuania Christmas is celebrated for several days. In Chester the more religious elements of this holiday and their strict observance are definitely on the wane. Only five families were found to observe the full Lithuanian ritual of Christmas.

In the Old World the festivities began on Christmas Eve with the appearance of the first star in the sky. Each person seated at the table was given a brightly colored wafer, called the plotkeles. This wafer had been previously consecrated in church. Each person shared his wafer with everyone present at this celebration. The plotkeles was a symbol of good will and harmony. After this ritual all sat down to the evening repast. Since December 24th is a fast day, no meat is served at this meal. In Lithuania the fish most commonly served on this occasion was the pike. In Chester it is the herring or some other type purchased at the local market. At this meal, fish soup, fried cabbage, and a traditional dish called kisjelius, which is made from oatmeal and served with cream and sugar, are served. Large, homemade loaves of dark rye bread are placed on the table. This bread is sprinkled liberally with poppy seeds and stamped with the image of the Christ Child. Hay or straw is placed underneath the tablecloth in memory of the night at Bethlehem.[13]

In Lithuania, Christmas Mass was celebrated at five o'clock on Christmas morning, but in Chester the Lithuanians attend this Mass at midnight. In the Old Country and in Chester, the churches are decorated with evergreens and flowers. In these churches there is always a crèche and usually it is shown against a background of rocks, trees, and houses depicting the town of Bethlehem. During the Mass in Lithuania old Christmas carols,

which have been handed down from past generations, were sung by the parishioners. These carols are held in high esteem and reverence. In Chester
these carols are sung but with decreasing significance. In Lithuania the
custom of gift-giving was not practiced, but in Chester the Lithuanians
have adopted this custom. As in several other European countries, it was
on St. Nicholas Day, December 6th, that the Kalėdū Diedukas, the old man
corresponding to Santa Claus, made his appearance and distributed presents
to the children.

In Lithuanian, Christmas Day was usually passed quietly as a family
affair, but the second and third Christmas Days, St. Stephan's Day and the
Day of John the Baptist, were occasions for much gaiety and merriment. In
certain areas of Lithuania, on December 28th, Holy Innocents' Day, there
were puppet shows, representing King Herod passing sentence on the children
of Bethlehem.

In Lithuania there was an amusing New Year's Eve custom. After the
evening meal, two or three masked men and women, carrying flaring torches,
called at some house in the village. They were entertained with the best
the house could afford; there was gay music and dancing. When they left
their host and hostess, also masked, the latter accompanied the group to
the next house. In this manner the torchlit procession grew to large numbers, eventually including most of the inhabitants of the village and the
people living on nearby farms.[14]

To commemorate the visit of the Three Kings to Bethlehem, three
crosses, usually made of evergreen, were fastened above the door of the
Lithuanian home, where they remained until January 6th, the day of Epiphany, and also of the Three Kings. In the evening of that day, men in
costume representing the Three Kings went from house to house and once
more there was feasting and merriment.

Very few Chester Lithuanians observe the poltkeles ritual of the
Christmas Eve supper. Some parents will carry out the full observance of
this custom for the benefit of their children. But as these American-born
children get older, there is less and less interest in this traditional
custom and, in fact, all things Lithuanian. Second-generation children
very rarely sing Lithuanian Christmas carols. Santa Claus and gift-ex-
changing in Chester are done on December 25th. Christmas is the one day
in the year when all the members of the family make every effort to be together. St. Stephen's Day and the Day of the John the Baptist are not
celebrated by second-generation, or, for that matter, by the first-generation members any more in Chester. Holy Innocents' Day and puppet shows
are not the common store of knowledge of second-generation Lithuanians.
The New Year's Eve customs, as described above, are never seen in Chester.
Three crosses symbolic of the Three Kings who visited Bethlehem, are not
displayed on doors. In their place, the customary American decorations
are observed during the Yule season. The Christmas greeting among Lithuanians, Linksmū Kalėdū, is seldom heard from second-generation Lithuanians.

Among peasant Lithuanians, as among practically all European peoples,
the pig and its products form a large portion of Christmas menus. It is
still quite a prevalent custom, especially in rural districts and in villages, for the thrifty household to slaughter a pig shortly before Christmas
and to prepare from it all sorts of food--sausages, head cheese, blood pud-
ding, pigs feet and bacon--to be eaten during the holiday season and the
ensuing winter months. According to some authorities, the popularity of
the pig is a survival from pagan times when a pig was considered the most
acceptable sacrifice to Frey, the beloved sun god of the Norsemen and Sax-

ons, and flesh of a pig was the daily food of the heroes in Valhalla. It is generally believed that our Christmas is a blend of a religious festival celebrating the nativity of Christ and of Yule, the mid-winter festival at which the heathen peoples of the North rejoiced in the returning sun.

Among the peasant Lithuanians the pig constituted a considerable portion of the Christmas bill of fare. The following courses made up a typical Christmas dinner menu: soup, commonly made from clear beef buillon or dried mushrooms; roast suckling pig with sauerkraut; roast potatoes; baked apples; a spring salad consisting of lettuce, sliced radishes, scallions, cucumbers, sour cream mixed in the salad (this was served after 1914); and applecakes.

At Christmas time, among the Chester Lithuanians, pig is seldom served for dinner. Three Lithuanian farmers lived outside the Chester city limits in Delaware County. The poor farmer is more apt to have roast pig for Christmas than the urban dweller. But even in rural areas, and more particularly among the more prosperous Lithuanian farmers, this meat appears with diminishing frequency at Christmas time. In Chester, the most common meat served for Christmas dinner is either chicken or turkey. In addition to this main course the Lithuanian housewife frequently serves with great pride homemade plain and smoked sausages, sauerkraut soup (very few Lithuanians nowadays make their own sauerkraut), cooked wheat served with sweetened water, cubed pieces of baked dough about an inch square in size, a mixture of ground poppy seed and sweetened water, and mushroom soup in which bits of baked herring and finely cut up beets have been added. In the earlier days after arrival in Chester, first-generation Lithuanians frequently went on mushroom gathering trips to the woods in the country. They were and still are regarded as "foods fit for the gods" to be dried and served at Christmas time. Mushrooms are dried in the oven and hung up in the shed or some room to dry. Despite the prohibitive price of mushrooms (grybai) of late, the number of Lithuanians who pick their own is becoming less and less every year. Most second-generation members may enjoy the hunt for mushrooms in the woods but when it comes to eating them, especially the fried variety, nausea destroys the appetite. These mushrooms are not the white variety which Americans ordinarily purchase in a market. The ones eaten by Lithuanians are large, yellow, and umbrella-shaped. Some of the older families are quite industrious and manage to collect a large supply of mushrooms for the winter. The same is true for berry picking, except that most second-generation children hate to pick them but cannot attain satiety with the parental supply.

Even after some forty or fifty years of residence in Chester, changes in food habits come about at a very slow pace. But acculturation in this area of life has made considerable modification in foods which appear on the daily typical Lithuanian table. The amount of change and the rapidity with which typical American foods and recipes are taken over into the Lithuanian culinary regime seem to be governed by the socio-economic status of the particular family. The better this position, the more the change to American foods. The poorer the family people, the slower the transition. A fairly reliable index of acculturation is how much and how well the immigrant speaks English. If he knows the language with a high degree of proficiency, the more he will like American foods. And the reverse is true. Lithuanian business men and professional men, for example, eat both kinds of food more or less indiscriminately but have an occasional yen for "a good old Lithuanian" dish. The immigrant who cannot speak English usually will show a strong preference for Lithuanian foods and a similar distaste and low opinion for American dishes. Thus, language alone is one of the chief instrumentalities by which the Lithuanian immigrant learns the finer connotations of American culture on the material level.

It is significant that members of the second-generation Lithuanian family, when visiting with their parents or relatives, show an increasing dislike for Lithuanian dishes. The more extensive acculturation of this generation undoubtedly lies behind this culinary preference. In some families the mother becomes quite upset when her children refuse outright to eat these traditional Lithuanian recipes at Christmas time. The conflict between the two generations on this occasion can be flamed to the point of abrupt exit from the parental home. The writer has been present at such gatherings. The spark initiating the bitter disappointment to the mother was provided when an American-born son brought a native-born friend of native-American family with him to such a dinner. Most Americans do not care to be invited again for the consumption of "slippery mushrooms and baked herring in beet soup." Another gastronomic coup de grâce was the diplomatic attempt on this same occasion by the guest to please his hostess by eating her hot sauerkraut liberally loaded with melted salt pork, some of which floated on top of the dish in small pieces. This episode is an illustration par excellence of conflict between two generations seated at the same table. Both generations have Lithuanian cultural backgrounds but the children have absorbed more of the American culture than have the parents. Such situations, when the parent works very hard and long to "give my son a nice Christmas," are nothing short of tragic.

Palm Sunday, the Sunday before Easter, was a day of great religious significance in Catholic Lithuania. On this day the "palm" was blessed. In Lithuania real palms were not obtainable and pussy-willows were used as substitutes. The peasants took gaily decorated pussy-willows to church to be blessed by the priest. On Good Friday the entombment of Christ was re-enacted with great solemnity and sorrow. The Easter service in Lithuania was a daytime one and was regarded as one of the most important among the numerous religious events on the calendar. After this service the people went home to an elaborate Easter dinner. Before sitting down to this meal family members and guests exchanged beautifully decorated eggs (called velykų kiaušinis or margutis) along with good wishes. In some rural districts it was the custom to give some of the food which had been blessed in church to the farm animals, on the theory that so doing would assure them good health for the year.[15]

Palm Sunday is also an important religious holiday among the Chester Lithuanian Catholics. Real palms are distributed to the parishioners. Easter dinner in many families is as important as the Christmas dinner. Gaily decorated eggs are still exchanged and eaten on Easter morning. The game of egg-breaking is still played by parents but more by the children. Some housewives achieve attractive coloring of eggs by boiling them in a solution of onion skins which have been saved for this special occasion. This gives them a deep reddish brown color. This game consists of testing the hardiness and solidarity of an egg. Before the child competes in this game, he choses an egg by tapping both ends against the teeth or some other hard object. Then the child holds an egg firmly in his fist while the parent cautiously taps his egg against the child's egg until one is broken. Blunt ends are matched with blunt ends and pointed ends with pointed ends. This game is a source of great delight to the young children. The champion's egg competes with more eggs later in the day. Among second-generation families this Easter egg-breaking custom has all but disappeared. However, the mothers still color the eggs for their children.

Another interesting holiday in peasant Lithuania was Thanksgiving Day.

A most joyous festival, the nubaigai, (from nubaigti, meaning to finish or to end), marked the culmination of the fall harvesting season. At that time landowners kept open house for all who had assisted in the harvesting and for their families. An abundant feast was prepared for the harvesters and dancing, games, singing, and merrymaking lasted until late at night. This celebration was one of the most anticipated of the year in the life of the peasant.

A large number of harvest customs and celebrations have been passed down to present generations. In the observance of these harvest customs the real essence of Lithuanian culture is revealed. Formerly, the Lithuanian farmers, at the harvest season, killed a cock and a hen without bloodshed. This was a survival of a harvest sacrifice. The fowl were then eaten by the family. Servants were not allowed to be present at this procedure. In Lithuania, the last sheaf of grain, dressed as an old woman, called the Boba (the old woman), was borne in triumphal procession to the farm. Sometimes the person who bound the last sheaf was wrapped up in it. At the farmhouse every effort was made by the farmer and his family to drench the Boba with water so as to ensure plenty of rain for next year's crops. The harvest usually was featured in this celebration, but the mode of presenting it was somewhat unique. The most beautiful girl walked at the head of the procession, carrying the wreath on a plate covered with a white linen cloth. As the reapers advanced toward the house, they sang an old song which told how they have rescued the master's crop from a hugh bison (probably symbolic of winter) that would have devoured it and how they have brought the rye safely into his barn. On entering the farm yard, they changed to songs in honor of the master and his family. Then the wreath was presented and the master thanked everyone and gave a gift to every girl in the procession. One of the harvesters usually delivered a speech at this juncture. According to tradition, the speech had to end with a meaningless jumble of Latin and French or Polish words. This latter usage was thought to have been a satire on the use of foreign languages by the great landed proprietors of Lithuania of the past. The following translation of an ancient Lithuanian harvest speech or poem is representative:

"From deep forest, from trackless swamps, pursued by famine
we wandered about in search of a valley, strewn with flowers,
silvered by rye, gilded by wheat. We wandered through dark
woods and birch groves, over treacherous bogs, over innumerable
bees' nests and over the lairs of bear. We suffered from cold
and rain and no one showed us any pity. At last an old bear had
the kindness to tell os: keep on going, go where your feet carry you, go where the finches fly and you will come to (here they
insert the name of their master) who lives on a farm surrounded
by tall maples, and who has immense acres sown with corn and
only a few labourers in the house. Go to him, help him to harvest his corn and he will give you enough to eat and drink. We
came to thee, pacious master, we have harvested thy corn and
now we bring thee a wreath, not of gold or silver, but of rye
like diamonds, of wheat like amber. Clarissime eminentissime
Vestra dominatis, oratis, vocatio, sinter terre vere gruski
garnuski lopatum, kofatum, co to ya pank statum..."[16]

For the second-generation members who live some distance from their parents, Christmas is the only family affair of any importance. Easter and Thanksgiving Day are of less importance. The observance of these holidays as two-generation family affairs depends upon the degree of attachment the member has for his parents and his distance from them.

94

With regard to the celebration of secular or national holidays by the first-generation, the following conclusions may be noted. Lietuvos Nepriklausomybės Šventė (Lithuanian Independence Day), which falls on February 16th, is not universally commemorated by all Lithuanians in Chester. Those few who want to observe this day go to the Social Club in Philadelphia, where the Lithuanians annually put on some appropriate program for this occasion.

Many reasons have been offered by the Chester Lithuanians for this disinterest in their national Independence Day. Several decades of living in America have deadened interest in the Old Country. Most of them say, "We are Americans now and our loyalties lie her. Besides, Russia now controls the mother country." This is the typical attitude. Support of causes takes money. Many Lithuanians are not willing to make any sizable financial donation toward the restoration of a free and independent Lithuania. At meetings of organizations which are dedicated to this cause, the average Lithuanian laborer, when he gives a twenty-five cent piece or half of a dollar, thinks that he has made a worthy contribution. During World War II Russia again seized control of the Baltic nations. Because of this fact a marked feeling of fultility permeates the minds of many of this foreign-born group. They believe that to overthrow the domination of the Soviet Union over Lithuania is like trying to hold back the sea with the palm of your hand. Years of living in the United States has banked the patriotic fires for the motherland. Many no longer have any close relatives there. Person after person stated, "I have all I can do to maintain my economic security here before I die." According to community gossip, twelve Lithuanians approved the control of Lithuania by the Soviet Union. This small group is labeled with the damaging epithet "pro-Russian." Among the majority this "Bolshevik group", as they are called, is experiencing pariah status. Careful and discrete investigation revealed that only two foreign-born Lithuanians openly stated that "Lithuania would be better off under Stalin." These two persons, who spoke good English and who read the New York Times (very unusual for this group of foreign-born), based their opinions on the belief that the era of small nations is doomed. They sincerely argued that small nations, such as Lithuania, could survive only when they are protected by some great power, such as the Soviet Union. These two Lithuanians are espousers of the doctrine of Realpolitik.

Perhaps the best barometer of genuine interest in the mother country is the amount of money these people contribute to various organizations which are working for the achievement of Lithuanian independence. Most of them stated that they simply could not afford to make any substantial donation for this purpose even though they had strong sentiments in that direction. But fervent chauvinistic speechmaking comes forth unflaggingly on this holiday in the Lithuanian community in Philadelphia and the larger urban centers, such as Chicago and New York City. With increasing acculturation the bulk of these foreign-born Lithuanians in Chester demonstrate diminishing interest in the country of their birth. World War II saw a renascence of nationalism which subsided during the post-war period. Intellectual displaced persons living in Chester have been partially responsible for this rivial of nationalistic sentiment.

Among the members of the second-generation Lithuanians there is a marked negative interest in the Lithuanian nationalistic holidays. This younger generation never attends such meetings in Chester or Philadelphia. Their lack of interest toward such holidays is to be explained by the fact of American birth, American education, and social relationships almost entirely in American social circles. Most of them do not even care if they never see the birthplace of their parents. In this respect the

95

cleavage between the two generations is apparently irreparable. In short, this generation, as compared with their parents, falls toward the more acculturated end of the continuum.

ORGANIZATION OF THE CHESTER LITHUANIAN-AMERICAN FAMILY

Whether the Lithuanian-American family in Chester is a patriarchy, matriarchy, or egalitarian in type is very difficult to say with any degree of accuracy and validity. As was pointed out in the discussion of the power structure in peasant Lithuania, the best that can be done is to characterize the family type from the point of view of the official culture.

The totality of rights of the husband vis-à-vis those of the wife in Chester are determined by the Catholic Church, the statutory law, prevailing opinion of the community, and the local mores. Since more than one-half of these foreign-born Lithuanians are nominally members of the local church, religion offers a strong buttressing of patriarchy. The local priest, when questioned on this matter, stated there are definite catechistic writings in the Catholic Bible which sanction male dominance in the family unit. In short, according to this view wives and children are subordinate to the father.[17] In litigation both the husband and wife possess equality before the law in such matters as inheritance and disposition of property. Public opinion supports the subordination of spouses and children. The local mores also support this positioning of family members. With the exception of the legal personality of the wife, all the other institutions of the Lithuanian social structure accord superior status to the married male. When all is told then, the Lithuanian family in Chester, from the standpoint of the official culture is a patriarchal organization.

As Pareto has well said, there is a wide gap between professed ideals and actions and everyday behavior. This is a particularly keen observation in the matter of the daily functioning of official patriarchy. A few examples will suffice to make this point clear. Take first the matter of family finance. All the men who were questioned on this point gave strong positive replies as to who carried and handled the family money. Yet in actual practice, 40 per cent of the married women carried and managed the financial details of the family. The curious thing is that ten men who stoutly claimed patriarchy in this respect did not actually either carry the daily money supply or pay the bills. In fact, one man who had just finished saying that he was the "boss of the money" asked his wife, who was on her way to the grocery store, for a dollar for some beer at the Club! Two men admitted quite openly that their wives were far superior to them in the matter of handling family finance. Another interesting aspect of finance is the way the pay check of youth under twenty-one years of age are regarded in the immigrant family. Not one case was found where the father permitted his gainfully employed child to keep all his earnings. Rather, parents, and more particularly the father, made unmistakable demands that the working child shall turn over all or a substantial portion of his earnings to his mother as part of his contribution to the support of the family. The underlying parental philosophy was that if one person works, all members of the family will eat. It does not need much imagination nor does it require scientific documentation to say that such a patriarchal ruling in regard to children's earnings frequently caused much bitter vituperation and conflict between the parent and the American-born child who had quite different attitudes about the subject.

In the Chester Lithuanian family the married men usually assumed total initiative in any legal matters affecting the family. There are several reasons for male dominance in this sphere. In the first place, there is a decided diffusion of Old World ideas. Men always handled legal affairs with the Russian officials in Lithuania. In Chester the family man had much more contact with the outside world, especially in his daily occupation. For this reason husbands had a much better command of the English language and things American than the wives. Three-fourths of the married women interviewed could not speak English. Illiteracy was common among the older married women. In fact, only two foreign-born men in Chester could be regarded as highly literate and well Americanized by any standards. Therefore, men took legal matters in their hands. Legal affairs were as a rule limited to such things as making out bills of sale, property titles, mortgages on real estate, and partnership papers. Only one man out of the total of ninety had been involved in court proceedings. This was for non-support of his family.

Another common test of patriarchy is, who disciplines the children? In Chester it was common practice for the mother to punish unruly children for minor infractions. Older and stronger children, especially boys, who had been found guilty of major deviations from the family norms, were dealt with by the father. In contrast to the so-called "enlightened American family," punishment in the immigrant family never took the form of discourse with the child so that he could see his wrong, but serious disobedience was met with solid, unforgettable strokes from a belt or stick.

In contrast to the cultural pattern in native-American families in Chester, it is common procedure for the working husband to sit down first at the table and to be served first by the wife. In all the writer's experience with the Lithuanian family over a period of some thirty years never once did he see the reverse of this custom at the table. In the early days after arrival in Chester this practice was quite automatic. Children accepted the situation. The hard-working father as a rule received the first dish of food and he ate ahead of all others seated at the table. This is the custom even when guests are at the table. It is, of course, possible that there were some exceptions to this practice. These eating habits are characteristic of the laboring classes. In the period before the first World War practically all immigrants belonged to this class. In later years these habits were changed toward more democratic practices due to Americanization and acculturation. But the customs described above were typical of Lithuanian immigrant laboring classes. American educated children play an important part in the change of Old World customs in this regard.

With respect to etiquette we may make the following observations. Immigrant Lithuanian men do not stand up when a woman enters a room or joins him at the table. The writer has never seen this happen in any Lithuanian home. The same holds for men assisting women who are about to sit at the table. Women seat themselves without the assistance of men. No matter what the situation, immigrant men, who are uneducated, do not remove their hats in the presence of women.

Still another indication of the male attitude toward women is seen in the matter of sexual intercourse and relationships. Evidence on this subject is not easy to procure. Out of thirty men, chosen because of their putative broadmindedness on the subject, only a third of them frankly answered questions on this subject. Because of the very personal nature of the investigation, the remainder refused to offer any information. Ten men did answer this part of the questionnaire. The gist of their replies was that their wives should permit them sexual relations whenever

they (the husbands) so desired. Only one man added that such relationships could be withheld when the wife is sick or indisposed from some other cause. These ten men also stated that their wives should not under any
circumstances, ever admit to anyone other than their husbands that they
enjoyed the sexual act (lytiškai santikiai).

When it came to interviewing wives on sexual matters, Lithuanian husbands did not permit such interviews in their absence. This is the prime
reason for the lack of cooperation from the wives. In addition, the potent modesty taboo on this subject originating from the European background
prevented cooperation. Two husbands told the writer, in very stern tones,
that he absolutely was not permitted to interview their wives about sexual
matters while they were not at home. Only two women were found who would
cooperate with the questions asked concerning sex. They did so only after
several meetings. Thirty married women, one after another, refused to be
questioned on the subject even when their husbands were at home. The two
who cooperated did so without the knowledge of the husbands. Only one
husband threatened physical violence if the questionnaire involved sexual
relationships. The two women who agreed to cooperate were interviewed in
Lithuanian in the most delicate manner concerning their sexual behavior.
The upshot of their statements was that they did not believe in male domi-
nence in this most intimate of human experiences. They offered the information with considerable modesty but were firmly opposed to any male pre-
rogatives dictated by the official culture. It must be remembered that
here again, as in the management of finances, there may be a wide gap between what is reported and what is every-day reality.

Finally, we may say a few words about patriarchy and parental influence in choice of marital partner. Generalizations as to whether the father or the mother had more to say about mate selection are meaningless. In
Chester, among the Lithuanians there was a distinct but largely inarticu-
late sentiment in favor of endogamous marriage with Catholic Lithuanians.
With the exception of five parents such a marriage was preferred. However,
intermarriage in the second-generation members has proceeded to such an
extent that most parents have resigned themselves to positions of non-
violent opposition. Acculturation is hastened in this way, as individuals
with divergent cultures meet and mingle their traditions, customs, and
blood.

In the foregoing observations of the every-day operations of the family power structure, it can be seen that there are some cases which support
unofficial matriarchy and some which point toward practical patriarchy.
Detailed analysis of family organization and function shows that the family type does not fall neatly into clean-cut categories. Any attempt,
therefore, to attach a convenient label to the Lithuanian family in Chester serves merely as an heuristic device, but it contains serious methodo-
logical weaknesses. From the standpoint of acculturation, the evidence
seems to point to a weakening of patriarchy. In some families it remains
purely as a fiction in the mind of the male. In others it is as strong as
it was in peasant Lithuania. In fewer still there was evidence of an egalitarian family. The American-born children prefer the latter type. In
the final analysis, much rests upon the nature and strength of the personalities involved in family interpersonal interaction. In the second-
generation Lithuanian family patriarchy is in the twilight zone. An emer-
gent democratic structure is in the making.

RELIGION AND SECULAR INFLUENCES ON THE FAMILY

In the European setting the emphasis was upon the sacred. In Chester the emphasis on the sacred is weakened. The traditional patriarchal monogamy is at the present time undergoing thorough reconstruction in urban civilization. The major factors which contribute to the undermining of the traditional family are the economic developments associated with modern industrialism and the growth of a secular attitude which challenges the authoritarian religious bases of the conventional family unit. The growth of the modern factory system, the evolution of modern industrialism, the entrance of women into industry, the spread of universal education, the emergence of a single standard for both sexes, the urban way of life, and the automobile and its effects upon the courtship mores and social life have all played their part. Along with these broad economic and institutional changes to the personal attitudes of those who seek marriage. Last but not least should be mentioned the impact of science and technology upon contemporary religion.[18]

Among the second-generation members the emphasis is upon the secular. This differential emphasis has been the root cause of much parent-youth conflict. All that we can say here is that secularism, which has been espoused to a greater extent in the second than in the first-generation Lithuanians, is traceable to the main currents in the American social order with its worship of the cult of success, the excessive preoccupation with materialistic goals and the cash nexus, individuation in personal life, and the apotheosis of science as an effective panacea for our leading social problems.

At this point let us make some concluding observations on the organization of the Lithuanian family in Chester. The family is the most intimate of all social groups. As Folsom has pointed out, the unity of any group depends upon the degree of similarity of values and attitudes held by the various members.[19] The Lithuanian family is no exception. The normal family consists of a "unity of interacting personalities," as Burgess put it.[20] It is held together by certain psychological factors. When these factors are attenuated, the family becomes disorganized. The second generation Lithuanian family members, while living with their parents are in a state of disorganization. Internal conflicts and external pressures loosen the bonds of the primary group. A breakdown in consensus is the result. Conflict may take the form of domestic discord, which may make the cooperative work of the family members difficult, although it may not proceed to the point of a break in the formal unity of the family. On occasion the tensions engendered by the fundamental lack of family harmony may lead to extreme disintegration in the form of alcoholism or desertion. Only two cases of the latter were discovered in Chester. Family quarreling due to the former cause was found in six cases. The disorganization of the family did go as far as desertion and divorce in the second-generation. In these latter cases there was the sociological and legal termination of the family.

According to Elliott and Merrill, the following factors characterize family organization.[21]

1. Unity of Objectives. An organized family unit has unity in its purposes or objectives. This means that the family members hold similar attitudes on the most vital of their cooperative efforts. Simiarly defined attitudes operate in such mutual concerns as the place of the family residence, the question of sexual relations, the disbursement of the family finances for various items, the care and discipline of children, their

schooling, religious life, and other matters of a very personal nature. The organized and effective family is the one in which the attitudes and values on these common objectives are given common definition by all family members. As has been pointed out, these common goals are not given a similar definition by the American-born youths of Lithuanian parents in Chester. These two generations do not define these situations in terms of common values.

2. Unity of Personal Ambitions. In Lithuania the individual members of the peasant family possessed life organizations and personalities which did not markedly deviate from those of their parents or the rest of society. Complete agreement of the personal ambitions of the second-generation members, especially the more educated ones, with the welfare and interests of the parental generation is very hard to maintain because of the development of the personality of American-born youth in an individualistic society. In Lithuania, the family was well organized because the individual members subordinated their interests and ambitions to the welfare of the family as an aggregate. Second-generation children, particularly when they attain young adulthood, find it increasingly difficult to adjust their personal ambitions for the good of the parental family unit. Family organization is threatened, for example, when second-generation children leave home early or marry outside the Lithuanian group and set up residence at some distance from the parents. In general, this generation is earnestly seeking professional and occupational positions which accord more status than that enjoyed by their parents. The degree of individuality which it is possible to achieve in American society cannot be compared to that which was possible in peasant Lithuania some half century or more ago. In the Old World the welfare of the family group was vital. The individual did not have a life apart from his family group. In Chester, such a complete merger of interests is difficult where each person attempts to live life as he sees it. Nevertheless, the degree to which there is a "consensus of opinion" among the family members in the Lithuanian family constitutes a measure of its effective organization. In many cases the household is one divided against itself. It perseveres because the members are willing and do accommodate their different views and personalities.

3. Unity of Interests. The members of the peasant Lithuanian family possessed substantially similar interests in all vital matters affecting the unit, since their lives were so largely circumscribed by the same kind of social surroundings. With respect to religion, occupation, education, and leisure time activities the family members participated as a unit. Such a close harmony of interests is clearly no longer possible in the modern urban life of Chester. In the American social milieu the various members of the family develop different interests by virtue of the statuses and roles they play in gesellschaft groups. A considerable identity of interest in religion, economic activities, education, and recreational outlets is characteristic of an organized family. In a disorganized family there is considerable dissimilarity in these interests. When the members of the family possess common definitions in these realms of life, the reciprocal relationships of family living function with more smoothness than when these interests lack basic similarity. Such is the fundamental nature of the conflict between the parental and second-generation Lithuanians.

FOOTNOTES

[1] Reprinted by the permission of the author.

[2] These rural-urban differences are taken from P. Sorokin and C. C. Zimmerman, Principles of Rural-Urban Sociology, New York, Henry Holt and Co., 1929, pp. 13-59.

[3] Cf. pp. 214-216.

[4] Cf. pp. 378-410.

[5] "Human Migration and the Marginal Man," American Journal of Sociology, Vol. 33 (May, 1928), pp. 881-893. The phrase marginal man was first used in this sense by Park. The idea has been developed further by E. V. Stonequist in The Marginal Man: A Study in Personality and Culture Conflict, New York, Charles Scribners and Sons, 1937, and "The Problem of the Marginal Man," American Journal of Sociology, Vol. 41 (July, 1935), pp. 1-12. Cf. also, M. A. Elliott and F. E. Merrill, Social Disorganization, New York, Harper and Bros., 1950, pp. 580-582.

[6] Op. cit., p. 892.

[7] Louis Wirth, The Ghetto, Chicago, University of Chicago Press, 1928, p. 265.

[8] Op. cit., p. 8.

[9] An Introductory Sociology, New York, American Book Co., 1934, p. 512.

[10] A case history in the possession of the author.

[11] For a more detailed analysis of this subject see H. E. Barnes, Society in Transition, New York, Prentice-Hall, Inc., 1942, especially Chaps. 1, 7, and 12; Ray E. Baber, Marriage and the Family, New York, McGraw-Hill Book Co., Inc., 1939, pp. 585-589; J. K. Folsom, The Family, New York, John Wiley and Sons, Inc., 1934, pp. 173-215; Ralph Linton, "The Natural History of the Family," in R. N. Anshen, (Editor), The Family: Its Functions and Destiny, New York, Harper and Bros., 1949, pp. 18-38; W. Goodsell, A History of Marriage and the Family, New York, The MacMillan Co., 1934, pp. 458-481; and J. H. S. Bossard, Social Change and Social Problems, New York, Harper and Bros., 1938, pp. 595-604.

[12] On bilingualism and marginal personality, see J. H. S. Bossard, op. cit., pp. 200-221; for an excellent summary of the writings on bilingalism, cf. Seth Arsenian, "Bilingualism in the Post-War World," Psychological Bulletin, Vol. 42, (February, 1945), pp. 65-86.

[13] For a more detailed account of Christmas customs in Lithuania see John Balys, Lietuviu Tautosakos Skaitymai, Tubingen, Patria, 1948, Part II, pp. 99-104.

[14] More details of Lithuanian New Year's Day customs are given in John Balys, op. cit., pp. 104-108.

[15] For more details on Easter in Lithuania see John Balys, op. cit., Part II, pp. 122-124. For pictures of decorated eggs see J. Baltrusaitis, op. cit., pp. 72-76.

[16] This quotation, full of grammatical errors, is taken from Age A. Benedictsen, Lithuania, _The Awakening of a Nation_, Copenhagen, Egmont H. Petersens, 1924, p. 66.

[17] For the official Catholic view on marriage see the text, _supra_, pp. 113-114.

[18] More detailed analyses of the causes of the rise of secularism are contained in H. E. Barnes, _Social Institutions_, New York, Prentice-Hall, Inc., 1946, pp. 608-613; R. E. L. Faris, _Social Disorganization_, New York, The Ronald Press, 1948, pp. 280-284; M. A. Elliott and F. E. Merrill, _op. cit._, pp. 343-366; A. G. Truxal and F. E. Merrill, _The Family in American Culture_, New York, Prentice-Hall, Inc., 1947, pp. 3-255; and F. C. Dietz, _The Industrial Revolution_, New York, Henry Holt and Co., 1927.

[19] For a good analysis of values and family organization, cf. Joseph K. Folsom, "Changing Values in Sex and Family Relations." _American Sociological Review_, Vol. 2, (October, 1937), pp. 717-726.

[20] Cf. E. W. Burgess, "The Family as a Unity of Interacting Personalities," _The Family_, Vol. 7 (March, 1926), pp. 3-9.

[21] _Op. cit._, pp. 331-332.

Chapter 9. THE RELIGIOUS LIFE OF AMERICAN LITHUANIANS

<u>Source</u> - Rev. Casimir Peter Sirvaitis. <u>Religious Folk-</u>
<u>ways in Lithuania and Their Conservation Among</u>
<u>the Lithuanian Immigrants in the United States.</u>
<u>(A Study With Conclusions on Acculturation).</u>
Abstract of a Dissertation in Sociology, The
Catholic University of America Press, Washing-
ton, D. C., 1952. The selection is from Part
Two, "Religious Folkways Among the Lithuanian
Immigrants in the United States," pages 26-49.[1]

Overview

In his research the Rev. Sirvaitis selected five Lithuanian centers
in the United States. These included Shenandoah, Pennsylvania, the oldest
Lithuanian community, with about 4,000 people of Lithuanian descent; Chicago, Illinois, the largest Lithuanian settlement, with about 100,000 of
Lithuanian descent; Mason County, Michigan, the largest Lithuanian agricultural colony, with about 1,000 Lithuanian families; Waterbury, Connecticut,
with about 5,000 of Lithuanian descent and Cleveland, Ohio, with more than
10,000 of Lithuanian descent. He lived in these settlements for about
three years and his techniques of study included direct observations and
planned interviews.

The purpose of his research was to ascertain to what extent Lithuanian religious folkways had been practiced and observed among American Lithuanian Catholics. He provided interesting information about Lithuanian
religious folkways in terms of family festivals (christening of children,
weddings, funerals), devotions, ecclesiastical feasts and holy days (such
as Advent, Christmas, Easter, the Feast of St. George and the Feast of St.
Casimir), venerated persons, and venerated objects and animals.

The Rev. Sirvaitis concluded that the conservation of Lithuanian religious traits and practices was influenced noticeably by the rising rate
of intermarriages between Lithuanians and other nationalities from 1920
until World War II and after. Lithuanian immigrants had lost various religious folkways, modified some, and acquired some American Catholic religious folkways. He pointed out, for instance, that many Lithuanian practices and beliefs related to the christening of a child had been completely
forgotten by American Lithuanians. One's name day was celebrated by only
a small number of American Lithuanians. In wedding arrangements they no
longer needed the help of the matchmaker, piršlys, who was so important in
old Lithuania. Many old Lithuanian beliefs and practices about the wake
and death had been forgotten by American Lithuanians.

Not having sufficient written sources on religious folkways among the
Lithuanians in the United States, the author was obliged to live in the
four selected Lithuanian centers from June 1946 to February 1947 to collect necessary material. In Shenandoah, Pennsylvania, he lived one month
and a half; spending the same period of time in Waterbury, Connecticut;

three months in Chicago, Illinois, and only two weeks in Custer, Michigan. In the fifth selected center, Cleveland, the author has lived since his arrival to the United States in 1939, excluding several years when he studied at the Catholic University, Washington, D. C. In general, the time especially assigned to collect material through interviews and observations extended to about three years.

I. FAMILY FESTIVALS

The Lithuanians came to this country for the most part single and young. They married in this country with partners of their own nationality, raised children and thus formed a family which was surrounded by a new American and urban environment.

There was a gradual diminution or modification of the awe and reverence of children toward their parents. The average size of the family is 3.5. The married sons and daughters of the immigrant Lithuanians usually do not live with their parents. Intermarriages between the Lithuanians and other nationalities were constantly on the rise in America from 1920 until World War II and after (to about 60 per cent of all marriages in Lithuanian parishes). Interfaith marriages comprise a little over twenty per cent of all marriages. About fifteen per cent of the Lithuanians marry before a justice of peace. The divorce rate among them is 38.4 per one thousand marriages. Desertion among Lithuanian immigrants is difficult to determine.

1. Christening of Children

The old Lithuanian mothers who came from Lithuania (almost all of them) believe that pregnant women must themselves behave well; otherwise their children will be affected. Some mothers while waiting for the birth of their child ask for a special Cincture of the Blessed Virgin Mary, and wear it for the purpose of having a safe delivery of their child. Some Lithuanian midwives before World War I always made the sign of the cross on the newly-born baby also before and after his bath. The water was blessed with the sign of the cross before the baby was washed; this was common among the old Lithuanian immigrants who were Catholics. It was done to protect their babies from harm. Some midwives used to attach a little holy medal to the swaddling clothes of the baby. Incensing the baby with holy herbs when it was frightened and disturbed was also practiced.

Godparents are selected from good friends and relatives and their financial status is usually taken into consideration. The large christening parties were in practice in all five Lithuanian settlements about thirty years ago. The godmother has to think good thoughts during baptism so that the baby will be good. The expenses of the dinner are paid by the father of the baby. The godfather distributes cigars to the men. In all five settlements during the baptismal dinner the godparents were advised to sit close so that the teeth of the baby would grow close to each other. But this was done "just for fun." Midwives receive small donations from the godparents and the guests. Some donations are given to the christened baby also. The godparents usually remember their godchild on various occasions.

Some Lithuanian families do not wash their baby after his baptism because of their respect for the sacred oils. The so-called blessing of mothers after the birth of a child was practiced about thirty or even twenty years ago but now it is disappearing in churches. Sometimes the baby's future is guessed by observing his more frequent actions. The old Lithuanian immigrant mothers taught their children prayers in Lithuanian. The second generation teach the prayers in English.

If the Lithuanian parishes have their own schools, the children learn their religion, catechism and prayers in these schools. Usually the sisters teach the children in English. In some parishes Sunday schools operate wherein the children attend for several years and learn religion.

The first Communion exercises are very solemnly performed in the Lithuanian parishes. The children are trained by the nuns. Many old ladies weep while seeing these ceremonies.

Confirmation is usually administered every third year. Lithuanian mothers are always glad to see their youngsters practicing their religion faithfully.

2. Weddings

The period of engagement of Lithuanian immigrants was comparatively very short. At the beginning they kept that old Lithuanian custom of arranging marriage with the help of a pirŠlys (matchmaker). After the agreement, the young man used to give some money to the girl to buy the wedding outfit. The present generation of Lithuanian Americans is entirely free from this custom of having a pirŠlys which was kept in Lithuania until World War II.

Now, the Lithuanian youth are trying to extend the period of acquaintance for about one to three years. The sons and daughters of the immigrant Lithuanians, in general, ask their parents to give their consent for marriage with their chosen partner. After this formality, the young man buys the engagement ring. The Lithuanian parents in general want their sons and daughters to marry partners of the Lithuanian nationality.

When the wedding day is set, the so-called wedding showers are arranged, usually the surprise type. At the same time, in some parishes the young couple go to the parish for premarital instructions. In recent years weddings are becoming more frequent on Saturdays. The wedding party takes place in the parish hall, in some restaurant, or in a hotel, or the parents' home. At most of the Lithuanian weddings the rue flower is still used for the decoration of plates and tables.

The parents often make the sign of the cross on their sons or daughters who are leaving home to be married. The ceremonies in church are performed as in every American Catholic church. If there is a Nuptial Mass the bride and bridegroom with their witnesses receive Holy Communion. In the vestibule, after the wedding, the couple are greeted by their relatives and friends and showered with rice or confetti.

At the beginning of the present century as well as nowadays the couple are met at the door by the mother of the bride or the bride groom with a tray on which are two glasses of wine, some bread and salt. Before the wedding party starts to eat, they make a loud noise with their knives and forks on the plates so that the couple will kiss. Before World War I there was a presentation of gifts, or a "buying" of the wreath with certain ceremonies, for instance, breaking of plates, singing special songs, and so forth.

Recently at some Lithuanian weddings the custom of throwing the bridal bouquet to the surrounding girls has made its appearance. In Chicago, there is a special ceremonial ending to a Lithuanian wedding continued until recently: the taking of the veil off the bride.

The couple, nowadays, after the wedding go on a honeymoon trip. The blessing of the young wife after the wedding is not in practice at present.

3. Funerals

The parish priests visit their sick parishioners usually once a month and bring them Holy Communion if they are asked to do it. The patients, in a Catholic hospital which usually has its own chaplain, can receive Holy Communion every day if they wish to do so. At present in none of the five settlements did the author find any singing of hymns during a sick call at home. The priest carries the Blessed Sacrament "incognito." While the priest administers the Sacraments to the sick, the other members of the family usually kneel and pray in the room.

At the hour of death the members of the family recite the prayers for the dying; often they recite the rosary or the litany for the dying. The crucifix and the candle are placed in the hands of the dying person and the holy names of Jesus, Mary and St. Joseph are invoked. Some families practice the sprinkling of the dying with holy water.

When the bystanders are sure that the sick person is truly dead, they let him rest a while and then the undertaker is called. About thirty years ago, in all five settlements under consideration the wake was held in the homes. Now there is a modern trend to have the wake at the undertaker's funeral parlor.

During the wake thirty years ago, the Lithuanians used to sing religious hymns. At present the singing, except in the wakes among the Lithuanian farmers in Iron, Michigan, has disappeared because of a general trend to adapt themselves to the present American customs. During the wake if the dead person belonged to any religious societies, the society members come to recite the rosary for the dead. The rosary is said on the last night of the wake by the priest.

Friends of the deceased bring flowers and wreaths and place them about the coffin. The offering of Mass cards is being used in increasing number.

The morning of the funeral Mass, the priest usually comes to the place where the body is lying in state and recites prayers from the Catholic ritual. As soon as the priest departs for the church, the last farewell to the body takes place. The priest, preceded by the crucifix and two candles carried by the altar-boys meets the body at the church door, and while the bell is tolled, he sprinkles the coffin with holy water and conducts the psalm Miserere; then the office for the dead is sung and the Mass with other ceremonies follows, for instance, the hymn Libera, psalm Benedictus and other prayers by the tomb in the cemetery. In Chicago, some funerals end with the Angelus sung by the priest and bystanders. About twenty years ago, the people who returned from the cemetery used to say the rosary for the dead. At present they say only a few prayers and at times none at all.

The thirtieth day after the funeral is commemorated by a Requiem High Mass very rarely. However, the anniversary is commemorated very often. In

Chicago, after the Requiem Mass, friends are invited to the house, say a rosary until the dinner is prepared. After dinner drinks are at times served.

The grave of the departed one, in general, is visited very frequently by the family for several months in all settlements.

II. DEVOTIONS, ECCLESIASTICAL FEASTS AND HOLY DAYS AMONG AMERICAN LITHUANIANS

1. Advent

In general Advent is not observed by American Lithuanians as strictly as it is observed in Lithuania. The so-called rarotinės Mišios (a traditional Advent Mass) was discontinued in American Lithuanian churches. Lithuanians in this country at present do not sing any traditional Advent hymns at home. It must be noted that altar breads--plotkelės (Christmas wafers) are still distributed to the parishioners before Christmas. In Chicago, about ninety per cent of the parishioners accept these altar breads.

2. Christmas

It seems that the feast of Christmas has become a greater feast among the Lithuanians in America than it is among the Lithuanians in their native land.

(1) Christmas Eve--Kūčia

The author can affirm that in every Lithuanian settlement it is possible to find some families of immigrant Lithuanians who fast according to the old Lithuanian way, not eating anything until the evening--kūčios. Great preparations are made for the feast of Christmas. Presents are bought and traditional courses are prepared; Christmas trees are adorned; porches or windows are illuminated; and cribs are installed. The traditional meal kūčia commences with the altar breads. Only some Lithuanian farmers in Custer, Michigan, up to the present day, still place hay on the table. Predicting one's future on the kūčia day is almost forgotten. The food of kūčia is not left on the table overnight as it is in some parts of Lithuania.

(2) Midnight Mass

In many Lithuanian churches there is a midnight Mass. About eighty to ninety per cent of the parishioners go to confession and receive Holy Communion at the midnight Mass or early in the morning. Some families exchange their presents on Christmas morning after the Mass. The youth are not forbidden to go to the movies on the "first day" of Christmas.

We may add that during the midnight Mass there is a procession to the crib and a Christmas hymn is sung in Lithuanian. Pastors and priests greet their parishioners during the Christmas Masses.

3. New Year's Day

On New Year's eve many Lithuanian church halls are crowded with parishioners who come to await the New Year. Usually a dinner is served and people dance and sing songs. At midnight greetings are extended to each other.

About this time some parish priests start their annual parish visit. During this visit the priests extend the crucifix to be kissed. They do not sing, but recite some prayers and bless the house, taking the parish census at the same time. The parishioners usually give a donation to the priest. The Easter confession cards are not distributed to the parishioners during this annual visit.

4. The Epiphany

The Masses on the feast of the Epiphany are said only in the morning since the people have to work this day. In Chicago, some families have reunions and special meals are prepared, similar to the meals prepared on kūčia--Christmas eve. In the morning chalk and incense are blessed in all the Lithuanian churches in Chicago and the chalk is distributed to the people after every Mass on the feast of the Epiphany. Some families mark their front door with the letters K M B. This sign beseeches a blessing for the occupants and welcomes guests.

5. Purification of the Blessed Virgin Mary

In all Lithuanian churches candles are blessed before Mass. In some churches, the people assisting at Mass hold candles and are helped by the altar-boys to light the candles several times as the custom requires. Some Chicago parishes hold services in the evening at about seven-thirty. The blessed candles are kept in a box and used for certain occasions, such as: death, lighting, and so forth.

6. Lithuanian Independence Day (February 16)

Almost every year on February sixteenth or rather on the Sunday nearest to this date, Lithuanian churches have a solemn High Mass for Lithuania. Catholic organizations at times with national Lithuanian organizations have solemn meetings consisting of speeches and a special program usually arranged with folksongs, folkdances, or a play. The younger Lithuanian generation, in general, is not willing to participate in these meetings.

7. Annunciation of the Blessed Virgin Mary

This feast is not a holy day of obligation in the United States. However, many Lithuanian women come to the morning Mass on this occasion.

8. Shrove Tuesday

Shrove Tuesday in America has lost its significance. However, the traditional potato pancakes are baked and sometimes Shrove Tuesday parties are arranged for the whole Lithuanian community.

On Ash Wednesday, ashes made from the palms of the previous Palm Sunday are blessed. They are distributed to the parishioners after Mass in the morning and again in the evening. Lithuanian Catholics like these ceremonies and willingly come to church to have their foreheads signed with the blessed ashes.

9. Lent

Before World War I the Lithuanian immigrant families tried to observe the Lenten fast as they did in Lithuania. At present some families do not eat meat during the first week and the last week of Lent. The rest of the Lenten fast is observed as it is announced by the church. In Aurora, Illinois, some women come to one family to sing Kalnus (Christ's Passion Hymns). It must be noted that Graudūs Verksmai (Passion Lamentations) are still sung in many Lithuanian churches and the Stations of the Cross are made both in English and Lithuanian.

10. Palm Sunday

In every Lithuanian church there is the blessing of the palms and a procession on Palm Sunday. The blessed palms are distributed to the people and many of the parishioners carry them home. Some families make ornamentations with these blessed palms and place them beside a holy picture. Some save them for incensing during thunder. Some others believe that if there is a blessed palm in the house, it will protect the house from thunderstorm.

11. Holy Week

In Chicago, the Holy Week ceremonies in church do not differ from those in Lithuania. On Holy Thursday, there is a procession to the so-called "prison." In some churches this "prison" is not considered a "prison" since it is very beautifully adorned with flowers.

During the services on Good Friday the people come on their knees from their pews to kiss the Crucifix. In some churches, there is a Three Hours service beginning at noon on Good Friday. The so-called "soldiers" who stood by the "Sepulchre" before World War I are not seen at present.

The Holy Saturday services are attended by many people since they come to get holy water. In some parishes they come to get some of the fire blessed in the morning. Some women take the holy water home and sprinkle all the rooms in their home on Holy Saturday; others consume some of the holy water when it is brought home. Certain families keep the holy water to sprinkle themselves on going to bed or getting out of bed in the morning.

Eggs are adorned and colored by some families in the Lithuanian settlements.

In all the Lithuanian churches the custom of blessing food on Holy Saturday is still continued but the number of people who bring the food is seemingly declining every year.

On the evening of Holy Saturday some churches have services, Compline with a sermon on the Passion of Christ. In a few churches the singing of religious hymns all during the night of Easter is still preserved.

12. Easter

Before the early Mass there are the Resurrection ceremonies in church which are performed in almost the same way as they were performed in Lithuania. The procession usually makes three rounds inside the church. Ceremonies, such as Matins are omitted because of a general tendency to shorten the services in the United States. About twenty years ago, some societies participated in the Easter procession.

There is no racing home after the services as is done in Lithuania. The sprinkling of the table with holy water, of the rooms and the drinking of some of it are still practiced by some families on Easter morning.

About thirty years ago, when immigrant Lithuanians were rather young and many of them not married, they played some games during Easter, for instance, "beating the girls with twigs," "sprinkling the girls with perfume," and so forth.

The women showed their corsages and hats on Easter morning in all the Lithuanian settlements. It is interesting to note that some Lithuanian families in Shenandoah have what is known as "Little Easter" (Velykėlės) which is held on Low Sunday.

13. The Feast of St. George

The author was told that only some of the Lithuanian farmers who settled about Custer, Michigan, continue the custom of venerating St. George as the protector of animals.

14. May Devotions

In many Lithuanian churches May devotions are held every evening about seven-thirty. There are no May devotions in the home at the present time.

Usually on the second Sunday of the month of May, Mother's Day is celebrated.

15. Memorial Day

On Memorial Day in all the Lithuanian settlements many people go to the cemeteries to decorate the graves of their dead relatives and friends. In Chicago special traditional services are arranged by all the Lithuanian parishes of the city in St. Casimir's Lithuanian cemetery.

16. Rogation Days

The Rogation Days are celebrated with special services only in some Lithuanian churches. The processions are made only inside the church with the school children participating.

17. Pentecost

In Waterbury some young birch trees are placed at the door of the Lithuanian church on Pentecost. This is done "in commemoration of Pentecost." In the church there is no other special ceremony. Some Lithuanian farmers around Custer, Michigan, still adorn their homes with birch trees on Pentecost. Thus custom among the city Lithuanians is not practiced.

18. Corpus Christi

The traditional Corpus Christi procession is made in the Lithuanian churches in Chicago, Illinois, after which herbs are blessed. Few churches have vespers sung every evening during the octave of Corpus Christi. Some churches have the procession on the Sunday within the octave.

19. St. John's Feast

The Lithuanian Knights in Chicago as well as in Cicero have an outdoor picnic on St. John's feast day, which usually takes place in the evening. They sing Lithuanian songs, roast wieners, dance and have fun. Lithuanians know the stories about papartis (fern) and the medical herbs which have curative power if they are collected before St. John's feast.

20. Assumption of the Blessed Virgin Mary

On the feast of the Assumption of the Blessed Virgin Mary flowers are still blessed in many Lithuanian churches.

21. Nativity of the Blessed Virgin Mary

The author was told that only once when Father I. Kelmelis from Lithuania had services in Custer, Michigan, were the grains blessed on the feast of the Nativity of the Blessed Virgin Mary. The other priests discontinued this custom.

22. October Devotions

Only in some Lithuanian churches is the rosary said during the month of October. At home, it is said by some Lithuanian farmers in Custer, Michigan.

23. All Souls' Day

The traditional procession with five stations performed on All Saints' Day and on All Souls' Day is identical with that in Lithuania. Before this feast, the priests distribute envelopes for the offerings for the dead and say Masses and recite the rosary for those whose names are in the envelopes. Some people go to the cemetery on All Souls' Day to visit their dead; however, they do not light candles on the graves.

It must be mentioned that before All Souls' Day, the children have Halloween parties in some homes or schools and visit their neighbors with their usual "Trick or treat."

24. Special Better-Known Feasts of the Saints

Every year the Lithuanian Knights commemorate the feast of St. Casimir. On the feast of St. Anthony many candles are usually lighted in honor of this Saint and Masses are offered for various intentions. The feast of St. Agatha is not observed in the Lithuanian churches in this country. St. Anne is venerated in America by the Lithuanians as she is in Lithuania. On the feast of St. Blaise in all the Lithuanian churches throats are blessed by touching the chin with two joined candles. Both old and young in great numbers receive the blessing.

25. Sunday and Holy Days of Obligation

The singing of the valandos (Little Hours of the Blessed Virgin Mary), reciting of the rosary and the reading of morning prayers in the Lithuanian churches on Sunday morning have been discontinued. The hymn Pulkim ant Keliu (Let Us Fall on Our Knees) which is sung before the High Mass in Lithuania is very much liked and preserved in the greater number of Lithuanian churches up to this day. The sermon is given during the Mass after the Gospel has been read and the announcements made. After High Mass benediction with the Blessed Sacrament is given. It must be noted that the old Lithuanian hymn of supplication Sventas Dieve (Holy God) and the conclusive hymn Garbinkime Svenciausiaji Sakramenta (Let Us Praise the Most Holy Sacrament) are still sung. Vespers are sung in a few Lithuanian churches.

In the greater part of the Lithuanian churches only one Mass is celebrated for the English speaking people. Usually the children's and youth Masses are marked with an English sermon and English announcements. During the High Mass the parish choir sings the Mass combined with some Lithuanian hymns.

During the summer time all the Lithuanian parishes have picnics in woods, or parks, or at some larger farms in the country.

Some Lithuanian farmers in Custer, Michigan, unable to attend Mass on Sundays say certain prayers during the noon hour.

In general, the attendance at Mass seems to have improved, if we look at the Lithuanian Catholics of the older generation and those of the present.

On Holy Days of obligation the Masses are celebrated earlier so that the parishioners who have to work that day will be able to attend Mass.

26. Religious Services During the Week and Atlaidai

Very many Lithuanian churches have various novena services held in English and Lithuanian.

The so-called Atlaidai (Days of Indulgence) in the Lithuanian churches of the United States are of two kinds; the Forty Hours Devotion and the feast of the church Patron.

Many priests, usually from other Lithuanian neighboring parishes as well as from some distant Lithuanian parishes, come to assist at the Forty Hours Devotion. A special missionary priest is often invited to give the sermons during the three days' devotion. Every evening the vespers of the Feast of Corpus Christi are sung by the choir or school children. A solemn procession is made in church at the conclusion of the Atlaidai and the Lithuanian hymn Garbeir Slove (Praise and Honor) is sung.

The feast of the Patron in some churches is commemorated by solemn vespers sung on the eve and on the evening of the feast, and a procession is also made.

III. OTHER RELIGIOUS FOLKWAYS AMONG THE LITHUANIANS IN THE UNITED STATES

1. God, Sacred Persons and Objects

(1) God. A strong thought about God's Providence with some elements of fatalism is still existent among Lithuanians of the first generation in this country. It seems, however, that their orientation is changing to a rather more firm belief in their own faculties and forces in the attainment of happiness in this world.

It must be noted that about thirty per cent of the Lithuanian immigrants in the United States are not practical Catholics. They are for the most part atheists who do not believe in God. The old Lithuanian Catholic greeting form is rarely used today. However, the prayers before and after meals have not disappeared among good Lithuanian Catholics up to this day.

Incidentally we remark that more vulgar and atheistic books by Lithuanians have appeared in the United States than throughout all Lithuania.

It must be noted that some old Lithuanian immigrants say certain special prayers until this day which they learned from their parents in their mother country. There is a rather widespread custom to have private novenas in honor of a mystery of faith, of the Mother of God, or of the Saints. The singing of religious hymns in homes has disappeared almost entirely.

The use of some old Lithuanian charms and spells which ended with the sign of the cross has greatly decreased in the United States. We remark here that the use of Sapninykas (Book explaining dreams) was very widespread among the American Lithuanians and it is still consulted by some.

Finally, it must be added that the consecration of the Lithuanians to the Sacred Heart of Jesus was repeated officially in this country in 1946.

(2) The Blessed Virgin Mary. It is possible to say that Mary's cult is continued by American Lithuanians as it is in Lithuania. The feasts of the Blessed Virgin are venerated and religious services in her honor are well attended. In Chicago, Lowlanders--Lithuanians from Lowland Lithuania--erected a shrine of the Blessed Virgin Mary--a replica from Siluva, Lowland Lithuania, and have novena services in her honor. The rosary Confraternities and Sodality of the girls list numerous members. The Miracles at Lourdes (Liurdo Stebuklai) a Lithuanian book written by Bishop P. Bucys is a widely read book among American Lithuanians of the older generation.

(3) Saints. The most popular Saint among the Lithuanians in the United States is St. Casimir and next to him probably St. Anthony. It

seems that the Lithuanians instinctively direct their thoughts and their hearts to this national Saint when they are in exile or in some foreign country and are confronted with many difficulties for the preservation of their nationality.

St. Anthony is invoked in prayers to restore health, to get a partner for marriage and to recover stolen or lost goods.

Among the other Saints, who are venerated by the American Lithuanians, we may include St. Therese of the Infant Jesus, St. Appolonia, St. Joseph and others.

Finally, we may say that the celebration of a birthday is very widespread among the Lithuanian Americans in all the settlements except Chicago where the celebration of the person's name day is still in vogue and observed not only by the old Lithuanian immigrants but also by American-born Lithuanians.

(4) Sacraments and Sacramentals. Since practicing Lithuanian Catholics in this country seem to be more inclined to a frequent reception of the Sacraments, it is safe to assert that a realization of the necessity of the Sacraments, for instance, Penance and Holy Eucharist, in the daily life of the American Lithuanians practicing their religion has increased more than it did among European Lithuanians. However, the external respect paid to the Holy Eucharist is different in the Lithuanian churches in the United States from that in Lithuania. It must be noted that the Lithuanians are generous in making offerings for Masses. The sacrament of Matrimony is considered by some Lithuanians as a private and civil thing. Not all Lithuanian children are baptized and the names of baptism for the present generation are entirely American. Confirmation is administered every third year. The American bishops are not met so solemnly as they are in Lithuania. Extreme Unction is administered more promptly in the United States among the Lithuanian Catholics than it is in Lithuania. The priesthood among the Lithuanians is considered as a high status, but probably, not so high as it is esteemed in Lithuania.

All Sacramentals, such as candles, holy water, palms, and other blessed articles as the rosary, scapulars and prayerbooks are venerated by the Lithuanian people in America as they are in Lithuania. The author did not witness any great difference.

(5) Shrines. Lithuanians have their own shrine in Chicago. It is the Shrine of the Blessed Virgin Mary who appeared in Šiluva, Lithuania. The solemnities at this Shrine are celebrated from September eighth through to the fifteenth; the days of the Atlaidai at the Shrine of the Blessed Virgin Mary at Siluva, Lithuania. The hymn which is sung at the Shrine of Šiluva is sung here at the Nativity of the Blessed Virgin Mary church before and after the services. There are some other churches which are furnished with the pictures of the Blessed Virgin Mary of Vilna--Ausros Vartai. They do not attract large groups of Lithuanian people.

(6) Churches. There are about one hundred and twenty Lithuanian churches in this country which are still centers of Lithuanian religious and national activity. In some churches there are Lithuanian inscriptions, American and Lithuanian national arms, Lithuanian art crosses, decorations with national colors and motifs, and various statues of their venerated Saints. All these churches are furnished with pews for the parishioners and heated in the winter. They are clean and neat. The Lithuanian churches in America are not decorated with wreaths, as is customary in Lithuania.

(7) Crosses and Statues. The Lithuanians do not erect wayside cross-es in this country. There are a few Lithuanian art crosses erected by the churches. However, small national Lithuanian crosses can be found in many Lithuanian homes.

(8) Cemeteries. A number of the Lithuanian parishes have their own cemeteries. The Chicago Lithuanian parishes have a beautiful common ceme-tery, called the Cemetery of St. Casimir. The tomb inscriptions are most-ly in Lithuanian with a request to the reader to say Amžiną atsilsį (the prayer "Eternal Rest"). Flowers are planted on all the graves. External respect for a Catholic cemetery has changed. As far as the author knows the cemeteries are not visited as often as they are in Lithuania.

2. Venerated Persons

(1) Priests. In 1942, there were three hundred and twenty-three Lith-uanian speaking priests in the United States. It is true that there is a cultural difference between the old immigrant priests and the young Ameri-can Lithuanian priests. A close relationship among them is rare. In gen-eral, all the Lithuanian American priests lead a rather active life, show-ing probably a greater initiative than the priests in Lithuania; Lithuanian American priests are rather humble and industrious.

Lithuanians in general show a respect to their parents. The older generation, however, believes more in the truthfulness of the priestly words than does the younger generation which is more critical.

(2) Nuns. Lithuanian nuns in America can be proud of their number (over 650) which is greater than the number of nuns in Lithuania proper. They perform various work in schools, missions, churches, hospitals, on their farms, and so forth. The people appreciate their work. These teach-ing Sisters try to transplant some Lithuanian cultural traits into the hearts of their pupils.

(3) Servants in the Church. Many Lithuanian churches in the United States do not have sacristans. The organist (male or female) plays the organ at all religious services whenever these services require music. Some respect is given to a good organist. In Lithuania this respect was more noticeable than in the United States. The pastor's housekeeper does not receive any special respect from parishioners.

(4) Davatkos - Devout Women. Devout, unmarried women are proportion-ally less numerous in the United States than they are in Lithuania. They wear somewhat more simple clothes and belong to various religious societies.

3. Venerated Animals and Objects

(1) Fire. Fire is still venerated by the Lithuanian people. Some Lithuanians of the second generation know of this respect for fire, by signing it with the sign of the cross in the morning, or on leaving the house, and not allowing any spitting into it, and so forth.

(2) Sun and Moon. "It is improper to point to the sun or the moon with one's finger"--some Lithuanian women told the author while he stayed in Shenandoah, Pennsylvania. Another woman affirmed that the sun "jumped three times on the morning of St. Peter's day in 1946." Before the war, the sky was unusually red and meteors were falling--they foretold great

calamity.

Some Lithuanians still say a prayer when they see a full moon. The farmers still believe in the effects of the different phases of the moon on plants and corn (Custer).

(3) Bread. The traditional respect for bread has somehow diminished in the United States even though the second generation is acquainted with this respect: they just do not practice it. There are no rye harvesting festivals in this country among the Lithuanian farmers.

(4) Earth. In general, Lithuanian immigrants know their traditions about the holiness of the earth; however, they do not practice any particular custom relating to these traditions.

(5) Water. A certain respect for water and old traditions about it are remembered by old immigrant Lithuanians. At present they recall it as something amusing.

(6) Rue Flower. The rue flower is almost as greatly respected by the Lithuanians in the United States as it is in Lithuania. It seems that this flower has acquired a new significance among the American Lithuanians. It signifies maidenhood in Lithuania; in the United States it signifies the Lithuanian nationality. Songs about rues are still sung by the Lithuanians in this country.

(7) Homes. No Lithuanian home building customs are practiced by the Lithuanian builders. The homes, however, are respected since "the crucifix and holy pictures are placed in them." Lithuanian farmers as well as the poorer families probably have more holy pictures than the urban and richer Lithuanians. Newly built homes are often blessed by the priest.

(8) Woods-Trees. We have seen what significance is attributed to the šermukšnis (rowan tree) in Lithuanian folklore. In the United States no particular significance is attached to it; it is planted in a few places and is liked "because it is a Lithuanian tree." Other venerated trees are remembered only during conversation.

(9) Bees. Customs related to bees are not practiced; however the old traditions are remembered. Deep respect for bees has almost disappeared entirely.

(10) Birds. The Lithuanians do not find, in this country, any of the birds which they venerated. No storks, cuckoos, larks or swallows are seen in their sections of the United States. However stories about these birds are remembered and passed down to their children.

(11) Thunder and Storm. During a thunderstorm some Lithuanians pray, light a candle, incense the room with holy herbs and make the sign of the cross. The old immigrant Lithuanians relate stories about the howling winds, but while telling you about them they themselves laugh at what they once believed.

(12) Bears. The Lithuanians do not have any customs concerning bears in this country.

(13) Serpents. Serpents (žalčiai) are not seen by the Lithuanians living in urban areas. However, snakes are recognized as having curative power, for instance, when whiskey is poured on them, and they are kept in bottles.

116

4. Evil Animals and Spirits

(1) The Goat or Goats. Goats are no more liked by the Lithuanians in this country than in Lithuania. Their connection with the devil is described in stories.

(2) The Toad or Toads. Even in this country old immigrant Lithuanians loathe the toad because it is so ugly. Some people remember stories from Lithuania about the toad as having, just like the goat, some connection with the devil.

(3) Goblin--Aitvaras. The American Lithuanians do not believe in Aitvaras (a certain kind of goblin) any more.

(4) Witches--Raganos. In ordinary conversation among Lithuanian women one may hear the name of ragana which is attributed to some woman who secretly does harm to other people. However, the author did not find any story professing that witches exist among the Lithuanian people in the United States.

(5) Devils. The author heard some stories about devils and their tricks which are current among the second generation of Lithuanians in this country. Some old Lithuanian immigrants begin to think that devils are nothing more than the people who do wrong.

(6) Lucifer. One story about Lucifer is related even today among Lithuanian Catholics and it is as follows: The Easter procession performed three times in church makes the chain of Lucifer stronger and thus he remains enchained until the next Easter. Some say that if you sharpen a knife on Sunday you make the chain of Lucifer weaker and you help free Satan from this chain.

CONCLUSIONS ON ACCULTURATION

Acculturation is the assumption of culture through contact. It is expressed by an assimilation into a group, in accommodation to a group, or in imitation of the cultural pattern of a group. We are especially concerned here with a particular acculturation of the Lithuanian immigrant group in their religious folkways to the American Catholic religious folkways.

The following agents and situations took part in this process of acculturation.

1. Churches

Organized and established Lithuanian churches were the first to introduce Lithuanian immigrants to American life.

2. Religious Organizations

Numerous Lithuanian religious organizations which usually were benefit organizations, at the beginning of the Lithuanian immigration, also helped Lithuanian immigrants to get acquainted with American life.

117

3. Cooperation and Conflicts with Other Religious Groups and Atheists

Because of some conflicts the Polish-Lithuanian organizations were gradually dissolved in almost all the Lithuanian settlements in which they had been formed. Thus the Lithuanians separated from the Poles and opened their doors rather to American influence. Some cooperation shown between Irish and the Lithuanian Catholics strengthened their religious convictions and friendly spirit. Conflicts with Lithuanian atheists taught Lithuanian Catholics greater tolerance.

4. Cooperation and Conflicts with Pastors

Discords between pastors and parish committees usually arose because of misunderstanding in the administration of church property. However, all these misunderstandings and accusations gradually decreased and old conflicts in their old form and degree do not occur among Catholic Lithuanians any more.

5. Elimination of Conflicts, Re-definition of Attitudes and a Greater Tolerance

After conflicts, quarrels, misunderstandings, widely spread gossip, a period of quiet work, rest and greater tolerance in regard to other groups and persons took place.

6. Imitation of Some Religious Folkways Practiced by American Catholics

To illustrate this acculturation process, we may point out some lost religious folkways and at the same time indicate the practice of many new religious folkways.

At present many practices and beliefs related to the christening of a child are completely forgotten by American Lithuanians. The churching of mothers after childbirth is also disappearing. Lithuanian girls receiving Holy Communion for the first time do not wear wreaths of rue. One's name day is celebrated only by a small number of immigrants especially in Chicago.

At their weddings, American Lithuanians do not need the help of piršlys (matchmaker) nor do they have the ceremonial betrothal. The parents (with some exceptions) discontinued the blessing of their sons and daughters going to church for the wedding. The Lithuanian brides do not weep any more when going to church nor do they chant sad words on that occasion. The brides do not wear rue flowers nor are they afraid of any charms. The ceremonial meeting of the couple after the wedding remains very simplified and they do not sing special wedding songs either. The conclusion of the wedding of the ceremonial hanging of the piršlys is not practiced nor are the other concluding ceremonies followed. The "wakening of the couple" has almost disappeared entirely as well as the blessing of the young wife in church. The after-wedding dinner is not prepared (with some exceptions).

Neighbors do not meet the priest who comes to visit the sick person with the Blessed Sacrament, nor does the priest carry the Blessed Sacrament

118

publicly. No one hears religious hymns on this occasion in the home of the sick person nor do any believe in signs which used to "foretell one's death." They have ceased to prepare the body in their homes by themselves and no longer do they sing religious hymns at the wakes in cities and towns. Many beliefs related to the wake and death are forgotten. In many cases the children have ceased to kiss their dead parent's hands or feet as they say the last farewell. They do not kneel any more at the moment of this farewell. The shedding of tears and the emotions are very well controlled. The coffin is not carried by pallbearers to the church even if the distance from the funeral home to the church is very short, nor is the Litany of All Saints sung. The priests do not sing the Miserere nor Benedictus in the funeral processions outside the church or at the cemetery.

These are only some religious cultural traits, taken from the christening of children, weddings and funerals, which the Lithuanian immigrants have lost or modified and which may serve in this abstract as an illustration of the acculturation process.

The following folkways may illustrate newly introduced ones.

The American Lithuanians started to practice "baby showers." They began to dress their babies for baptism in the so-called baptismal gown. During the ceremonies of baptism, the American born godparents are asked and answer the liturgical questions in English. The third generation of the Lithuanian children are not taught Lithuanian prayers at home. They began to celebrate the First Holy Communion exercises very solemnly in church and at home, followed by banquets. The children, in general, go to Holy Communion rather frequently. The teaching of the catechism is arranged by the decrees of the local Bishop and is well carried out by the pastors.

Lithuanian boys and girls started to have numerous dates as well as long engagement periods before their weddings. They infrequently ask for the consent of their parents before their wedding. Wedding showers began to take place with attached ceremonies. Rather long instructions by the parish priests before marriage became the custom. American-Lithuanian brides began to observe different customs and superstitions while going to the altar for the wedding ceremony, and a great number of marriages are performed with the Nuptial Mass. On the church steps the couple kiss each other after the wedding and they are showered with confetti.

Thus the Lithuanian immigrants have lost some of their religious folkways; some of these folkways have been modified; others have had their origin in this country by imitating the American Catholics or Americans in general. Some of these folkways were replaced by American folkways retaining, however, some Lithuanian characteristics.

7. Substitution of Some Religious Folkways for Some More
Common American Folkways

In the acculturation process some Lithuanian and American folkways were often combined preserving certain Lithuanian characteristics and practicing an American custom; for instance, the conclusion of a Lithuanian wedding in Chicago, Illinois, with English songs and Lithuanian simplified ceremonies may be called a sort of creative assimilation.

8. Great Amalgamation as a Means of Participation

The author has found that sixty-six per cent of marriages concluded in Lithuanian churches in investigated settlements are of mixed nationalities. Thus about sixty-six Lithuanian young men and women of every hundred who marry in Lithuanian churches are amalgamated with different nationalities. It is clear, therefore, that the Lithuanian cultural traits are fusing in all directions and the Lithuanians are "disappearing" very rapidly.

9. Participation

A very limited participation of particular Lithuanians and their families in some American family festivals and community activities is noted in the first years of their arrival. Later this participation becomes more friendly and more frequent. The second Lithuanian generation participates in various American activities more often than in Lithuanian national activities since English is their native language with all its implications, and American ways are their ways in general.

The impending change in the composition of the membership[2] of Lithuanian parishes makes it entirely possible that the still remaining small segregation will gradually disappear.

FOOTNOTES

[1]Reprinted by the permission of the author and the publisher, the Catholic University of America Press.

[2]This conclusion is valid only when we do not take into consideration Lithuanian Displaced Persons who immigrated to the United States recently and who increased the percentage of pure Lithuanian stock in some parishes a great deal.

Chapter 10. THE LITHUANIAN IMMIGRANT PRESS

Source - Danute-Dana J. Tautvilas. The Lithuanian Press in America, (Thesis -
M.S.), Catholic University of America
Library, Washington, D. C., 1961. The
selection is from Chapter V, "First
Steps 1874-1904," Chapter VI, "Lithuanian Press Between 1905-1945," Chapter VII, "Growth of Lithuanian Press
in Post war Period," pages 38-66 and
from Table 6, pages 94-102.[1]

Overview

The history of the Lithuanian press began officially on August 16,
1879 with the publication of the weekly newspaper, Gazieta Lietuwiszka
(Lithuanian Newspaper) in New York City. This four page newspaper ceased
publication in 1880. Between 1880 and 1886 several other Lithuanian newspapers were published but were also short lived. However, a new Lithuanian newspaper, Vienybe Lietuvininku (The Unity of Lithuanians) began to
be published in 1886 in Plymouth, Pa. This newspaper continues to be published in Brooklyn, N. Y. under the title Vienybe (The Unity). Pennsylvania, where the earliest Lithuanian immigrants settled in significant
numbers, especially in the coal mining communities, had other Lithuanian
newspapers, such as Saule (The Sun), first published in Mahoney City, July
11, 1888, Garsas (The Sound), first published in Shenandoah on October 13,
1892 and Nauja Gadyne (New Era), first published in Mt. Carmel on January
23, 1894. The chief characteristic of the Lithuanian press in the period,
1874-1905, was instability because of the lack of journalistic or literary
skills of the publisher-owners and editors and their inability to satisfy
the expectations of their subscribers.

In the next period, 1905-1945, which corresponded to the period of
the main Lithuanian immigration, there was a significant growth in Lithuanian newspapers and periodicals. During this period, 17 new Lithuanian
newspapers and 65 new Lithuanian periodicals appeared in large cities
where Lithuanians settled. One of the most important publications was a
Lithuanian Roman Catholic newspaper, Draugas (The Friend), which was established in Wilkes Barre, Pa. on July 27, 1909. In 1912 the newspaper
moved to Chicago and from 1916 on it became a daily Lithuanian newspaper.
Chicago also had another large daily Lithuanian newspaper, The Naujienos
(The Lithuanian News), a socialist newspaper, which was first published as
a daily newspaper on August 1, 1914.

At the end of 1945, 13 Lithuanian newspapers and five periodicals
continued to be published in the United States. The Lithuanian press as
a product of immigration continued to be noticed in the post-World War II
period. During the period 1946-1960, American Lithuanians, former displaced persons, established 4 new Lithuanian newspapers and 33 new magazines. The total number of Lithuanian newspapers and periodicals published
in the United States in 1960 was 10 newspapers and 48 magazines.

FIRST STEPS 1874-1904

The history of Lithuanian press in the U.S.A. begins with the year 1874, when M. Tvarauskas tried to publish the first Lithuanian newspaper Gazieta Lietuwiszka (Lithuanian Newspaper). However, this idea did not materialize until August 16, 1879 when officially the first issue of this weekly newspaper was published in New York, N. Y. This publication primarily was intended for Lithuanians living in the U. S.A. It was published by M. Tvarauskas with the aid of St. Casimir's Society of New York, Rev. P. Koncius and a Franciscan monk A. Zeytz. At that time the publisher found only 132 subscribers. The newspaper had four pages. After six months (i.e. in the beginning of January 1880) the publication ceased to exist. There were 16 issues published altogether.[2]

In October 1881, M. Tvarauskas published a new Lithuanian weekly paper entitled: New Yorko Gazieta Lietuwiszka (New York Lithuanian Newspaper). However, after 14 issues, this newspaper was discontinued on April 9, 1892.[3]

As soon as financial problems to publish another Lithuanian newspaper were solved, M. Tvarauskas published a weekly paper Unija (The Unity) in Brooklyn, N. Y. in October 1884. Only fifteen issues of this publication came out and then it was discontinued. J. Sliupas edited it for some time.[4]

The press was and still is a powerfully strong bond between all the Lithuanians scattered about the American soil. Therefore, the Lithuanians in America published a score of papers. General information about Lithuanian newspapers and periodicals during 1885-1904 period was compiled from the following sources:

Ayer and Sons. Annual American Newspapers and Periodicals Directory. Philadelphia: Ayer and Sons, 1890-1904.

Bagdonavicius V., Jonikas P., and Balciunas J. Kovos Metai del Spaudos. Chicago: Lithuanian Press Club, 1957.

Lietuviu Enciklopedija. Boston: Lithuanian Encyclopedia Publishers, Vols. I-XII, 1953-1957.

Park, Robert E. The Immigrant Press and Its Control. New York: Harper and Bros., Publishers, 1922.

Ruseckas, Petras. Pasaulio Lietuviai. Kaunas, Lithuania: Draugija Uzsienio Lietuviams Remti, 1935.

Szlupas, John. Lithuania in Retrospect and Prospect. New York: Lithuanian Press Association of America, 1915.

On July 2, 1885, J. Sliupas published a bi-weekly paper Lietuviskas Balsas (Lithuanian Voice). It had four pages. The number of subscribers and the subscription price is unknown. It was one of the first Lithuanian newspapers published regularly until April 17, 1889.[5]

In 1886, J. Paukstis established a new newspaper Vienybe Lietuvininku (The Unity of Lithuanians) published weekly in Plymouth, Pa. This newspaper still exists in Brooklyn, N. Y. under the title Vienybe (The Unity). According to the information of some old Lithuanian residents, the first Lithuanian immigrants in Plymouth, Pa. settled in 1869.

On July 11, 1888, a new paper Saule (The Sun) was published in Mahonay City, Pa. It was the first regular Lithuanian newspaper in the U. S. A. This newspaper still exists. In the beginning it was published weekly and later on semi-weekly. Articles and news items are published in an old fashioned Lithuanian language.

In 1892, Lietuviu Mokslo Draugyste (the Lithuanian Education Society) in Shenandoah, Pa. published a literary monthly magazine Apszvieta (Education). After 15 issues this magazine was discontinued in 1893, because of lack of sufficient support from subscribers.

On October 13, 1892, a new weekly newspaper Garsas (The Sound) was published in Shenandoah, Pa. It was edited by T. Astramskas. In 1893, this publication was discontinued.

A weekly newspaper Lietuva (Lithuania) was published in Chicago on December 13, 1892. No information could be found how many subscribers it had. This paper existed until 1920.

In 1893, Lithuanian residents in Boston, Mass. published a newspaper Bostono Lietuviskas Daikrastis (Boston Lithuanian Newspaper). It appeared irregularly. After seven issues it was discontinued.

On January 23, 1894, one more Lithuanian newspaper Nauja Gadyne (New Era) was published in Mt. Carmel, Pa. It was intended for Lithuanian workers in that area. This weekly newspaper existed for two and a half years. It was discontinued after 49 issues on June 13, 1896.

In order to fight against atheism which started to spread among some Lithuanian immigrants, a Catholic periodical Valtys Devynioliktojo Amziaus (The Boat of the 19th Century) was established in Plymouth, Pa. in April 4, 1894. This periodical was edited by Rev. A. Burba. For unknown reasons it was discontinued after three issues.

On January 15, 1895, a humorous bi-weekly periodical Perkunas was published in Shenandoah, Pa. There is no information how many issues of this periodical were published and when it was discontinued.

A weekly newspaper Garsas Amerikos Lietuviu (Voice of Lithuanians in America) was published on October 2, 1895 in Shenandoah, Pa. and later on it continued to be published in Elizabeth, N. J. This publication was discontinued in 1899.

To give some information about Lithuanian literature, education, and a general idea about politics, the monthly magazine Tevyne (Fatherland) was begun in Mt. Carmel, Pa. on January 1, 1896. Later on it became a weekly newspaper and had about 15,000 subscribers. From 1908, it was published in Boston, Mass. No information could be found in the available sources when this publication was discontinued.

On February 2, 1896, a Catholic newspaper Rytas (The Morning) was established in Waterbury, Conn. It was edited by Rev. J. Zebris and published weekly. Its circulation is unknown. After two years, the publication ceased to exist.

A periodical Kardas (The Sword) was published in Baltimore, Md. on April 1, 1896. It was a socialist newspaper. No information could be found on how many subscribers it had. After forty issues, this publication was discontinued for an unknown reason.

In 1896, R. P. Kuncmanas established weekly newspaper Pensylvanijos Darbininkas (Pennsylvania Worker) in Shenandoah, Pa. In 1897, the title of this paper was changed to Darbininkas (The Worker). After three years of existence, it was discontinued in 1899.

A weekly newspaper Amerikos Lietuvis (Lithuanian in America) was established in Chicago, Ill. in 1897. The publishers and editors were J. Grinius and J. Laukis. Only three issues of this newspaper came out.

On September 27, 1897, one more Lithuanian publication Pasaule (The World) was published in Elizabeth, N. J. However, after seven months, it was discontinued.

In 1898, a scientific monthly magazine Galybe (The Might) was published in Baltimore, Md. Only few issues of this magazine came out.

In 1898, a quarterly magazine Dirva (The Field) was established in Shenandoah, Pa. The publisher and editor was Rev. A. Milukas. No information could be found in the available sources how many subscribers it had. However, it is a known fact that the most part of publishing expenses were paid by the publisher and editor Rev. A. Milukas. It was discontinued on August 12, 1902.

In 1899, Rev. M. Kriauciunas and J. Tananevicius established a weekly newspaper Katalikas (The Catholic Weekly) in Chicago, Ill. This publication covered political and religious news. In 1914, when World War I broke out, this publication became a daily newspaper, in order to give more information to readers about events in Europe. From 1916 it was published weekly until April 1917, when it was discontinued.[6] In the beginning it had about 1,500 subscribers. In 1914-1916, this publication had a circulation of more than 9,000.[7]

A monthly Catholic magazine Tarnas Baznycios (Servant of the Church) was published in Waterbury, Conn. in 1899. This magazine was edited by Rev. A. Gricius. It was discontinued in 1900.

On February 4, 1899, a weekly paper Viltis (The Hope) was published in Shenandoah, Pa. It was intended for Lithuanian workers in that area. In 1901, it came to an end because of lack of sufficient support from the subscribers.

In 1899, a weekly humorous newspaper Linksma Valanda (Gay Hour) was begun in Mahonay City, Pa. However, after two years of existence, it was discontinued in 1901.

On February 7, 1900, a magazine Kurejas (The Creator) was begun in Chicago, Ill. Its slogans were: freedom, equality, and brotherhood. After 19 issues, this magazine was discontinued.

A weekly newspaper Ateitis (The Future) was published in Pittsburgh, Pa. on September 14, 1900. It was discontinued in 1901.

In the beginning of 1901, a socialist periodical Darbininku Viltis (Workers' Hope) was published in Pittsburgh, Pa. It was discontinued in 1905.

On January 31, 1901, a Catholic weekly Zvaigzde (The Star) was published in Brooklyn, N. Y. This newspaper was edited by Rev. Varnas and Rev. A. Milukas. Its circulation is unknown. After nine and a half years of existence, this publication was discontinued in 1910.

A weekly paper Darbininku Viltis (Workers' Hope) was published in Shenandoah, Pa. on January 10, 1903. This new publication was established instead of periodical Viltis (The Hope) which was discontinued in January 1901.

In 1904, a socialist weekly newspaper Spindulys (The Beam) was published in Brooklyn, N. Y. No information about the subscribers could be found. After three years of existence, this publication was discontinued.

During this period, the native country of Lithuanian immigrants was enslaved and ruled by the Russian government. There were violent outbursts against the rule of the Russians. Lithuanians had known the dangers of book smuggling and the delights of secret societies dedicated to the cause of liberty when Lithuanian press in Lithuania was prohibited (1864-1904). They had known the pain of prison and exile, the public whipping post, and hanging. Many of her sons had fled to North or South America in pursuit of that liberty of conscience and freedom of life that was denied in occupied Lithuania. Therefore, the first Lithuanian immigrants established newspapers and periodicals in their native language devoted to American-Lithuanian life. All the above mentioned publications were aimed to meet this requirement. Lacking sufficient support from the subscribers, many of those publications were discontinued after few issues or several years. Some of them continued to be published because of the generosity of publishers and their supporters.

During 1874-1904 period, 29 Lithuanian newspapers and periodicals were published. At the end of 1904, ten Lithuanian newspapers and periodicals continued to be published, namely: Spindulys (The Beam) and Zvaigzde (The Star) published in Brooklyn, N. Y.; Katalikas (The Catholic Weekly) and Lietuva (Lithuania) published in Chicago, Ill.; Linksma Valanda (Gay Hour) and Saule (The Sun) published in Mahanoy City, Pa.; Tevyne (Fatherland) published in Mt. Carmel, Pa.; Ateitis (The Future) and Darbininku Viltis (Workers Hope) published in Pittsburgh, Pa.; Vienybe Lietuvninku (The Unity of Lithuanians) published in Plymouth, Pa.

For a sequence of Lithuanian publications in this period see Table 6.

LITHUANIAN PRESS BETWEEN 1905-1945

In the beginning of the year 1905, the Lithuanian press in the U. S. A. was already established. However, the chief characteristics of the Lithuanian press were still instability and general disorder, as was true of the press of all recent immigrants; because the publishers-owners, and editors hardly possessed any journalistic or literary qualities. Its main purpose was to inform the readers of both American events and of events in the native country. Sometimes, however, earlier publications did not satisfy the mood and expectations of the subscribers. Therefore, new publications were established. As time marched on, the more important papers and periodicals developed considerably with the help of various Lithuanian societies.

General information about the new Lithuanian newspapers and periodicals which appeared in 1905-1945 is given below, compiled from the following sources:

Ayer and Sons. Annual American Newspapers and Periodicals

Directory. Philadelphia: Ayer and Sons, 1905-1945.

Common Council for American Unity. "Lithuanian Publications in the United States," _List of Foreign Language Publications_. New York, 1926-1945.

Gineitis, K. _Amerika ir Amerikos Lietuviai_ (America and American Lithuanians). Kaunas, Lithuania: Spindulys, 1925.

Lavinskas, F. _Amerikos Lietuviu Laikrasciai_ (American-Lithuanian Newspapers). Long Island City, 1956.

Lietuviu Enciklopedija. Boston: Lithuanian Encyclopedia Publishers, Vols, I-XIV, 1953-1958.

Park, Robert E. _The Immigrant Press and Its Control_. New York: Harper and Bros., 1922.

Sapoka, A. (ed.). _Lietuvos Istorija_ (The History of Lithuania). Kaunas, Lithuania: Knygu Leidimo Komisijos Leicinys, 1936.

Simutis, A. _Pasaulio Lietuviu Zinynas_ (Lithuanian World Directory). New York: Lithuanian Chamber of Commerce, Inc., 1953.

On February 9, 1905, a socialist weekly newspaper _Keleivis_ (Traveler) was established in Boston, Mass. by A. Zvingilas. At the end of 1907, it had 1,000 subscribers. After World War I, its popularity increased and circulation reached about 23,000. This newspaper still exists and at present, it has about 6,000 subscribers. Now it is an organ of the Association of Lithuanian Socialists. Publisher: Keleivis Publishing Company.[8]

In February 1905, the Lithuanian Socialist Society in America established a political, economic and literary weekly newspaper _Kova_ (The Fight) in Philadelphia, Pa. At the beginning it had about 2,000 subscribers. In 1914, its circulation reached about 4,000. This publication was discontinued in 1918.

In the beginning of May 1905, a humorous periodical _Pleperys_ (Chatterbox) was published in Philadelphia, Pa. After several issues it was discontinued.

A monthly magazine _Vaistininkas_ (Druggist) was published in Boston, Mass. in November 1905. After several issues it ceased to exist.

In December 1906, a humorous periodical _Dilgeles_ was published in Philadelphia, Pa. It was discontinued after few issues.

A satirical periodical _Kapsas_ was published in Philadelphia, Pa. in 1907. Only a few issues of this periodical came out.

In January 1907, a monthly literary magazine _Amerikos Lietuvis_ was published in Worcester, Mass. After 13 issues, it was discontinued.

In May 1907, a fraternal periodical _Spindulys_ (The Beam), edited by Rev. A. Dilionis, was published in Pittsburgh, Pa. No information is available about the number of subscribers and the year when it was discontinued.

A weekly newspaper Lietuviu Zinios (Lithuanian News) appeared in Mc-Kees Rock, Pa. in 1909. After three years of existence, it was discontinued in 1911.

In February 1909, a humorous periodical Dagis appeared in Boston, Mass. After 12 issues, it was discontinued in December 1910.

In July 1909, a monthly magazine of general news Dalgis was published in Philadelphia, Pa. After several issues, it ceased to exist.

On July 27, 1909, a Lithuanian Roman Catholic weekly newspaper Draugas (The Lithuanian Friend), edited by Rev. A. Kaupas, was established in Wilkes Barre, Pa. In 1912, its publication was transferred to Chicago, Ill. From 1916, it became a daily Lithuanian newspaper. This publication still exists and at present it is one of the largest Lithuanian daily newspapers in the U. S. A. It is edited by L. Simutis. At the present time it has a circulation of more than 60,000. Publisher: Lithuanian Catholic Press Society.[9]

In January 1910, a literary magazine Laisvoji Mintis (Free Thought) was established in Scranton, Pa. It represented a group of free-thinking Lithuanians. This magazine was edited by J. Sliupas. It was discontinued in 1915. Only 60 issues of this magazine were published.

A humorous periodical Pipiras (Pepper) was published in Boston, Mass. in 1910. It was edited by J. Mickevicius. After few issues it ceased to exist.

In 1910, a fraternal magazine Lietuvaite (Lithuanian Woman) was published in McKees Rock, Pa. After few issues this magazine ceased to exist.

Thus, at the end of 1910, the following Lithuanian newspapers and periodicals continued to be published:

1. Amerikos Lietuvis, a monthly literary magazine.

2. Dagis, a humorous periodical.

3. Dalgis, a monthly magazine of general news and literature.

4. Draugas, a Lithuanian Roman Catholic weekly, religious and general news.

5. Darbininku Viltis, a weekly socialist newspaper.

6. Katalikas, a weekly newspaper which covered religious and political news.

7. Keleivis, a socialist weekly newspaper, political, literary and general news.

8. Kova, a political, economic, and literary weekly newspaper.

9. Lietuva, a political and general news weekly paper.

10. Laisvoji Mintis, a political, economic, and literary monthly magazine intended for the freethinking readers.

11. Lietuviu Zinios, a weekly general newspaper.

12. <u>Saule</u>, a weekly newspaper published in an old fashioned Lithuanian language.

13. <u>Tevyne</u>, a political, literary, and educational monthly magazine.

14. <u>Spindulys</u>, a religious and general news periodical.

15. <u>Zvaigzde</u>, a fraternal and general news weekly paper.

16. <u>Vienybe Lietuvninku</u>, a weekly newspaper.

In 1911, a monthly fraternal magazine <u>Aidai</u> (Echos) was published in Waterbury, Conn. Only few issues of this magazine came out.

A socialist weekly newspaper <u>Laisve</u> (Freedom) was established in Boston, Mass. in 1911. After some time, its publication was transferred to Brooklyn, N. Y. From 1919, this newspaper began to represent the communist ideology. At present, it publishes articles which are in line with Soviet propaganda. Now it is a semi-weekly paper published in Richmond Hill, Long Island by Laisve, Inc. It has a circulation of more than 5,000.[10]

In May 1911, an anarchistic bi-monthly periodical <u>Laisvoji Zmonija</u> (Free People) was published in Chicago, Ill. However, after few issues, it ceased to exist.

In 1911, a fraternal monthly magazine <u>Upelis Ramybes</u> (The River of Peace) appeared in Waterbury, Conn. Only several issues of this magazine came out.

On November 22, 1911, a satirical monthly magazine <u>Tarka</u> was published in Brooklyn, N. Y. After 24 issues, this magazine ceased to exist.

In January 1912, a weekly newspaper <u>Kelione</u> (Journey) was published in Worcester, Mass. No information is available about the circulation and the date when this paper was discontinued.

A socialist monthly magazine <u>Lietuviu Zurnalas</u> (Lithuanian Journal) appeared in Chicago, Ill. in February 1912. It was discontinued at the end of 1914.

On July 17, 1912, a bi-weekly periodical <u>Vakaru Varpas</u> (The Western Bell) was published in Omaha, Neb. After several months, it ceased to exist.

In 1913, a satirical periodical <u>Dievo Rykste</u> (God's Switch) was published in Chicago, Ill. Its circulation and the date when it was discontinued is unknown.

A humorous periodical, <u>Spitolninkas</u>, was published in Waterbury, Conn. in 1913. Only a few issues of this periodical came out.

In January 1914, a fraternal periodical <u>Galvocius</u> (The Thinker) was published in Chicago, Ill. After several issues it was discontinued.

In January 1914, a progressive weekly newspaper <u>Ateitis</u> (The Future) was published in Boston, Mass. From 1915, its publication was transferred to Chicago, Ill. and then it appeared three times per week. It was discontinued in 1918.

In 1914, a humorous monthly periodical Sake (The Fork) was published in Chicago, Ill. Only a few issues of this periodical came out.

On March 14, 1914, a socialist periodical Zarija (Glowing Fire) was published in Chicago, Ill. Its circulation is unknown. It was discontinued at the end of 1918.

An illustrated literary magazine Jaunoji Lietuva (Young Lithuania) was established in Chicago, Ill. in 1914. It appeared monthly. After two years it was discontinued.

In February 1914, a monthly magazine Veidrodis (The Mirror) was published in Chicago, Ill. It was intended for Lithuanian theatre workers. This magazine was discontinued in 1915.

On February 19, 1914, a socialist weekly newspaper Naujienos (The Lithuanian News) was established in Chicago, Ill. From August 1, 1914, it became a daily newspaper. At present, it is one of the largest daily newspapers. It is edited by P. Grigaitis and published by the Lithuanian News Publishing Company. It has a circulation of more than 43,000.[11]

A weekly newspaper Amerikos Lietuvis was published in Worcester, Mass. on April 19, 1914. Its circulation is unknown. After one year of existence, this newspaper was discontinued.

In May 1914, a progressive weekly newspaper Darbininku Balsas (Workers' Voice) was published in Baltimore, Md. Only few issues of this paper came out.

On October 21, 1914, newspaper Zaibas (The Lightning) was published in Grand Rapids, Mich. After several issues, it ceased to exist.

In February 1915, a political and educational monthly magazine Musu Draugas (Our Friend) was published in Chicago, Ill. No information is available about the circulation and the date when this magazine ceased to exist.

In 1915, a literary monthly magazine Pazanga (Progress) appeared in Chicago, Ill. Only several issues of this magazine came out.

A satirical monthly magazine Rimbas was published in Rockford, Ill. on June 27, 1915. After several issues this magazine was discontinued.

On July 7, 1915, a periodical Pazvalga was published in Boston, Mass. It was established instead of the magazine Laisvoji Mintis (Free Thought) which was published in the beginning of 1915 and after few issues ceased to exist. Later on, the magazine Pazvalga merged with the magazine Jaunoji Lietuva which appeared in 1914. No information is available about the circulation and the date when this magazine was discontinued.

On August 19, 1915, a Catholic semi-weekly newspaper Darbininkas (The Worker) was established in Boston, Mass. by St. Joseph's Lithuanian Society. In the beginning, the newspaper was edited by Rev. Kemesis. In 1951, it merged with the newspapers Amerika and Lietuviu Zinios. After that, its publication was transferred to Brooklyn, N. Y. At present, the newspaper Darbininkas, edited by S. Suziedelis, is published semi-weekly. It has a circulation of more than 10,000. The publisher is Franciscan Fathers.[12]

A fraternal weekly newspaper Santaika appeared in Cleveland, Ohio on November 25, 1915. Only several issues of this paper came out.

In November 1915, a humorous periodical Zvirblis (The Sparrow) was published in Forest City, Pa. Only a few issues of this periodical came out.

At the end of 1915, a religious monthly magazine Tautos Rytas (Nation's Morning) was published in Brooklyn, N. Y. It was discontinued after a few issues.

After reorganization of the paper Santaika at the end of 1915, a new weekly newspaper Dirva (The Field) was established in Cleveland, Ohio on August 26, 1916 by the Ohio Lithuanian Publishing Company. This newspaper still exists and at present it is published semi-weekly. It is an organ of the Lithuanian American National Alliance published by American Lithuanian Press and Radio Association "Viltis."[13]

On April 21, 1916, a socialist, political and literary monthly magazine Naujoji Gadyne (The New Era) was established in Philadelphia, Pa. by Lithuanian Socialist Aliance of America. It was discontinued in October 1917.

In October 1916, a monthly magazine Moteru Balsas (Women's Voice) was published in Philadelphia, Pa. by the Women's Alliance Society. The number of subscribers is unknown. It was discontinued in December 1921.

In 1916, a fraternal monthly magazine Moteru Dirva (The Women's Field) was established in Worcester, Mass. by the Lithuanian Roman Catholic Women's Society. No information is available about the circulation and the date when this magazine was discontinued.

On May 17, 1917, a fraternal weekly newspaper Garsas (The Sound) was established in Wilkes Barre, Pa. This paper still exists and at present, it is an organ of the Lithuanian Roman Catholic Alliance of America. It has a circulation of about 9,000.

A humorous periodical Dilgele (The Nettle) was published in Worcester, Mass. in September 1917. It was discontinued in July 1919.

In November 1917, a fraternal periodical Atgimimas was published in Lawrence, Mass. It was an organ of the American-Lithuanian National Church. No information is available about the circulation and the date when it was discontinued.

At the end of 1917, a monthly bulletin Apzvalga (Review) appeared in Philadelphia, Pa. It was published by the Lithuanian Socialist Society. It was discontinued after several issues.

In 1918, a monthly magazine Amerikos Ukininkas (American Farmer) was published in Hart, Mich. After a few issues, it was discontinued.

On November 27, 1918, a weekly newspaper Lietuva (Lithuania) was published in Chicago, Ill. by a group of Lithuanian patriots. It was discontinued in May 1920.

In 1919, a Marxist ideology monthly magazine Proletaras (Proletarian) was published in Chicago, Ill. It was discontinued in 1923.

In February 1920, a fraternal periodical Darbo Valanda ir Perkunas (Working Hour and Thunder), edited by Rev. Kemesis, was published in Cleveland, Ohio. Only several issues of this periodical came out.

In June 1920, a monthly magazine Ukininku Sinios (Farmers' News) was published in Scottsville, Mich. It was discontinued after several issues.

In September 1920, an agricultural monthly magazine Artojas (The Plowman) was published in Cleveland, Ohio. Only a few issues of this magazine came out.

On September 23, 1921, a national weekly newspaper Tevynes Balsas (Motherland's Voice) was published in Wilkes Barre, Pa. It was discontinued in 1922.

At the end of 1921, a humorous periodical Perkunas (Thunder) was published in Boston, Mass. Only a few issues of this periodical came out.

A literary periodical Zinios (News) was published in Chicago, Ill. on December 17, 1921. After a few issues, this periodical ceased to exist.

In January 1922, a literary monthly magazine Moksleiviu Keliai (Students' Road) was published in Valparaiso, Ind. Only a few issues of this magazine appeared.

On March 2, 1922, a progressive weekly newspaper Darbininku Tiesa (Workers' Truth) was published in Brooklyn, N. Y. It was discontinued after 36 issues.

In October 1922, a weekly newspaper Telegramas appeared in Chicago, Ill. Its publisher is unknown. This paper ceased to exist at the end of 1923.

In November 1922, a fraternal monthly magazine Sviesa (The Light) was published in Chicago, Ill. by the Lithuanian Protestant Society. It was discontinued in December 1933.

In November 1923, a weekly newspaper Aidas (Echo) was published in Cleveland, Ohio. Its circulation is unknown. It was discontinued in November, 1932.

On December 25, 1923, a weekly newspaper Varpas (The Bell) was published in Chicago, Ill. instead of the paper Telegramas. No information is available about the circulation and the date when it was discontinued.

In 1923, a socialist periodical Lietuviu Zinios (Lithuanian News) was published in Chicago, Ill. It ceased to exist in November 1924.

In July 1924, a humorous periodical Bite (Bee) appeared in Boston, Mass. Only a few issues of this periodical came out.

A political and literary monthly magazine Vadovas (The Leader) was first published in Chicago, Ill. on July 24, 1924. No information is available about the publisher and the date when it was discontinued.

In 1924, a fraternal periodical Meile Kataliku (The Love of Catholics) was published in Du Bois, Pa. It was intended for Catholic families and their children. It was discontinued after several issues.

A medical and health periodical Gydytojas (Physician) appeared in Chicago, Ill. in 1924. It was published by Lithuanian physicians. Only a few issues of this periodical came out.

A commercial bulletin Amerikos Lietuviu Vaizbos Buto Zinios appeared in Boston, Mass. on October 6, 1925. It was published by a group of Lithuanian business men. It ceased to exist in 1926.

In 1925, a fraternal bi-weekly paper Taradaika was published in Chicago, Ill. by the Lithuanian Knight Society. It was discontinued in 1926.

In 1927, a periodical Chicagos Zinios (Chicago News) was published in Chicago, Ill. After several issues, it was discontinued at the end of 1927.

In 1928, Margutis, a monthly magazine of music, folklore and humor was established in Chicago, Ill. This magazine still exists and at present is published by L. Vanagaitis, D.B.A. Margutis Publications. The number of subscribers is unknown.[14]

In 1928, a group of business men published a monthly magazine Tarpininkas in Boston, Mass. Only a few issues of this magazine came out.

In 1928, a political and literary periodical Gyvenimas (Life) appeared in Chicago, Ill. It ceased to exist in 1930.

On October 25, 1929, a fraternal weekly newspaper Sandara (The League) was published in Chicago, Ill. It still exists and at present is an organ of the Lithuanian National League of America. It has a circulation of more than 26,000.[15]

In October, 1929, a non-partisan periodical Atzala (The Shoot) was published in Shaft, Pa. No information is available about the circulation and the date when it was discontinued.

In 1930, a progressive periodical Liaudies Tribuna (Peoples Platform) was published in Chicago, Ill. Only a few issues of this periodical came out. Its publisher is unknown.

In June 1931, a fraternal periodical Detroito Kurieras was published in Detroit, Michigan. It ceased to exist after a few issues. The publisher is unknown.

In August 1931, a fraternal monthly magazine Tautos Balsas (Nation's Voice), edited by Rev. M. Valadka, was published in Scranton, Pa. by the Lithuanian National Catholic Church Society. After 12 issues, this magazine was discontinued.[16]

On November 18, 1931, a progressive weekly newspaper Nauja Gadyne (New Era) was published in Brooklyn, N. Y. by the Lithuanian Labor Society. This paper was discontinued in 1936.

A fraternal periodical Giedra was published in Wilkes Barre, Pa. in 1932. This periodical ceased to exist after several issues.

On December 1, 1933, a Catholic weekly newspaper Amerika, edited by Rev. Pakalniskis, was published in Brooklyn, N. Y. On April 15, 1951, it merged with the semi-weekly paper Darbininkas (The Worker) published in Brooklyn, N. Y. by the Franciscan Fathers.

In August 1933, a literary and political monthly magazine Ismintis (Wisdom) was established in Boston, Mass. It was published and edited by R. Zidziunas and E. Simanavicius. No information is available about the circulation and the date when it was discontinued.

In October 1933, a periodical Siuvejas (The Tailor) was published in Brooklyn, N. Y. Publisher and editor was J. Buividas. Only a single issue of this periodical came out.

In 1934, a liberal magazine Pazanga (Progress) appeared in Chicago, Ill. It was published and edited by Dr. A. Karalius and De. Montvidas. Only several issues of this magazine came out.

In 1936, a fraternal periodical Jaunimas (The Youth), edited by J. Poska, was published in Chicago, Ill. It was intended for the Lithuanian youth. After one year of existence, it was discontinued.

In 1937, a religious monthly magazine Pasiuntinys (Messenger) was established in Chicago, Ill. It was published and edited by Rev. S. Draugelis and J. Poska. No information is available about the number of subscribers and the date when it was discontinued.

In July 1937, a periodical Teisybe (The Truth) appeared in Lawrence, Mass. It was published and edited by S. L. Zapenas. After several issues, it ceased to exist.

In February 1938, a political and literary monthly magazine Lietuviu Naujienos (Lithuanian News), edited by J. Gustis, was published in Philadelphia, Pa. This magazine still exists. At present, it is published by J. Gustis and the Friends of American Lithuanian News. Its circulation is unknown. It covers political, literary, and group interest news.

In 1939, a political and literary monthly magazine Lietuva (Lithuania) appeared in New York, N. Y. It was published and edited by J. Tysliava. This magazine was discontinued in October 1941.

In 1940, a religious monthly magazine Syvturys (Lighthouse), edited by Rev. Tamosiunas and J. Gylys, was established in Chicago, Ill. It was published by the Lithuanian Mission Society. No information is available about the circulation and the date when it was discontinued.

In 1942, Viltis (The Hope), a Lithuanian literary and arts magazine in English was established in San Clemente, Ca. It still exists and at present is published 6 times per year. The publisher and editor: V. F. Beliajus. Circulation--1,600.

During the period 1905-1945, 17 new Lithuanian newspapers and 65 new periodicals appeared in larger cities where Lithuanians were closely and firmly united and were well organized. The Lithuanians in America published many newspapers. They were devoted to bring Lithuanians closer together and to establish cooperation among different groups in their patriotic activities. The Lithuanian press is a really powerful bond between all the Lithuanians scattered about on the American soil.

At the end of 1945, 13 Lithuanian newspapers and 5 periodicals continued to be published in the United States of America, namely:

Newspapers:

1. Darbininkas (The Worker), a Lithuanian Catholic semi-weekly paper published in Brooklyn, N. Y.

2. Dirva (The Field), organ of the Lithuanian American National Alliance of America published weekly in Cleveland, Ohio.

3. Draugas (The Lithuanian Daily Friend), a Lithuanian Roman Catholic daily paper published in Chicago, Ill.

4. Garsas (The Sound), a fraternal weekly paper, organ of the Lithuanian Roman Catholic Alliance of America published in Wilkes Barre, Pa.

5. Kristaus Karaliaus Laivas (Ship of Christ the King), a fraternal weekly paper published in Chicago, Ill., by the Marian Fathers.

6. Keleivis (Traveler), socialist weekly paper published in Boston.

7. Laisve (Freedom), a Marxist weekly paper published in Brooklyn, N. Y.

8. Naujienos (The Lithuanian News), a liberal daily paper published in Chicago, Ill.

9. Sandara (The League), a fraternal weekly paper published in Chicago, Ill.

10. Saule (The Sun), general news weekly paper published in Mahanoy City, Pa.

11. Tevyne (Motherland), a fraternal weekly paper published in New York by the Lithuanian Alliance of America.

12. Vilnis (The Surge), a Marxist daily paper published in Chicago, Ill.

13. Vienybe (Unity), general news weekly paper published in Brooklyn, N. Y.

Periodicals:

1. Margutis, music, folklore, and humor monthly magazine published in Chicago, Ill.

2. Muzikos Zinios (Music News), quarterly, published in Cicero, Ill. by Lithuanian Organist Alliance of America.

3. Lietuviu Naujienos (Lithuanian News), group interest, published in Philadelphia, Pa.

4. Viltis (The Hope), a literary monthly magazine published in San Clemente, Ca.

5. Zvaigzde (The Star), a literary monthly magazine published in Chicago, Ill. by the Jesuit Fathers.

GROWTH OF LITHUANIAN PRESS IN POSTWAR PERIOD

It is probably not a mere coincidence that nationalist movements have so frequently originated and been supported from outside. In many cases Lithuanian national consciousness has manifested itself first of all in the exile, the refugee, and the immigrant. The Lithuanians refer to the United States of America as "the second birthplace of their nationality." National consciousness is inevitably accentuated by immigration. Loneliness and an unfamiliar environment turn the wanderer's thoughts and affections back upon his native land. The strangeness of the new surroundings emphasizes his kinship with those he has left.

This general effect is intensified in those whose race is still struggling for political recognition. The most able members of such an immigrant group are apt to be men exiled for their patriotic activities. In the new country they have more freedom to work for their cause than they had under a hostile government at home, and they naturally encourage their fellow immigrants to help them.

The data all point to the fact that the Lithuanian press is a phenomena of immigration. If there were no non-English-speaking arrivals, in a few years there would be no immigrant press. The Lithuanian press, if it preserves old memories, is at the same time the gateway to new experiences.

General information about the new Lithuanian newspapers and periodicals which were established in the United States after World War II is given below, compiled from the following sources:

Ayer and Sons. Annual American Newspapers and Periodicals Directory. Philadelphia: Ayer and Sons, 1945-1959.

Common Council for American Unity. "Lithuanian Publications in the United States," List of Foreign Language Publications. New York, 1945-1959.

Hunter, Edward. In Many Voices--Our Fabulous Foreign-Language Press. Norman Park, Georgia: Norman College, 1960.

Lietuviu Enciklopedija. Boston: Lithuanian Encyclopedia Publishers, Vols. I-XXI, 1953-1960.

Ruzancovas, A. (ed.). Knygu Lentyna (Bookshelf). Danville, Ill.: Lithuanian Bibliographic Service, Nos. 38-118, 1951-1960.

Simutis, A. Pasaulio Lietuviu Zinynas. New York: Lithuanian Chamber of Commerce, Inc., 1953.

Aidai (Echoes), a cultural monthly magazine published by the Franciscan Fathers in Kennenbunkport, Me., On October 4, 1949. Later on, its publication was transferred to Brooklyn, N. Y. This magazine first was established in Munich, West Germany in 1945.[17]

Apzvalga (Review), irregular periodical published by the Free Lithuanian Society in San Diego, Ca. in 1959.

Atspindziai, an independent periodical published and edited by V. Meskauskas in Chicago, Ill. on April 23, 1952.

Cicero Lietuvis (Cicero Lithuanian), irregular periodical published by the Cicero Lithuanian Society in 1959.

Darbas (The Work), a liberal literary and political quarterly magazine was established in Boston, Mass. in 1947. At present, it is published in Brooklyn, N. Y. by the Lithuanian Labor Society, Inc. Its circulation is unknown.

Eglute (The Little Tree), a cultural illustrated monthly magazine for children was established in Lawrence, Mass. in the beginning of 1950. Later on, the publication of this magazine was transferred to Putnam, Conn. At present, it is published by the Lithuanian Cultural Society and edited by Dr. A. Serksnas. It has a circulation of more than 1,200.[18]

Evangelijos Zodis (Gospel's Word), a religious monthly magazine established by the American Lithuanian Lutheran Church Council in Chicago, Ill. in 1951. It is edited by Rev. A. Trakis.

Gabija, a literary periodical published by the Lithuanian Press Society in Brooklyn, N. Y. in 1951. No information is available about the circulation and the date when it was discontinued.

Girios Aidas (Echo of the Forest), a silviculture magazine established in Chicago, Ill. in 1950. It is published two times a year by the Lithuanian Foresters in Exile. The magazine is edited by Prof. J. Kuprionis. Its circulation is unknown.

Kalifornijos Lietuvis (California Lithuanian), an illustrated cultural monthly magazine established in Los Angeles, Ca. in 1946. In 1949, it merged with the Lietuviu Dienos (Lithuanian Days) magazine. At present, this magazine is published by A. F. Skirius. Each issue contains 40-50 photographs, representing Lithuanians' life in the Western World. Sixteen printed pages are in Lithuanian language and 8 pages in English. It has a circulation of more than 15,000.[19]

Karys (The Warrior), a historical, literary, and military science monthly magazine published in Brooklyn, N. Y. in November 1950. It is intended for the veterans of Lithuanian descent and for Lithuanians in the wide world. This periodical first was established in Kaunas, Lithuania in 1919. At present, it has a circulation of more than 1,600. Subscription six dollars per year.[20]

Knygu Lentyna (Bookshelf), a Lithuanian bibliography bi-monthly bulletin published in Danville, Ill. in July 1949. At present, it is published by V. Saulius and edited by A. Ruzancovas and B. Kviklys. It has a circulation of more than 300.

Kibirksteles (The Spark), an illustrated periodical, irregular, published by the Nuns of the Immaculate Conception in Putnam, Conn. This periodical is intended for the young Lithuanian girls. It was established in 1953.

Laisvoji Lietuva (Free Lithuania), a bi-weekly newspaper of group interests published by the Lithuanian Regeneration Association in Chicago, Ill. on August 17, 1953. Its circulation is unknown.

Laiskai Lietuviams (Letters to Lithuanians), a religious monthly magazine published by the Jesuit Fathers of Della Strada in Chicago, Ill. in 1950. This magazine still exists and at present is edited by Rev. J.

Vaisnys. Its circulation is unknown.[21]

Lietuva (Lithuania), a political magazine published by the Lithuanian Freedom Committee in New York in 1952. It is edited by the editorial board and appears irregularly. Its circulation is unknown.

Lietuviu Kelias (Lithuanians' Road), a weekly newspaper established by the Liberal Lithuanian Association in Brooklyn, N. Y. on February 16, 1950. Later on, its publication was transferred to Watertown, Conn. After 36 issues, this weekly paper ceased to exist on November 17, 1950.

I Laisve (Toward Freedom), Lithuanian quarterly of politics. It was published in Brooklyn, N. Y. in 1953. In 1959, its publication was transferred to Cicero, Ill. At present, it is edited by Dr. V. Vardys. Its circulation is unknown.

Litcanus, a political and cultural quarterly magazine in English established by the American-Lithuanian Student Association, Inc., in Brooklyn, N. Y. on November 24, 1954. It has a circulation of more than 5,000 and informs foreigners about Lithuania.[22]

Metmenys, a cultural quarterly magazine for young Lithuanian generation published by V. Kavolis in Cicero, Ill. in 1959. Its circulation is unknown.

Musu Vytis (Our Knight), a literary and cultural bi-monthly magazine begun by the Lithuanian Student Scouts Association in Chicago, Ill. in 1951. This magazine still exists. Its circulation is unknown.

The Marian, a religious monthly magazine in English established in Chicago, Ill., 1948. It is published by the Congregation of Marian Fathers and edited by Rev. F. J. Jancius. Its circulation is unknown.[23]

Naujoji Ausra (New Dawn), a cultural periodical published by the Lithuanian Cultural Institute in Chicago, Ill. in December 1947. After 13 issues, this periodical was discontinued in November 1949.

Nemunas, a cultural illustrated periodical, edited by L. Dovydenas, published in Chicago, Ill. in May 1950. Later on, its publication was transferred to Scranton, Pa. After 6 issues, it was discontinued.

Rytas (Morning), a weekly newspaper published by the Lithuanian Catholic Information Bureau in Brooklyn, N. Y. in 1951. After some time, it ceased to exist.[24]

Seja (The Sowing), a liberal political and literary monthly magazine published in Melrose Park, Ill. in May 1953. It still exists and at present is edited by G. Lazauskas. Its circulation is unknown.

Sportas (Sports), a bi-monthly sports magazine, edited by K. Cerkeliunas, published by the American-Lithuanian Sports Society in Brooklyn, N. Y. in 1959. Its circulation is unknown.

Studentu Gaires (Students' Road), a quarterly magazine for Lithuanian students published by the Lithuanian Student Association in Chicago, Ill. in 1959. Its circulation is unknown.

Tautos Praeitis (The Past of a Nation), a Lithuanian historical magazine, irregular, published by the Lithuanian Historical Society in Cicero,

Ill. in 1959. Its circulation is unknown.

Teisininku Zinios (Jurists News), a jurisprudence quarterly magazine established by the Central Committee of Lithuanian Jurists in Chicago, Ill. in 1955. This magazine still exists. Its circulation is unknown.[25]

Technikos Zodis (Technical News), a science and technology monthly magazine established in Chicago, Ill. in April 1951. At present it is published by the Lithuanian Engineers and Architects Association. Its circulation is unknown.

Tevynes Sargas (Fatherland's Guard), a political, cultural, and social science periodical established in Brooklyn, N. Y. in 1951. It is published by the Lithuanian Christian Democratic Association and edited by the editorial board. Its circulation is unknown.[26]

Uzuolanka, a literary and cultural monthly magazine established in Chicago, Ill. in February 1952. It is published by the "Nemunas" Society and edited by A. Vilainis-Sidlauskas. Its circulation is unknown.

Zinios (News), a weekly newspaper, edited by P. Lisauskas, published in Brooklyn, N. Y. on October 1, 1950. After certain period of time, it ceased to exist.

Varpas (The Bell), a political and literary magazine, irregular, published by the Lithuanian Bell Publication Fund in New York, in 1953. No information is available about the circulation and the number of issues which were published.[27]

Vetykla (Winnowing), a humorous periodical published in Chicago, Ill. in 1955. Only one issue of this periodical came out.

During the period 1946-1960, 4 new Lithuanian newspapers and 33 new magazines were published in Brooklyn, Chicago, Cicero, Los Angeles, Melrose Park, Ill., New York, and Putnam, Conn. They were devoted to American Lithuanians, former displaced persons, who came to this country their second home.

In November 1960, 28 of these Lithuanian magazines and 1 newspaper continue to be published. A total number of Lithuanian papers and periodicals which are published in the United States of America in 1960 are: 10 newspapers and 48 magazines.

The Lithuanian press in America arose spontaneously out of its environment. In a very real way, these papers were missionaries of the American way of life, giving rise to a restlessness and a vigor that inevitably extended the freedoms enjoyed in the United States. This is the heritage of all foreign-language newspapers and periodicals that makes it impossible for them to be content with silence or neutralist attitude toward the plight of the captive peoples of the world. The Lithuanian newspapers and periodicals learned how to mobilize public opinion and how to exercise political pressure. Initially, they were torn between two poles, a sense of belonging and loyalty to the country where their editors and their readers were born, and a sense of belonging and loyalty, too, to the country which received them so openly.

TABLE 6

LITHUANIAN NEWSPAPERS AND PERIODICALS LISTED IN SEQUENCE OF THEIR APPEARANCE IN THE U.S.A. 1879-1959

No.	Title	Year	City and State
1	GAZIETA LIETUWISZKA (Lithuanian Newspaper)	1879	New York, N.Y.
2	APSZWIETA (Education)	1892	Shenandoah, Pa.
3	UNIJA (Union)	1884	Brooklyn, N.Y.
4	LIETUVISZKAS BALSAS (Lithuanian Voice)	1885	Brooklyn, N.Y.
5	WIENYBS LIETOWNINKU (Lithuanian Unity)	1886	Plymouth, Pa.
6	SAULE (The Sun)	1888	Mahaney City, Pa.
7	NEW YORKO GAZIETA LIETUWISZKA (New York Lithuanian Paper)	1891	New York, N.Y.
8	GARSAS (The Sound)	1892	Shenandoah, Pa.
9	LIETUVA (Lithuania)	1892	Chicago, Ill.
10	BOSTONO LIETUVISKAS BALSAS (Boston Lithuanian Voice)	1893	Boston, Mass.
11	GARSAS AMERIKOS LIETUVIU (American-Lithuanian Voice)	1894	Shenandoah, Pa.
12	NAUJA GADYNE (New Era)	1894	Mt. Carmel, Pa.
13	VALTIS DEVYNIOLIKTOJO AMZIAUS (The Boat of 19th Century)	1894	Plymouth, Pa.
14	PERKUNAS (The Thunder)	1895	Shenandoah, Pa.
15	TEVYNE (Fatherland)	1896	Mt. Carmel, Pa.
16	RYTAS (The Morning)	1896	Waterbury, Conn.
17	KARDAS (The Sword)	1896	Baltimore, Md.
18	PESYLVANIJOS DARBININKAS (Pennsylvania Worker)	1896	Shenandoah, Pa.
19	LITHUANIAN WEEKLY MAGAZINE	1896	Brooklyn, N.Y.
20	AMERIKOS LIETUVIS (American Lithuanian)	1897	Brooklyn, N.Y.
21	LIETUVISKAS KNINGINAS (Lithuanian Library)	1897	Shenandoah, Pa.

TABLE 6--Continued

No.	Title	Year	City and State
22	PASAULE (The World)	1897	Elizabeth, N.J.
23	GALYBE (The Might)	1898	Baltimore, Md.
24	DIRVA (The Field)	1898	Shenandoah, Pa.
25	NAUJA DRAUGIJA (New Society)	1898	Brooklyn, N.Y.
26	KATALIKAS (The Catholic)	1899	Chicago, Ill.
27	TARNAS BAZNYCIOS (Church Servant)	1899	Waterbury, Conn.
28	VILTIS (The Hope)	1899	Shenandoah, Pa.
29	LINKSMA VALANDA (Merry Hour)	1899	Mahaney City, Pa.
30	KUREJAS (The Creator)	1899	Chicago, Ill.
31	ATEITIS (The Future)	1900	Pittsburgh, Pa.
32	DARBININKU VILTIS (Workers' Hope)	1901	Pittsburgh, Pa.
33	ZVAIGZDE (The Star)	1901	Brooklyn, N.Y.
34	LIETUVIS (Lithuanian)	1901	Shenandoah, Pa.
35	SPINDULYS (The Beam)	1903	Brooklyn, N.Y.
36	KELEIVIS (The Traveler)	1904	Boston, Mass.
37	KOVA (The Fight)	1905	Philadelphia, Pa.
38	PLEPERYS (Chatterbox)	1905	Philadelphia, Pa.
39	VAISTININKAS (Druggist)	1905	Boston, Mass.
40	TIESOS DRAUGAS (Truth's Friend)	1906	Brooklyn, N.Y.
41	DILGELES (The Nettles)	1906	Philadelphia, Pa.
42	KAPSAS	1907	Philadelphia, Pa.
43	AMERIKOS Lietuvis	1907	Worcester, Mass.
44	SPINDULYS (The Beam)	1907	Pittsburgh, Pa.
45	JAUNIMO SAPNAI (Youth Dreams)	1907	Unknown
46	PIRMYN (Forward)	1908	Minersville, Pa.
47	LIETUVIU ZINIOS (Lithuanian News)	1909	McKees Rock, Pa.

TABLE 6--Continued

No.	Title	Year	City and State
48	DAGIS (The Thistle)	1909	Boston, Mass.
49	DALGIS (The Scythe)	1909	Philadelphia, Pa.
50	DRAUGAS (The Friend)	1909	Wilkes Barre, Pa.
51	LAISVOJI MINTIS (Free Thought)	1900	Scranton, Pa.
52	PIPIRAS (The Pepper)	1910	Boston, Mass.
53	LIETUVAITE (Lithuanian Woman)	1910	McKees Rock, Pa.
54	AIDAS (Echo)	1911	Waterbury, Conn.
55	LAISVE (Freedom)	1911	Boston, Mass.
56	LAISVOJI ZMONIJA (Free Mankind)	1911	Chicago, Ill.
57	SVIESA (The Light)	1911	Waterbury, Conn.
58	UPELIS RAMYBES (River of Peace)	1911	Waterbury, Conn.
59	TARKA (The Grater)	1911	Brooklyn, N.Y.
60	KELIONE (Journey)	1912	Worcester, Mass.
61	LIETVIU ZURNALAS (Lithuanian Magazine)	1912	Chicago, Ill.
62	VAKARU VARPAS (The Western Bell)	1912	Omaha, Neb.
63	DIEVO RYKSTE (God's Switch)	1913	Chicago, Ill.
64	SPITOLNINKAS	1913	Waterbury, Conn.
65	GALVOCIUS (The Thinker)	1914	Chicago, Ill.
66	ATEITIS (The Future)	1914	Boston, Mass.
67	SAKE (The Fork)	1914	Chicago, Ill.
68	ZARIJA (The Glowing Fire)	1914	Chicago, Ill.
69	JAUNOJI LIETUVA (New Lithuania)	1914	Chicago, Ill.
70	NAUJIENOS (News)	1914	Chicago, Ill.
71	VEIDRODIS (The Mirror)	1914	Chicago, Ill.
72	AMERIKOS LIETUVIS	1914	Worcester, Mass.
73	DARBININKU BALSAS (Workers' Voice)	1914	Baltimore, Md.

TABLE 6--Continued

No.	Title	Year	City and State
74	ZAIBAS (The Lightning)	1914	Grand Rapids, Mich.
75	MUSU DRAUGAS (Our Friend)	1915	Chicago, Ill.
76	PAZANGA (The Progress)	1915	Chicago, Ill.
77	RIMRAS	1915	Rockford, Ill.
78	DARBININKAS (The Worker)	1915	Boston, Mass.
79	PAZVALGA	1915	Boston, Mass.
80	VYTIS (The Knight)	1915	Chicago, Ill.
81	ZVIRBLIS (The Sparrow)	1915	Forest City, Pa.
82	NAUJOJI GADYNE (New Era)	1915	Philadelphia, Pa.
83	SANTAIKA	1915	Cleveland, Ohio
84	TAUTOS RYTAS (Nation's Morning)	1915	Unknown
85	MOTERU BALSAS (Women's Voice)	1916	Philadelphia, Pa.
86	MOTERU DIRVA (Women's Field)	1916	Worcester, Mass.
87	GARSAS (The Sound)	1917	Brooklyn, N.Y.
88	DILGELES	1917	Worcester, Mass.
89	ATGIMINAS	1917	Lawrence, Mass.
90	LIETUVOS ATSTATYMAS (Restoration of Lithuania)	1917	Brooklyn, N.Y.
91	APZVALGA (Review)	1918	Philadelphia, Pa.
92	AMERIKOS UKININKAS (Farmer of America)	1918	Hart, Mich.
93	LIETUVA (Lithuania)	1918	Chicago, Ill.
94	DARBAS (The Work)	1919	Brooklyn, N.Y.
95	MEILE IR SEIMYNA (Love and Family)	1919	Chicago, Ill.
96	PROLETARAS	1919	Chicago, Ill.
97	DARBO VALANDA IR PERKUNAS (Working Hour and Thunder)	1919	Cleveland, Ohio
98	KOVA (The Fight)	1920	Philadelphia, Pa.

TABLE 6--Continued

No.	Title	Year	City and State
99	UKININKU ZINIOS (Farmers' News)	1920	Scottsville, Mich.
100	PASIUNTINYS	1920	Chicago, Ill.
101	ARTOJAS (Plowman)	1920	Cleveland, Ohio
102	BANGA (The Wave)	1921	Chicago, Ill.
103	TEVYNES BALSAS (Fatherland's Voice)	1921	Wilkes Barre, Pa.
104	PERKUNAS	1921	Boston, Mass.
105	ZINIOS (News)	1921	Chicago, Ill.
106	KRISTAUS KARALIAUS LAIVAS (The Boat of Christ the King)	1921	Chicago, Ill.
107	MOKSLEIVIU KELIAI (Students' Road)	1921	Valparaiso, Ind.
108	DARBININKU TIESA (Workers' Truth)	1922	Brooklyn, N.Y.
109	TELEGRAMAS (Telegram)	1922	Chicago, Ill.
110	SVIESA (The Light)	1922	Chicago, Ill.
111	APSVIETIMAS (Education)	1923	Unknown
112	AIDAS (Echo)	1923	Cleveland, Ohio
113	VARPAS (The Bell)	1923	Chicago, Ill.
114	LIETUVOS ZINIOS (News of Lithuania)	1923	Chicago, Ill.
115	VADOVAS (The Leader)	1924	Chicago, Ill.
116	BITE (The Bee)	1924	Boston, Mass.
117	MEILE KATALIKU SEIMYNU (The Love of Catholic Families)	1924	Du Bois, Pa.
118	GYDYTOJAS (The Physician)	1924	Chicago, Ill.
119	AMERIKOS LIETUVIU VAIZBOS BUTO ZINIOS	1925	Boston, Mass.
120	RIMBAS	1925	Unknown
121	TARADAIKA	1925	Chicago, Ill.
122	CHICAGOS ZINIOS (Chicago News)	1927	Chicago, Ill.
123	MARGUTIS	1928	Chicago, Ill.

TABLE 6--<u>Continued</u>

No.	Title	Year	City and State
124	TARPININKAS	1928	Boston, Mass.
125	GYVENIMAS (Life)	1928	Unknown
126	SANDARA	1929	Chicago, Ill.
127	ATZALA (The Shoot)	1929	Shaft, Pa.
128	LIAUDIES TRIBUMA (Peoples Platform)	1930	Chicago, Ill.
129	DETROITO ZINIOS (Detroit News)	1931	Detroit, Mich.
130	TAUTOS BALSAS (Nation's Voice)	1931	Scranton, Pa.
131	TIESOS BALSAS	1931	Scranton, Pa.
132	NAUJA GADYNE (New Era)	1931	Brooklyn, N.Y.
133	GIEDRA	1932	Wilkes Barre, Pa.
134	AMERIKA	1932	Brooklyn, N.Y.
135	ISMINTIS (Wisdom)	1933	Boston, Mass.
136	SIUVEJAS (The Tailor)	1934	Brooklyn, N.Y.
137	PAZANGA	1934	Chicago, Ill.
138	JAUNIMAS (The Youth)	1936	Chicago, Ill.
139	PASIUNTINYS (Messenger)	1937	Chicago, Ill.
140	TEISYBE (The Truth)	1937	Lawrence, Mass.
141	LIETUVIU NAUJIENOS (Lithuanian News)	1938	Philadelphia, Pa.
142	LIETUVA (Lithuania)	1939	New York, N.Y.
143	SVYTURYS (Lighthouse)	1940	Chicago, Ill.
144	VILTIS (The Hope)	1942	Norwalk, Conn.
145	AIDAI (Echo)	1944	Brooklyn, N.Y.
146	KALIFORNIJOS LIETUVIS-LIETUVIU DIENOS (Lithuanian Days)	1946	Los Angeles, Ca.
147	DARBAS	1947	Boston, Mass.
148	NAUJOJI AUSRA (New Dawn)	1947	Chicago, Ill.
149	LIETUVOS TEISIMINKAS (Lawyer of Lithuania)	1949	Detroit, Mich.

TABLE 6--Continued

No.	Title	Year	City and State
150	NEMUNAS	1950	Chicago, Ill.
151	GIRIOS AIDAS (Forest Echo)	1950	Chicago, Ill.
152	ZINIOS (News)	1950	Brooklyn, N.Y.
153	EGLUTE	1950	Lawrence, Mass.
154	EVANGELIJOS ZODIS (Gospel's Word)	1951	Chicago, Ill.
155	GABIJA	1951	Brooklyn, N.Y.
156	KARYS (The Warrior)	1951	Brooklyn, N.Y.
157	RYTAS (Morning)	1951	Brooklyn, N.Y.
158	PELEDA (Owl)	1951	Chicago, Ill.
159	LUI CHRISTI	1951	Brooklyn, N.Y.
160	TECHNIKOS ZODIS (Ingineering Word)	1951	Chicago, Ill.
161	MUSU DIENOS (Our Days)	1951	Unknown
162	TEVYNES SARGAS (Fatherland's Guard)	1951	Brooklyn, N.Y.
163	ATSPINDZIAI (Reflections)	1952	Chicago, Ill.
164	LIETUVA (Lithuania)	1952	New York, N.Y.
165	LITERATUROS LANKAI (Literature Sheets)	1952	Unknown
166	JAUNIMO ZYGIAI (Youth's Deeds)	1952	Unknown
167	STUDENTU GAIRES	1952	Unknown
168	LITHUANIAN CONSULTATIVE PANEL	1952	Unknown
169	LIETUVISKOS KNYGOS MEGEJAS	1952	Unknown
170	SEJA (Sowing)	1953	Chicago, Ill.
171	VARPAS (The Bell)	1953	Brooklyn, N.Y.
172	I LAISVE (Toward Freedom)	1953	Brooklyn, N.Y.
173	JAUNIMO MINTYS (The Thought of Youth)	1953	Chicago, Ill.
174	LITHUANIAN CATHOLIC YOUTH BULLETIN	1953	Unknown
175	MUSU VYTIS (Our Knight)	1953	Boston, Mass.

TABLE 6--Continued

No.	Title	Year	City and State
176	LAISVOJI LIETUVA (Free Lithuania)	1953	Chicago, Ill.
177	GAUDEAMUS	1953	Unknown
178	AMERIKOS LIETUVIU BENDROUMENE	1954	Cleveland, Ohio
179	GIMTOJI KALBA (Native Language)	1954	Chicago, Ill.
180	EVANGELIJOS SVIESA (Gospel's Light)	1955	Unknown
181	APZVALGA	1958	Unknown
182	CICERO LIETUVIS	1959	Cicero, Ill.
183	ATZALYNAS	1959	Unknown
184	SPORTAS (Sports)	1959	Chicago, Ill.
185	TAUTOS PRAEITIS	1959	Unknown
186	TRIMITU AIDAI	1959	Unknown

FOOTNOTES

[1] Reprinted by the permission of the author.

[2] P. Ruseckas, Pasaulio Lietuviai (Kaunas, Lithuania: Draugija Uzsienio Lietuviams Remti, 1935), p. 43.

[3] A. Milukas, "Gazieta Lietuwiszka," Lietuviu Enciklopedija, ed. J. Puzinas, VII (1956), 43.

[4] P. Ruseckas, p. 43.

[5] A. Sapoka, Lithuania Through the Ages (Munich, West Germany: Lithuanian Press, 1948), p. 15.

[6] J. Prunskis, "Katalikas," Lietuviu Enciklopedija, ed. J. Puzinas, XI (1957), 154.

[7] N. W. Ayer and Sons, Annual American Newspapers and Periodicals Directory (Philadelphia: N. W. Ayer and Son's, Inc., 1915-1916), pp. 1276 and 1283.

[8] J. Prunskis, "Keleivis," Lietuviu Enciklopedija, ed. J. Puzinas, XI (1957), 335.

[9]Simutis, p. 34.

[10]Common Council for American Unity, "Lithuanian Publications in the U.S.A." List of Foreign Language Publications in the U.S.A. (New York: 1959), p. 3.

[11]P. Grigaitis, "Naujienos," Lietuviu Enciklopedija, ed. P. Cepenas, XX (1960), 71.

[12]Common Council for American Unity, List of Foreign Language Publications in the U.S.A., p. 4.

[13]B. Gaidziunas, "Dirva," Lietuviu Enciklopedija, ed. J. Girnius, V (1955).

[14]Common Council for American Unity, List of Foreign Language Publications in the U.S.A., p. 3.

[15]Ibid., p. 2.

[16]F. Lavinskas, Amerikos Lietuviu Laikrasciai (Long Island City, 1956), p. 88.

[17]Simutis, p. 33.

[18]Common Council for American Unity, List of Foreign Language Publications, p. 3.

[19]J. Prunskis, "Kalifornijos Lietuvis," Lietuviu Enciklopedija, ed. J. Puzinas, X (1957), 317-18.

[20]Simutis, p. 35.

[21]J. Prunskis, "Laiskai Lietuviams," Lietuviu Enciklopedija, ed. J. Girnius, XIV (1958), 88.

[22]"Lituanus," Lietuviu Enciklopedija, ed. J. Girnius, XVI (1958), 308.

[23]Simutis, p. 36.

[24]Ibid., p. 37.

[25]Common Council for American Unity, List of Foreign Language Publications, p. 2.

[26]Simutis, p. 38.

[27]A. Ruzancovas, Knygu Lentyna (Bookshelf) (Danville, Ill.: Lithuanian Bibliographic Service, No. 1 [115], 1960), p. 21.

Chapter 11. THE LITHUANIAN IMMIGRANTS IN
AMERICAN POLITICS

Source - John P. White. Lithuanians and
the Democratic Party. A Case
Study of Nationality Politics in
Chicago and Cook County. Ph.D.
Thesis in Political Science, the
University of Chicago, 1953. The
selection is from Chapter II,
"The Lithuanian Community of
Chicago," pages 20-48.[1]

Overview

White decided to study Lithuanians in Chicago because he believed
them to be a politically significant nationalistic group. The United
States Bureau of Census figures indicated they were eighth in the list of
nationalities of the foreign-born in Chicago in 1940. Further, their numbers were being increased by the influx of Lithuanian displaced persons
who were attracted to the largest Lithuanian community in the United
States. The Lithuanians were high in the list of ethnic importance to the
Democratic party in Chicago and Cook County, ranking just behind the Poles,
Italians and Czechs. At the top were the Irish, who were the entrenched
elite political group.

White found that Lithuanians resided in the following community areas
of Chicago: Lower West Side, Roselawn, Brighton Park, Bridgeport, New
City, Chicago Lawn and West Pullman. The oldest Lithuanian colony in Chicago was Bridgeport. This was one of the original Irish settlements in
Chicago and it produced a number of important Irish politicians. It was
the domain of Richard J. Daley, who became famous as Mayor of Chicago.
The newest, most populous and the most politically significant Lithuanian
community came to be Chicago Lawn. The Lithuanians were concentrated
heavily in the southeastern part of Chicago Lawn, centering around Marquette Park.

Lithuanian political activity in Chicago has been conducted through
the Lithuanian Democratic League, which depended in large degree upon the
churches, schools, clubs, lodges and other social groups to maintain its
political power. Democratic Lithuanian politicians were eager to seek any
kind of endorsement from Lithuanian pastors because of the importance of
the Church in Lithuanian life, even though formally members of the clergy
were non-political. They were also eager to win votes from more than 300
Lithuanian fraternal orders, clubs and associations, such as the Knights
of Lithuania and the American Legion posts in the Lithuanian community,
but not from the Lithuanian Chamber of Commerce. That group leaned toward
the Republican side. Democratic Lithuanian politicians also sought the
backing of the influential Lithuanian press, particularly The Naujienos
and The Draugas.

Political Importance of the Group

Criteria for Selection.--In choosing the Lithuanian group, the writer was motivated by a belief that it is a politically significant nationalistic group. Of course, the same could be said of a number of groups, but several factors dictated the selection of the Lithuanians in preference to other more numerous and politically more powerful groups.

The first such factor involves access to the group. In the type of study contemplated, it is vital to be able to get the facts about the internal structure and functioning of the group on the political scene. However, the nationalistic group is decidedly an "in-group" which tends to be suspicious and hostile toward strangers. Therefore, when the writer was assured of the full cooperation of the Lithuanian Democratic organization, this meant that material not ordinarily available could be utilized.

Another factor which facilitates the study of the Lithuanian group is its political organization. In the Democratic party, the recognized agency for the Lithuanian group is the Lithuanian Democratic League of Cook County, Inc., which is a federation of the Lithuanian Democratic clubs throughout the county. Most of the important nationalities in Cook County lack such a unified organizational structure, and so are more difficult to study.

Of course, regardless of any practical advantages such as those just mentioned, it is necessary that the group studied should be politically significant. There would be no point in studying a group having no importance in Chicago politics, for in such a case there would be no political interaction between the group and the party, and this interaction is the major subject of the proposed investigation. We may utilize two major criteria in determining the political significance of a given nationalistic group: (1) the numerical strength, in terms of foreign-born and second generation members of the group, and (2) the importance of the group in the electoral strategy of the party, as indicated by actions and policies of the party leaders.

Numerical Strength of the Lithuanian Group.--In seeking an unbiased appraisal of the actual numerical strength of a group, the only source we have is the United States Bureau of the Census. Unfortunately, the latest available figures are those derived from the 1940 census.

Table 3 shows that the Lithuanian group ranks eighth in the list of nationalities of the foreign-born in Chicago, or did in 1940. It must be pointed out that there has been a large influx of Lithuanian displaced persons into Chicago since the conclusion of World War II. No one knows exactly how many of these persons are living in Chicago at the present time, but it is known that the number is constantly being increased by the migration of displaced persons whose first American home was elsewhere, but who are drawn to Chicago because it contains the largest Lithuanian community in the United States. The Lithuanian consulate of Chicago estimates that between 10,000 and 12,000 Lithuanian displaced persons are now in Chicago. It might be added that other Eastern European nations have also sent a number of "DP's" to Chicago, thus aiding a general and long-term trend in favor of "New" immigrants over those from northern and western Europe.

The Second Generation.--Statistics on the foreign-born population do not tell the whole story of nationality groups, since they do not include data on the second generation--the sons and daughters of the immigrants.

TABLE 3

TABLE 3

LEADING NATIONALITIES OF FOREIGN-BORN
WHITE POPULATION OF CHICAGO[a]

	1940		1930	
	Number	Percentage[b]	Number	Percentage
Poland. . . .	119,264	17.7	149,622	17.5
Germany . . .	83,424	12.4	111,366	13.0
Russia. . . .	66,950	10.0	78,462	9.2
Italy	66,472	9.9	73,960	8.6
Sweden. . . .	46,258	6.9	65,735	7.7
Ireland . . .	35,156	5.2	47,385	5.5
Czechoslovak.	33,596	5.0	48,814	5.7
Lithuania . .	26,254	3.9	31,430	3.7
Austria . . .	26,091	3.9	24,646	2.7
Canada. . . .	21,573	3.2	29,836	3.5

[a]Source: U. S. Bureau of the Census, Sixteenth Census: 1940, Vol.
II, Character of the Population (Washington: Government Printing Office,
1943), Part 2, p. 642.

[b]Percentage given is that of the entire foreign-born population of
Chicago.

While no complete enumeration of this foreign-stock element is available,
census figures do include reports on a 5 per cent sample which was questioned as to its parentage. As defined by the Bureau of the Census,

> The term "foreign white stock" is used to indicate the com-
> bined total of two classes, namely, the foreign-born white
> and the native white of foreign or mixed parentage. The
> "foreign white stock", therefore comprises those persons who
> were born abroad or who had at least one parent foreign born,
> that is, those persons of the first and second, but not sub-
> sequent, generations.[2]

Table 4 shows that when the second generation is added to the immigrant total, there is not a great deal of change in the rank order of the
nationalities, although the Lithuanian group then falls behind the Austrians and into ninth place. It should also be noted that the figures
given are for Chicago only, and do not include data on Cook County as a
whole. The Census Bureau sampling of the foreign-stock population was
carried on only in selected municipalities.

Political Interpretation of Census Data.--Census figures on nationality groups often require interpretation and qualification before being
used in political analysis, as we suggested in Chapter I. For political
purposes, several of the leading groups in the census figures are much

TABLE 4

LEADING NATIONALITIES OF FOREIGN WHITE STOCK IN CHICAGO*

	1940		1930	
	Number	Percentage	Number	Percentage
Poland. . . .	359,984	19.2	401,316	18.3
Germany . . .	291,824	15.6	377,975	17.2
Italy	185,012	9.9	181,861	8.3
Russia . . .	158,990	8.5	169,736	7.7
Ireland . . .	134,876	7.2	169,568	7.7
Sweden . . .	110,198	5.9	140,913	6.4
Czechoslovakia	91,656	4.9	122,089	5.6
Austria . . .	63,691	3.4	55,462	2.5
Lithuania . .	59,274	3.2	63,918	2.9
Canada . . .	53,618	2.9	73,786	3.4

*Source: U. S. Bureau of the Census, Sixteenth Census: 1940. Country of Origin of the Foreign Stock, 1940 (Washington: Government Printing Office, 1943).

smaller than the statistics indicate, while others are probably larger.

An important element in Chicago's population is composed of Jews. The number of foreign-born and second generation Jewish foreign stock cannot be ascertained, since there is no Jewish nationality category in the census data. However, since persons of Jewish religion or descent appear to be concentrated in the same area that "Russian" foreign stock is predominant, it may be assumed that a large proportion of the Russian total is Jewish. Undoubtedly there are considerable numbers of Jews included in the totals for Germany, Poland, Czechoslovakia and Austria, but again this cannot be definitely ascertained.

In addition to the size of a nationality group, party strategists also take into account traditional loyalties of certain groups. Usually, the Chicago Democrats make little attempt to secure the allegiance of the Swedes and other Scandinavians, although Cermak made some gestures in their direction. Gottfried points out that Cermak was influential in securing several elective and appointive offices for Scandinavian Democrats.[3] Such experiments were feasible during the early New Deal era, when the Democrats controlled practically all the patronage in the county. However, at the present time the Democrats do not seem to regard the Scandinavians as a profitable object of their efforts. The Democratic ward committeeman in the Ninth ward told the writer that he "never wasted any jobs" on the large Scandinavian element in his ward, since they always voted Republican anyway.[4] On all levels, the party leadership must decide if their limited supply of patronage and nominations should be drawn upon to "recognize" a given group, and they will do so only if there is reasonable hope of success.

<u>Nationalistic Groups and the Democratic Party</u>.--Such examples demon-
strate the necessity for keeping in mind and applying our definition of
nationalistic groups as given in Chapter I. Applying that definition to
the groups active within the Democratic party, we can arrive at a revised
list of foreign-stock groups which will represent the nationalistic groups
of importance to the party. The following list, roughly in the order of
importance, is suggested:

1. Poles
2. Italians
3. Bohemians (Czechs)
4. Lithuanians
5. Slovaks
6. Greeks

In view of the variation of this list from the census list of foreign-
stock groups, some explanation must be made to account for the difference.
We will discuss several important groups individually, but in general omis-
sions are due to the following considerations: (1) A group is omitted because it is not really a discrete social group, but is an artificial construct of the census-takers; or (2) Where a group does not carry on the
interest group activities identified with the nationalistic group. This
may be due to the traditional Republicanism of the group, in which case
there is a mutual lack of interest on the part of the group and the party,
or it may be because the group does not find it necessary to fight for
recognition from the party. Some of the older groups, such as the Germans,
are certain to be granted at least occasional representation on the Democratic ballot without any organized effort on their part. In such cases,
patronage appointments are also of little or no importance, since there is
no need or desire to maintain a nationalistic political organization. A
group such as this is not considered a nationalistic group by the party,
and will not be so considered in this study. The patterns of political
interaction characteristic of nationalistic politics are absent in the
case of well established "have" groups, and the nominations granted such
groups are not of great symbolic importance to the group represented. They
are merely periodic evidence that the party recognizes the established position of the group and does not wish to discriminate against it.

These "non-nationalistic" groups cannot, of course, be expected to
react as markedly to recognition or lack of it as the "underdog groups,"
as Lubell calls them.[5] In short, they are not primarily a problem for the
party strategist specializing in nationalistic politics, and they must be
appealed to mainly on other grounds.

Turning to a comparison of the census list given in Table 4 with our
"Democratic" list, we see that the first omission, after that of the Germans, is the Russian group. As we have already pointed out, there is no
organized Russian nationalistic activity in the Cook County area. The number of ethnic Russians cannot be determined, but it is undoubtedly small.
In fact, even "ethnic Russians" is an unsatisfactory term, since there are
nationality divisions involved in addition to the Jewish-Gentile dichotomy.
Some of Chicago's "Russians" are Ukrainians, and are intensely nationalistic and anti-Russian. Assuming, however, that most of the census "Russians" are really Jews, it is undeniable that Jews are a politically important group. Many Jews are active in Chicago politics, and the top
Democrat, National Committeeman Jacob Arvey, is himself a son of Lithuanian
Jewish immigrants.[6] The Jewish group, however, is a special case, exhibiting characteristics not common to the nationalistic groups. For one
thing, Chicago's Jews came originally from widely varying national back-

152

grounds, and in some cases Jewish politicians place primary emphasis on their country of origin rather than on their Jewish heritage. A. J. Sabath is the outstanding example of this, since he was known quite as well in his role as a Bohemian as he was for his Jewish religion. Another factor is that the eternal problem of anti-Semitic prejudice acts as a deterrent on any tendencies to over-publicize the fact of Jewish origin, in contrast to the attitude of the ordinary nationalistic politician, who is likely to trumpet his ethnic background from the house-tops, since anti-foreignism is not as strong as anti-Semitism. The Jewish group does not carry on the organized "recognition" activity we have identified with nationalistic politics, and for that reason, we have not included them in our list of nationalistic groups.

We have already discussed our reasons for omitting the Irish from the list of nationalistic groups. The Irish predominate in the leadership of the Democratic party, so there is no need for a recognition struggle. The Irish are the entrenched elite group against which the under-dog groups must struggle for political advancement.

As we have noted, the Swedes and other Scandinavians are more or less written off by the Democrats. The feeling seems to be mutual, since the Scandinavians evidently make no attempt to secure favors from the Democrats.

We have also divided the Czechoslovaks into Bohemians and Slovaks and classified them separately. While the census figures give us no clue as to the break-down between Bohemians and Slovaks, it is obvious that the great majority are in reality Bohemians. This is indicated by the fact that Bohemians have been for many years considered an important factor in Chicago politics, while little has been heard from the Slovaks.

The Austrian group was heavily over-represented in census figures during the days of the ramshackle Austro-Hungarian empire. One commentary on the "Austrians" of Chicago illustrates the point well:

> The census classified a large swarm as "Austrian." They
> were really Poles, supplemented by Dalmatians, Croatians,
> Slavonians, Bosnians, Herzegovinians. In such numbers they
> came, year by year, that in 1910 the census-takers recorded
> an increase of more than 120,000 of these "Austrians" in
> Chicago. In addition, 24,000 were credited to Hungary.[7]

Presumably, the later figures on Austrians adhere more closely to actual ethnic lines, but, possibly because of the high degree of assimilation of the ethnic Austrians, they do not compose an important nationalistic group in Chicago, not being active as a group in either major party.

The Lithuanians.--Prior to the time that Lithuania regained its independence as an aftermath of World War I and the Russian Communist revolution, there was no United States Census classification for Lithuanians, despite their very sizable representation in the United States. The author of a study of linguistic condition in Chicago in 1903 pointed out the inadequacy of census data in dealing with the Lithuanians:

> The Lithuanians, who in language and sentiment form a dis-
> tinct people, and are represented by thousands of immigrants,
> are nowhere mentioned. In Chicago they were told by the
> enumerators that, there being no provision for Lithuanians,
> they might be either Poles or Russians. Whether in other
> places they were classified under Poland or Russia, or both,

it is impossible to say. For the enumerators are not always
so impartial in such cases . . .[8]

Even the inclusion of a Lithuanian category was no guarantee that the situation would be remedied, as the same author points out:

> For the school census of 1896, the innovation was made of
> classifying the Lithuanians separately, and several Lith-
> uanian enumerators were appointed. In 1898 the separate
> classification was retained, but no Lithuanian enumerators
> appointed, and the number dropped from 2,897 to 1,411, al-
> though, as a matter of fact, the Lithuanians had been pour-
> ing in constantly, as they have been since then.[9]

Buck came to the conclusion that despite any census figures to the contrary, there were at least 10,000 Lithuanian-speaking persons in Chicago
in 1903, and probably over 14,000.[10]

While the lack of a Lithuanian category in census data no longer
exists, Chicago Lithuanian leaders still maintain that the actual number
of Lithuanians is larger than census figures indicate. They cite the fact
that the naturalization papers of most of the older Lithuanians state they
were citizens of Russia or Poland or even of Germany. Since the United
States government had once officially stamped these people as being of
these non-Lithuanian nationalities, they have often allowed this "official"
pronouncement to go unchallenged whenever questioned by census-takers as
to nationality, even though they may have been Lithuanians by ancestry and
by preference.

Speculation as to possible inaccuracies in the census reports on the
number of Lithuanians in Chicago could be carried on indefinitely, but with
little utility. We could discuss, for instance, the "Polonized" Lithuanians, who, speaking Polish as well as Lithuanian, and usually living in a
Polish community, voluntarily report themselves as Lithuanian Poles, or
simply as Poles, if the former characterization will not be accepted by an
interviewer. But no conclusive answers could be reached, and in any case
it is unlikely that any appreciable difference in the ranking of the Lithuanians among other nationality groups of Chicago would result.

It appears that accurate figures would show that at the present time
there are 100,000 Lithuanian-Americans, more or less, in Cook County. This
is necessarily only an estimate, based on the figure of about 60,000 listed as residing in Chicago proper in 1940, plus accretions of ten to twelve
thousand post-war immigrants, plus an undetermined number from the County
outside Chicago.

It seems clear that while the Lithuanian group is certainly not the
largest nationality group, or even one of the largest, it is numerically
significant, and especially so to the Democratic party. As we have pointed out, some nationality groups which are more heavily represented in census data are actually of less importance to the Democratic party, for one
reason or another, than the Lithuanians.

But the crucial fact that proves that the Lithuanians are a group
which is a suitable subject for our case-study of nationality politics in
Cook County is that the Democratic party does in fact recognize the Lithuanians as a group with which it is advisable to deal politically. The
character of this party-nationalistic group relationship is the main interest of this study. If, as it appears, this relationship is sufficiently

typical, it is not necessary that the group used as a subject be so large as to be decisive in the affairs of the party.

Lithuanian Neighborhoods

The Neighborhood Pattern.--While Chicago's Lithuanians are scattered throughout the city, in the sense that some of them are to be found in practically every census tract, more than a third of them are concentrated into five neighborhoods, or "colonies," as they are sometimes called in the Lithuanian press.

Assuming that the distribution of persons of Lithuanian stock is roughly similar to the distribution of foreign-born Lithuanians, we can use census data on Lithuanian immigrants to illustrate this point.

Table 5 shows that roughly half of Chicago's foreign-born Lithuanian-Americans live within only twenty-five of the city's 935 census tracts. If we plot on a ward map of Chicago the census tracts where Lithuanians are the leading foreign-born nationality, and where foreign-born persons constitute at least 20 per cent of the total population, we see that five well-defined areas are mapped out, one in each of the following wards: Ninth, Eleventh, Twelfth, Thirteenth, and Twenty-First.

However, the three areas in the Eleventh, Twelfth, and Twenty-First wards are in reality not isolated from each other but are connected by census tracts where Lithuanians, while not the leading nationality, are quite numerous.

Bridgeport: The "Old Neighborhood."--The oldest existing Lithuanian colony is found in Bridgeport, just north of the Chicago Stock Yards. Bridgeport lies wholly within the Eleventh ward, and comprises most of the area of that ward. It was one of the original Irish settlements in Chicago, and produced a number of important Irish politicians.[11] But as was so often the case, the coming of the "new" immigrants saw the gradual departure of the older ethnic elements. The Lithuanians were among the latecomers to Bridgeport. As recently as 1930, the Lithuanians were not the leading nationality group, that distinction having passed from the Irish to the Poles.[12] However, between 1930 and 1940, the number of foreign-born Lithuanians in Bridgeport increased to the point where they comprised about a third of the total foreign-born population.[13]

While it is only in recent years that the Lithuanians have become the leading nationality in Bridgeport, there has already been a tendency for many Lithuanians to leave there. The area is an old one, and definitely not fashionable. Consequently, those economically able to find better living conditions have tended to move south and west into Marquette Park or Roseland. On the other hand, many of the Lithuanian displaced persons who came to Chicago after World War II have taken up residence in Bridgeport. But even to those Lithuanians who have moved away, Bridgeport continues to be "the old neighborhood" and trips back to the area from new homesites are common. Along the "main street" of Bridgeport, which is South Halstead Street, the Lithuanian area is well marked off. From about Thirtieth to Thirty-Fifth Streets on Halstead, many of the stores and offices bear Lithuanian names, and signs are written in Lithuanian or in the odd hodge-podge resulting from the addition of Lithuanian endings to English words. One block east of Halstead, down most of the length of the South Side, lies Peoria Street. But between Thirty-First and Thirty-Ninth Streets, this thoroughfare is called Lituanica Street.

TABLE 5

DISTRIBUTION OF PERSONS BORN IN LITHUANIA
BY COMMUNITY AREA, CENSUS TRACT, AND WARD*

Community Area	Census Tract	Ward	Number
Lower West Side	500	21	224
	501	21	864
	506	21	552
	502	21	67
Roselawn.	687	9	110
	688	9	679
Brighton Park	740	22	129
	743	12	62
	745	12	522
	746	12	439
	747	12	719
	748	12	949
	749	12	343
	750	12	59
Bridgeport	770	11	384
	771	11	938
	772	11	168
	773	11	520
	774	11	26
	777	11	296
	778	11	99
	779	11	197
	780	11	593
New City	782	11 and 12	540
	783	14	632
Chicago Lawn	846	13	1,534
	847	13	502
West Pullman	715	9	261
Total	. . .	. . .	12,408

*Includes only census tracts where Lithuanians are the leading nationality, or second nationality in areas adjacent to heavily Lithuanian tracts.

Sources: Sixteenth Census, Statistic for Census Tracts and Community Areas, Chicago, Ill., and Ward Map, City of Chicago, Sept. 19, 1947, issued by Board of Election Commissioners.

Though the original Irish Bridgeporters have largely vanished, the Irish politicians have not. Bridgeport is the heart of the domain of Dick Daley, one of Chicago's most powerful Irish politicians. Despite their numerical strength in Bridgeport, the Lithuanians show few signs of developing a political leadership which could challenge the Irish oligarchy.

The departure of many of the better-educated and more enterprising Lithuanians has deprived the area of some of its best potential Lithuanian leadership.

The Lower West-Side.--Just across the Chicago river from Bridgeport lies the Lower West Side. Although considered a distinct community area, the Lower West Side has from the earliest days had close ties with Bridgeport since the pioneer settlement in the general area ranged along both banks of the river.[14] Lithuanians in this general area constitute only the fourth largest nationality group, behind Poles, Czechs, and Yugoslavians. For the most part, the Lithuanians are concentrated in two areas surrounding the two Lithuanian churches in the area. Politically, the Lithuanians have not been very active in this area, outside of those who participate in activities in the nearby Bridgeport community. A Lithuanian Democratic club formerly existed in the Twenty-First ward, which includes the Lower West Side, but that club is now dormant.

Brighton Park.--The community area of Brighton Park, lying mostly within the Twelfth ward, is dominated by two nationalistic groups, the Poles and the Lithuanians, with the former in the lead. As in the case of Bridgeport, the two nationalities together make up a healthy majority of the total foreign-born and foreign stock population. As of 1940, the Poles had 45.8 per cent and the Lithuanians had 29.3 per cent of the total foreign-born population.[15] It might be noted that the juxtaposition of Poles and Lithuanians is something more than accident, since from the earliest days of Lithuanian settlement in Chicago this has often been the case.[16] While the Lithuanians are not usually considered to be Slavs, their relationship to the Poles dates back to the medieval union of Lithuania and Poland.

Chicago Lawn and Marquette Park.--Probably the most important Lithuanian community, from a political standpoint, is located in the Community Area designated as Chicago Lawn. However, the Lithuanians are heavily concentrated in the south-eastern part of Chicago Lawn, centering around Marquette Park, and the Lithuanian neighborhood is usually referred to by the name of the park.

The Marquette Park section of Chicago Lawn is one of the more recently developed parts of the area, is for the most part a pleasant lower middle-class suburb, with a high percentage of modern housing. Consequently, it has acted as a magnet for Lithuanians whose economic status permits them to move from older areas. Many business and professional men of the Lithuanian community live in Marquette Park. This is important to bear in mind as we study the political activities of Lithuanians in various parts of the city.

Roseland.--Another fairly recent Lithuanian settlement is in the Community Area of Roseland, in the Ninth ward. As of 1940, only two census tracts found the Lithuanians in first place, and these tracts are much smaller in population than those in Marquette Park. Nevertheless, the Lithuanian community here is well established. Unlike most Lithuanian colonies, the one in Roseland is not located in an area with a high percentage of Slavic residents. Roseland has for many years been heavily populated by Scandinavian and Dutch elements.[17] Politically, this has meant that the Lithuanians find themselves in a rock-ribbed Republican environment. The Scandinavians and Hollanders of Roseland have supplied the biggest obstacle in the path of the Democratic ward organization.[18]

Another group of Lithuanians is found further south in the Ninth ward, in the Community Area of West Pullman, which is heavily populated by Poles and Italians and which is dependably Democratic.

Other Areas.--The Community Areas just discussed do not constitute an entire list of those in which the Lithuanians have significant numbers. In all, Lithuanians are among the first five nationalities in twelve of the seventy-five Community Areas of Chicago. In addition to those previously discussed, the list includes Garfield Ridge, Archer Heights, New City, West Elsdon, Clearing, West Lawn, Mount Greenwood, and North Lawndale.[19] However, since we are concerned in this study with the political activities of the Lithuanian group, we will not discuss these other areas in detail, since for political purposes only the areas discussed individually are of much importance.

Community Organization

Political Importance.--While it is not the purpose of this study to undertake a sociological analysis of the Lithuanian community, it is necessary to mention a few of the Lithuanian community organizations which play a part in the conduct of nationalistic political activity. The nationalistic politician is forced to make efficient use of various community organizations in order to give at least the appearance of community solidarity behind the political demands of the nationalistic leadership.

A more important consideration, perhaps, is the fact that the existence and vitality of sub-groups within the nationality community may be viewed as a kind of barometer of the cohesion of the group. It must be remembered that in every Lithuanian organization the shared attitude of Lithuanian nationality is being reinforced and elaborated. This means that inter-action of Lithuanians as Lithuanians is being increased. Truman, using Lundberg's terminology, stresses the importance of the "degree of integrative interaction," and says that

> The frequency, or rate, of interaction will in part determine the primacy of a particular group affiliation in the behavior of an individual and . . . will be of major importance in determining the relative effectiveness with which a group asserts its claims upon other groups.[20]

A nationalistic political organization, such as the Lithuanian Democratic League, must depend to a very large degree, upon the schools, churches, clubs, lodges, and other social groups to maintain the group interaction political activity must be based. It would be a hopeless task for a nationalistic political organization to attempt to "represent" a nationality which had little or no social interaction. That is one reason why there is no "Russian Democratic (or Republican) League," despite the census figures which show a large number of "Russians" in Cook County.

The Churches.--The role of the Church in Lithuanian life can hardly be overemphasized. Lithuanians are overwhelmingly Roman Catholic in their faith, although there is one Lithuanian Protestant Evangelical church in Chicago. On the other hand, there are ten Lithuanian Roman Catholic parishes in Chicago proper, as well as one each in Chicago Heights, Cicero, and Waukegan.[21] These churches are truly pillars of the Lithuanian community. One Lithuanian, writing in 1913, expresses the situation of the Chicago Lithuanians very well:

They [the Lithuanian Churches] are all strong fortresses

and guardians of the nationality of the Lithuanians of
America. . . . It is thanks to the church and the school
that many hundred thousands of Lithuanians have not been
absorbed in the great nation. As long as the Lithuanians
construct and maintain their churches and their schools,
the name and nationality of the Lithuanians will be maintained in the country of George Washington.[22]

Chicago's Lithuanian churches are in every sense Lithuanian. Their
pastors are either Lithuanian secular priests or members of Lithuanian
religious orders.[23] These churches maintain parochial schools, taught by
Lithuanian nuns, in which the Lithuanian language is a part of the curri-
culum. At least some of the church sermons are delivered in that language.

Due to the high prestige enjoyed by the Church, it is not surprising
that members of the clergy are regarded as very desirable political allies, if they can be obtained. Formally, the members of the Roman Catholic clergy are non-political, and they are often placed in a somewhat difficult situation when urged by one party or the other to take sides in a
political controversy.[24]

It appears, nevertheless, that Lithuanian pastors have sometimes been
involved to some extent in political activities. According to one of the
original incorporators of the Lithuanian Democratic League, one of the
three men who presented the plan to the Democratic high command was a Lithuanian priest, one Father Baltutis.[25] This illustrates one of the prime
political functions of the Catholic clergy: serving on endorsement committees. When a political group wishes to present its case for the nomi-
nation of a given candidate, it is considered highly desirable to have a
representative of the clergy on the committee. In all fairness, it must
be said that there is no evidence that such endorsements have been weight-
ed heavily in favor of one or the other party. In a sense, they are more
or less character references. But the lending of their voices to the demands of nationalistic groups does make the clergy a party to those demands.

However, the political activities of the clergy are not the only considerations in determining the importance of the Church in nationality
politics. As a social center and in general a nucleus of community activities, the Church is important to nationalistic political organizations.
For example, the Ninth ward Lithuanian Democratic Club has its headquarters
at the parish hall of All Saints' Church at 10806 South State Street.[26]
This hall is used not only for regular meetings, but also for Democratic
political rallies. The Lithuanian Democrats also hold rallies at the parish hall of Nativity Church at Sixty-Eighth and Washtenaw Streets.[27]

It should be emphasized that all this does not mean that the Church
is embroiled in politics, in the sense of throwing its weight on the scales
of political controversy between the two parties. It is certain that if
the Republicans wished to rent parish halls for political purposes they
could do so. The Church acts merely as a kind of conductor for the social
and political interaction of Lithuanian groups. The attitude of the Church
is simply that it is favorable toward the interaction of Lithuanian groups
of various kinds, and this is surely not surprising in view of the nation-
alistically-oriented parish organization. The unstated policy of the
Church in this regard has very definite political consequences, in that it
tends to strengthen nationalistic politics in general, without intent to
favor either party. The fact that the Lithuanian Democrats are better organized and can thus make better use of the facilities offered by the
Church is not the responsibility of the Church.

159

<u>Fraternal Orders, Clubs, and Associations</u>.--The Lithuanians of Chicago have a wide range of voluntary organizations, covering everything from philatelists to funeral directors. In all, there are over 300 such clubs and associations.[28] We will discuss briefly only several which are important from a political standpoint.

Probably the most active fraternal group is the Knights of Lithuania, which is nominally a youth organization, but which has a "senior division" for older members. It is a Catholic organization carrying on the usual fraternal activities, and its membership is open to both men and women. Due to the large concentration of Lithuanians in Chicago, members from this area have been important in the national leadership of the lodge. Jack L. Jatis, one of the leaders of the Lithuanian Democratic League, is a former national president of the order, and has held other high offices in it. This group is understandably non-political in the sense that it does not openly support any political party or candidate, but since it is an important group in the community, it can be an important element in many political schemes. For instance, when the leaders of the Lithuanian Democratic League determined to take the initiative in forming a nation-wide "Lithuanians for Stevenson" club during the 1952 presidential campaign, they decided to use the Knights of Lithuania national convention as a starting point for their organizational efforts. Accordingly, Jack Jatis and Albert G. Preibis, the latter being president of the League, went to Dayton, Ohio to attend the national convention so that they could make the necessary personal contacts with Lithuanian leaders from various parts of the country.[29]

There are two American Legion posts in the Lithuanian community, the Darius-Girenas Post No. 271, and the Don Varnas Post No. 986. Both are prosperous and powerful, and so are important to the nationalistic politician as sources of endorsements and general support.

As the representative of the businessmen among the Lithuanians, the Chamber of Commerce is another important group. It appears that the Chamber of Commerce leans toward the Republican side, just as most other similar groups of businessmen do. In fact, County Treasurer John B. Brenza told the writer that the Lithuanian Republicans made up for their lack of political organization to a great extent by their control of the Chamber of Commerce.[30] Nevertheless, the Lithuanian Democrats regularly call on the Chamber of Commerce for endorsements and for service on committees presenting petitions to the Democratic Central Committee. The Chamber of Commerce seems willing to take on such tasks, evidently on the theory that Lithuanians should be supported, regardless of party.

<u>The Lithuanian Press</u>.--As the greatest Lithuanian center in the United States, Chicago has naturally become the hub of Lithuanian publishing activities. Seventeen periodicals in the Lithuanian language are regularly published in Chicago.[31]

The two daily newspapers published in Chicago have a nation-wide circulation, which enables them to operate on a daily basis despite the fact that competition for the limited local readership might otherwise have forced one of them out of business. Each paper represents a distinct political point of view.

<u>Naujienos: The Lithuanian Daily News</u>.--This paper was first published in 1914, as a Socialist organ. Its somewhat heavy ideological and theoretical character was noted by Park, writing in 1922, when he said that "The reading matter of the <u>Naujienos</u> consists only of such literature as Nietz-

sche's Thus Spake Zarathustra and propaganda articles."[32] As a Socialist
periodical, Neujienos was violently anti-clerical, and even in fairly recent years the Church has suspected it of hostility. As one Lithuanian
told the writer,

> When I was a kid in the Lithuanian school, the nuns always
> told us it was wrong to read Naujienos because it was athe-
> istic and against the Church. They told us good Catholics
> wouldn't even have it in the house.[33]

However, in reality Naujienos has mellowed with the years. It did
not join the left-wing Socialists who formed the Communist party, but remained loyal to the Socialist party. When the Lithuanian Federation dis-
affiliated from the Socialist party during one of the innumerable schisms
which finally reduced the party to its present state of futility, Naujienos
had no place to go politically except into the Democratic party.

The present editor, Dr. Pius Grigaitis, has held the position from
the very first year of publication. As a young law student, he left his
Lithuanian home for St. Petersburg and the Imperial University there. After the 1906 revolution, in which he took an active part, he was forced to
flee the Czar's domain. After completing his studies in Switzerland he
came to the United States.[34]

Dr. Grigaitis told the writer that Naujienos generally supports the
Democratic party because it most closely approximates the Social-Democratic
ideals for which the paper has always stood.[35]

Draugas: The Lithuanian Daily Friend.--The other daily paper in the
Lithuanian language is Draugas. It represents the other side of the cleri-
cal-laical political battle that was imported from the old country by the
Lithuanian immigrants. Draugas is published by the Lithuanian Catholic
Press Society, and as such is considered to present an official Church position on important issues. This impression is strengthened by the fact
that several Catholic priests are staff members.

Probably the most important preoccupation of Draugas is its bitter
opposition to the Soviet occupation of Lithuania, and to the international
Communist movement in general. However, on this issue there is little to
choose between Draugas and Naujienos. As a Socialist paper, Naujienos is
quite as hostile as Draugas toward the Community rulers of Lithuania,
since the Lithuanian Social Democrats were among the first victims of the
Communists after their occupation of Lithuania.

In Chicago politics, Draugas has tended to favor the Democratic party, but without the tendencies toward ideological identification involved
in the stand taken by Naujienos. Further, Draugas has taken a more intensely nationalistic stand on the "recognition" issue. It has been frank
to say that it will always support Lithuanian candidates, regardless of
party. An example of this attitude was an article which appeared in Draugas on May 24, 1951. The Draugas correspondent predicted that the Lithuanian Democrats would not oppose Anthony Olis, a Lithuanian Republican,
in his campaign for re-election to the Sanitary District board. Draugas
commented:

> It appears to me that it is the first time in Lithuanian
> history that such an intelligent and practical plan was
> decided upon--not caring whether it be a Republican or
> Democrat but primarily that it be a Lithuanian![36]

It should be added that even <u>Naujienos</u> has never found it advisable to oppose Lithuanian Republicans, though it has not been as enthusiastic about them as <u>Draugas</u>.

<u>Conclusion</u>.--The foregoing discussion of the Lithuanian community may serve to set the stage for our discussion of the political activities of the Lithuanian group. Summing up this brief survey, we may note that the Lithuanians are considerably concentrated into a number of neighborhood areas, the economic levels of which vary considerably. As a political factor, the Lithuanians are a significant group, as evidenced by their numbers and by the fact that the Democratic party includes them in its nationality strategy. Finally, if we are to take the existence of numerous and diversified community institutions as an indication, it would seem that the Lithuanian community possesses the vehicles for the "integrative interaction" which is probably essential to the success of the type of interest group activity represented by nationalistic politics.

FOOTNOTES

[1] Reprinted by the permission of the author.

[2] Bureau of the Census, <u>Country of Origin of the Foreign Stock</u>, <u>op</u>. <u>cit</u>., p. 76.

[3] Alex Gottfried. "A. J. Cermak, Chicago Politician." Unpublished Ph.D. dissertation. Department of Political Science, University of Chicago, 1952, p. 507.

[4] Leslie V. Beck, personal interview.

[5] Samuel Lubell, <u>The Future of American Politics</u>. (New York: Harper & Brothers, 1950), <u>p</u>. 38 and <u>passim</u>.

[6] Colonel Arvey illustrates the de-emphasis on national origin which some Jewish politicians practice, in contrast to Sabath's nationalistic attitude. The President of the Lithuanian Democratic League, A. G. Preibis, told the writer that he was not aware of Arvey's Lithuanian ancestry until a few months ago, when Arvey casually mentioned it in a conversation. Personal interview.

[7] Carl D. Buck, <u>A Sketch of the Linguistic Conditions of Chicago</u> (Chicago: University of Chicago Press, 1903), p. 6.

[8] <u>Ibid</u>.

[9] <u>Ibid</u>., p. 6n.

[10] <u>Ibid</u>., p. 13.

[11] Louis Wirth and Margaret Furez, <u>Local Community Fact Book, 1938</u> (Chicago: Chicago Recreation Commission, 1938), p. 60.

[12] <u>Ibid</u>.

[13] Louis Wirth and Eleanor Bernet, <u>Local Community Fact Book of Chicago</u> (Chicago: University of Chicago Press, 1949), p. 60.

[14] Ibid.

[15] Ibid., p. 66.

[16] Istorija Chicagos Lietuviu (Chicago: Spauda Lietuvos, 1900), p. 8.

[17] Wirth and Furez, op. cit., p. 49.

[18] Leslie V. Beck (Democratic ward committeeman), personal interview.

[19] Wirth and Bernet, op. cit., passim.

[20] David B. Truman, The Governmental Process (New York: Alfred A. Knopf, 1952), p. 35.

[21] Chicago Vadovas (Guide to Chicago in Lithuanian) (Chicago: Lithuanian Chamber of Commerce, 1952), pp. 155-160.

[22] A. Kaupas, "L'Eglise et les Lituaniens aux Etats-Unis d'Amerique," Annales des Nationalities, II (1913), 233-234, quoted in Robert E. Park, The Immigrant Press and Its Control (New York: Harper and Brothers, 1922), p. 54.

[23] Both the Jesuits and the Marian Fathers maintain Lithuanian religious communities in Chicago. Chicagos Vadovas, p. 164.

[24] The efforts of the Church to appear neutral are illustrated by a discussion which took place at a meeting of the Lithuanian Democratic League which the writer attended. Several precinct captains were discussing the question of the political allegiance of the nuns at a certain Lithuanian convent. One man, who lives in the neighborhood, said that their political affiliation could not be determined. It seems that the Mother Superior is in the habit of sending ten or twelve nuns to vote in each primary election, although the number of nuns in the convent is much larger, and they all vote in a general election. However, in the primary it inevitably happens that half the nuns who appear vote Democratic and half Republican, thus baffling the precinct captains of both parties, who like to have their voters neatly pigeonholed in their canvass books as friend or enemy.

[25] Jack L. Jatis, personal interview.

[26] Steve Dombro, personal interview.

[27] Southwest Lithuanian Democratic Club handbill advertising rally held on Oct. 21, 1948.

[28] Chicagos Vadovas, p. 154.

[29] Albert G. Preibis, personal interview.

[30] John B. Brenza, personal interview.

[31] Chicagos Vadovas, pp. 184-186.

[32] Park, op. cit., p. 113.

[33] A. G. Preibis, personal interview.

[34] Pius Grigaitis, letter to A. F. Wells, dated January 20, 1949.

[35]Grigaitis, personal interview.

[36]*Draugas*, May 24, 1951. Translated from the Lithuanian.

PART III.   THE LATER LITHUANIAN IMMIGRANTS

Chapter 12. LITHUANIAN IMMIGRATION TO THE U.S.A.
AFTER WORLD WAR II

Source -   Danute-Dana J. Tautvilas. The Lithuanian
Press in America, (Thesis-M.S.), Catholic
University of America Library, Washington,
D. C., 1961. The selection is from Chap-
ter III, "Lithuanian Immigration to the
U.S.A. After World War II," pages 24-31.[1]

Overview

Lithuanians who emigrated to the United States after World War II
were refugees from the Soviet Russian political, religious and social oppression. When the war ended, there were about 60,000 Lithuanians in
Western Europe who were unable to return to their homeland. They became
known as displaced persons and more than 30,000 found an opportunity to
emigrate to the United States as the result of the Displaced Persons Act
passed by Congress. They had lost relatives and friends through Soviet
deportations and many had relatives and friends still in Lithuania. They
yearned for the liberation of Lithuania and were strongly inclined to
cling to their culture wherever they emigrated - the United States, Canada, Australia, England, France, Germany, Sweden, or other countries.

Lithuanian immigrants after World War II generally found themselves
welcomed in the United States, although they experienced linguistic, monetary and other adjustments. Unlike the majority of the earlier Lithuanian
immigrants, many of them were members of the Lithuanian intelligentsia,
including professionals such as engineers, scientists, artists, writers,
lawyers and former government employees. Many of them could not use immediately their professional skills and had to take unskilled jobs.

These more recent Lithuanian immigrants sought to express their intellectual, aesthetic and social interests in closely knit group activities through their associations, clubs, scholarly periodicals, etc. They
truly hoped that Lithuania some day would be a free country to which they
might return and resume their life patterns. Their life in their new
country left them perplexed as to their cultural destiny.

For a long time Lithuania has been fighting her occupants for the restoration of her lost freedom. The struggle is a part of that worldwide,
anti-communist crusade, carried on directly by the oppressed peoples who
are now being counted by the hundreds of millions. During the past twenty
years, the whole civilized world has been searching for the answers to the
problem of freedom and slavery. If freedom in the world became accessible
to some people, it was refused to millions of others. From the shores of
the Baltic, along the Carpathians, and to the Adriatic Sea the Red Imperi-
alists, having broken all their honored commitments and international
agreements, maintain control over millions of once-free peoples by means
of armed forces and brutal terror.

The Lithuanian Nation fights its battles on two different fronts: at home and abroad. The fight itself, however, is one--just as the very idea of freedom is one and indivisible. The struggle at home is in direct opposition to the Soviet occupant. The resistance is passive as well as active. In the first case, one attempts to preserve the Lithuanian national culture; in the second, one tries to prohibit the destruction of property and the extermination of the Lithuanian people by the enemy.

A large segment of the country's population fled to the Western World as a result of the Soviet onslaught into Central Europe in 1944, and is carrying on the struggle through diplomatic channels in all parts of the world. All politically and ideologically minded people, young and old alike, are part of that struggle.

The Lithuanian immigrants to the United States of America after Second World War were refugees from political, religious, and social oppression, as have been many of the previous American immigrants. However, there is an important distinguishing characteristic among them. The majority of them have come to America as a result of the war which, at the same time that it made them refugees, put their previously free and independent homelands under Soviet domination. Many of the earlier immigrants came here because of oppression, but it was usually oppression of the particular minority to which they belonged. There is no precedent for the situation of these immigrants (known as Displaced Persons) whose whole countries were overcome by disaster at the time of their emigration. And these countries were intensively conscious of their national aspirations. Many of them had been enjoying political independence only since the First World War.

A very important thing to remember in trying to understand these Lithuanian immigrants is that they do not come from the "old country," they come from the "enslaved country." They are not homesick only for their friends and relatives overseas; they are also homesick for their nation. This is clearly seen in the literature produced by the Lithuanian immigrants which is full of longing for Lithuania and deals almost completely with the past and future hopes rather than with the present. The feeling of national belongingness among exiles is perhaps even more intense than "free home nationalist" was. Therefore, they feel it a duty to do what is possible to liberate their country and then to rebuild it. Many hope to return to live there after liberation, when it comes. This nationalistic feeling of duty is intensified by the sense of moral duty which always falls upon those who have been lucky in a situation where others were not. Because they got away and others did not, the former have a moral obligation to fulfill. Most of these Lithuanian immigrants have lost relatives and friends through Soviet deportations; all have some who still are in Lithuania, and occasionally a letter slips through the censors which gives a glimpse of life in the homeland.

Many people take it for granted that the immigrant, the refugee, has come here with the intention of adopting as quickly as possible the customs and the ways of his new country, the United States, and that he is anxious to relinquish his native values and customs. But a person of this opinion is disconcerted when he finds that even when given the opportunity to become assimilated, the immigrant clings to his old culture, does not attempt to become dissolved in the melting-pot, refuses to be integrated.

People from countries where nationalism is allowed to express itself and where there is political freedom do not feel the same obligation as do the Lithuanian immigrants and other displaced persons toward their native land. For in Lithuania there is a drive to make the people lose their national consciousness and become not only physically but also spiritually a part of the Soviet Union. Because there they are not free to protest, because any expression of Lithuanian national consciousness there may lead to death, the job of protesting devolves upon those Lithuanians who are in free countries.

National aspirations and the moral sense of duty naturally cause the Lithuanian immigrant to resist assimilation; in addition, the factors which have in the past caused national cohesion among immigrants are present also today. It is a natural human trait to love what is familiar, and for that love to increase when in strange surroundings. The familiar is also secure and thus national grouping gives security and protection where the new community is hesitant to welcome newcomers or even is hostile to them. It is true that the Lithuanian immigrants after World War II generally found a very warm welcome in the United States. There was general sympathy for their position, as expressed by the Displaced Persons Act passed by Congress in 1948 (Public Law 774).[2] Although for the past hundred years the traditional Golden Gate of immigration had been closing gradually, and though the sentiment was becoming more and more hostile to further immigrant influx, there was change for a period of time immediately after World War II. The United States, one of the few nations not greatly damaged by the war, felt its responsibility towards a ravaged world.

But even with the warmest welcome, their lack of knowledge of the English language, their monetary status, and the fact that they were newcomers limited the opportunities for adjustment in the American community for these immigrants. Unlike the majority of the earlier Lithuanian immigrants, many of them are members of the Lithuanian intelligentsia: educated people, professions, specialists, people familiar with higher culture.[3] Here they usually find themselves in the cheaper dwelling areas of large cities. The Americans most of them meet are people of lower culture with little education. Very few newcomers can utilize their education in obtaining jobs. Thus, many are forced to leave their skills and professions and do manual labor in the factories. Engineers and scientists generally find that they can use their training in obtaining jobs, but lawyers, former government employees, liberal arts people in general, usually cannot. Thus people from the upper and middle classes of Lithuania find themselves forced into a lower-class environment in the United States. They do not find much in common with their neighbors at home and at work, and therefore quite naturally seek fellowship elsewhere among their fellow immigrants. In the activities of the nationality groups a person can use the talent and ability which is stifled elsewhere. And so the intellectuals write for magazines and newspapers published here in their language, form the leadership of exile political groups, join clubs of various kinds, express here their need for action.[4] Immigrants not belonging to the intelligentsia also prefer to remain with their national fellows. There is acceptance here--a small, rather compact community where they do not feel strange. Social clubs and athletic groups form. Talent can show itself and be appreciated for the arts are encouraged and supported, and there is opportunity (for those who wish to take it) for participation in various ways. Lithuanian choruses, choirs, and exhibition folk-dancing groups are seen by many American audiences, as well as by Lithuanian ones.

A large number of young people seek higher education in the colleges and universities, and among the students, therefore, another section of the national community has developed. Its leaders are generally the older students who had begun their higher education in Germany and Austria and are finishing it here. At this time, most of them have already completed their college study, and the younger group is taking over. The students are members of the Lithuanian Students' Association, Inc.[5] In cities where a large number of Lithuanian students are found--New York, Boston, Chicago, Detroit, Cleveland, and others--these organizations plan activities of a cultural, social, and political nature. The Lithuanian student travels a great deal, considering his financial status, for that is the only way he can keep some sort of liaison with the other members of the scattered student community. The students are very important because they form the future intelligentsia of a nation.

The nationality group struggles for its existence and the whole struggle is based on one premise that there will be a time to return to a free Lithuania. Exile politics has little meaning or influence on the international scene, for exile governments have nothing to govern. Their sole purpose now is to serve as a reminder that the status quo in the countries behind the Iron Curtain must not be accepted as satisfactory.

When World War II finally came to an end, there were about 60,000 Lithuanian Displaced Persons in Western Europe (France, Germany, Italy, Austria, and the Scandinavian countries), 24 per cent of whom were children: 34 per cent--women; and 42 per cent--men.[6]

These people found themselves in the West because:

1. they fled from the Russian communists on account of their political and religious persecutions;

2. they were taken as forced-labor by the Germans;

3. they were deported to concentration camps in Germany.

Most of them were unable to return to their homeland--Lithuania. Therefore, they became known as displaced persons, who were looking for an opportunity to immigrate to some other country.[7]

The majority of them found residence in the United States. This new immigration, by no means primarily political, was distinct from the earlier one, in that many of the educated class were transplanted to America. One could find many scholars and men of science immigrating to the United States.

About 40,000 of Lithuanian Displaced Persons had a chance to immigrate to the United States. Specially, after 1948 when the Displaced Persons Act was passed by Congress.

After World War II, the first group of Lithuanian immigrants came to the United States in 1946, but their number was small.[8] They were the ones who had close relatives in the U.S.A. or had been here before.

Larger immigration of Lithuanians to the U.S.A. started in 1948, when the doors were finally opened to Displaced Persons. The first ship (General Black) with Displaced Persons (immigrants) landed in New York on October 30, 1948. Among various nationalities there were 148 Lithuanians who were the first group to reach the shores of America under the Displaced Persons Act.[9] In two years (1948-1950), in accordance with the Displaced Persons Act, 27,807 Lithuanian immigrants came to the United States.[10]

In 1950 there were more than 1,000,000 Americans of Lithuanian descent in the United States of America.[11] Among them there were over 30,000

Lithuanian Displaced Persons who came to the United States after Second World War.[12] Even now there are some Lithuanians who immigrate to the United States of America from some other countries (Australia, England, Germany, France, Canada, and some others, but their number is small.[13]

Looking into the future, the fate of the Lithuanian immigrant (Displaced Person) seems clear. If a change in world affairs does not come fairly soon to lift the Soviet yoke from the shoulders of the oppressed countries and make it possible for some to return to Lithuania, there will be few in America who will still feel a loyalty as strongly as they do now. That might mean death of an old and venerable nation and of a beautiful language and culture, thus causing a loss to the human family. In the absence of any immediate better hope, we can at least hope for a better future.

FOOTNOTES

[1] Reprinted by the permission of the author.

[2] "Lietuviai Ateiviai," Lietuviu Enciklopedija, Vol. X (1957), 65.

[3] Ibid., p. 67.

[4] "Lietuviai Ateiviai," Lietuviu Enciklopedija, 67-69.

[5] Ibid.

[6] "Lietuviai DP," Lietuviu Enciklopedija, Vol. V (1955), 148.

[7] Ibid.

[8] "Lietuviai Ateiviai," Lietuviu Enciklopedija, 66.

[9] Ibid.

[10] Ibid.

[11] Communism Exterminates Nations; The Red Tide Overwhelms Lithuania (Dayton: Federation of Lithuanian-American Roman Catholic Societies, 1950), p. 4.

[12] Simutis, p. 104.

[13] "Lietuviai DP," Lietuviu Enciklopedija, V, 157.

Chapter 13. LITHUANIAN REFUGEES AND THEIR
OCCUPATIONAL ADJUSTMENT

Source - Aleksandras Plateris, "Occupational
Adjustment of Professional Refugees -
A Case Study of Lithuanian Profession-
als in the United States," Lituanus,
Fall-Winter, 1964, 27-44.[1]

Overview

Plateris investigated the occupational adjustment of Lithuanian professional refugees in Chicago who included lawyers, gymnasium teachers,
army officers, physicians, dentists, engineers, architects, chemists, economists, business school graduates, agronomists, veterinarians, university
professors, priests, pharmacists, musicians, artists, writers, foresters
and merchant fleet captains. Some were able to resume their occupations
or similar work but the majority, especially the older generation, could
improve their positions only slightly during the first six years of their
lives in the United States. Whereas older professionals in Lithuania were
better situated than the younger ones, in the United States some older
professionals were adversely affected. Plateris reported cases of university professors, high court justices and army generals working as janitors
in Chicago factories. On the other hand, many of the younger refugees
were able to improve their occupational status by acquiring new skills or
new professions.

Lithuanians in professions having a special routine, such as physicians, engineers or priests, found satisfactory positions rather early.
Lawyers and teachers, by contrast, found great difficulty in working in
their old occupations because they were in culture bound occupations where
they lacked the expertise either in the American language, law or other
specific requirements. Lithuanian dentists, more than physicians, were
hindered by American regulations which did not allow them to practice without American graduate studies.

Plateris brought up factors which influenced the adjustment of Lithuanian professionals to the new circumstances. The extreme indigency of
life in German camps made the Lithuanians appreciate American prosperity.
Facilitating their adjustment was the impact, in various ways, of the
large number of Lithuanians already living in Chicago. Finally, there was
the desire of the refugees and their children for higher education as a
means of getting ahead.

The Lithuanian Refugees

Immigration by Lithuanians to the United States took place in two
general periods. The first period includes the latter part of the nineteenth century and the beginning of the twentieth; it ended when World War
I began. Between World War I and World War II, comparatively few Lithu-

anians settled in the United States. During the second period of immigration, in the late fourties and early fifties, the number of immigrants was much smaller than during the first period. The two groups of immigrants differed considerably. The first consisted predominantly of economically underprivileged unmarried persons of both sexes, mostly farm laborers, looking for better opportunities; the second group was composed of refugees from Soviet tyranny, both families and unattached individuals. A large proportion of these refugees consisted of professional persons and their families. As the refugees fled their country in order to escape persecution, various groups of the population of Lithuania were represented among them in direct proportion to the perceived probability of being persecuted. The more prominent members of a persecuted group are more likely to attract the attention of the persecutors; therefore, it is natural that professional people would be overrepresented among the refugees. Persons belonging to other occupations, all the way down the socio-economic scale, were also found among them, but were proportionally less numerous.

Once the refugees arrived in the United States, whatever their previous occupation, all had to start anew. Almost all, except those possessing easily transferable skills, had to take any work they were able to obtain, usually that of unskilled laborers. Manual labor did not have the same implication for various strata of the refugees. Those who had done such work all their lives resumed their previous occupation, with the difference that now their work was much better paid. Their position was comparable to that of the earlier immigrants who had entered this country for economic reasons. The situation of the professionals, however, was quite different: their occupational status declined and, usually, so did their income. Some of them were eventually able to resume either their former occupation or some similar work, but the majority, especially the older generation, could only slightly better their positions during the first half-a-dozen years of their lives in the United States.

A study of occupational adjustments of Lithuanian professionals was conducted in Chicago, where a large group of Lithuanians settled.[2] The occupational adjustments of the Lithuanian refugees are described as they were found to be at a particular moment, late in 1954, when most of the refugees had lived in the United States for two to five years. At that time, the factors determining the occupational adjustments of various professional groups had already become apparent, and there has been no basic change since then. During the period of ten years that has elapsed since the completion of this study, many persons included in the study have either retired or died; many others, especially among the younger ones, have improved their occupational status by acquiring new skills or a new profession. However, the very fact that some professionals had to change their profession or to repeat their graduate work in American universities in order to improve their job opportunities lends support to the differences in occupational potentialities of different professional groups as described here. In 1954 the specific occupational potentialities had already become clear, but few persons had yet had the opportunity to acquire and use new professional or semiprofessional skills. Hence, for those interested in the fate of individual professional groups as such, the situation in 1954 is more interesting than that at a later date. Moreover, information about the occupational potentialities of the Lithuanian refugee professionals may apply to other refugee groups, past or future, possible differences in adjustment may be due to different levels of prestige enjoyed by the cultures of various nations and to the type of welcome various groups of refugees receive in this country.

Collection of Data

The population of the study was limited to graduates of universities, other institutions of higher learning, ecclesiastic seminaries, and army officers' schools. Moreover, the study dealt only with persons who had received their degrees before leaving Lithuania, i.e., not later than in 1944, the year most refugees left their native country.

The data were gathered in two distinct phases: first, lists were prepared of all persons belonging to the above--efined population, then a sample of four professional groups were interviewed. In each professional group of refugees, there were one or more individuals in a central position, having either extensive information about other members of their profession, or ready-made lists, as many such groups had their associations.

Eventually, lists of nineteen professional groups were compiled, indicating (1) the name, (2) the address, (3) the age, and (4) the present occupation of each individual, although in some cases the information was not complete. The lists comprised 757 persons, belonging to the following professions: 111 lawyers; 84 gymnasium teachers; 82 army officers; 78 physicians; 60 engineers, architects, and chemists; 60 economists; 46 dentists; 46 agronomists; 40 priests; 31 university professors; 23 pharmacists; 17 musicians; 15 business school graduates; 14 actors; 14 writers; 13 veterinarians; 11 artists; 10 foresters; 2 captains of the merchant fleet.

The present occupation of the respondents was classified into four categories: (1) work in their original profession; (2) semiprofessional work in a profession similar to the original one, but on a lower level (here, the typical cases were lawyers working as real estate salesmen, physicians working as hospital interns, and engineers employed as draftsmen); (3) white collar work, including office clerks, sales clerks, and self-employed small businessmen; (4) manual labor. It was not possible to ascertain whether these lists were exhaustive, but in view of the close ties between fellow professionals, it can be assumed that the number of those who were omitted was small.

Each professional group had its own adjustment problems; the more intensive investigation, therefore, had to be limited to several selected groups. Since the present occupation of almost all 757 persons was known, it was decided to concentrate on the two extremes: those occupationally best adjusted and those least well adjusted. Four professional groups were selected: for the best adjusted groups, the physicians and engineers, and for the least well adjusted, the gymnasium teachers and lawyers. Random samples of 40 were taken of the physicians and of the lawyers, and those 80 persons were contacted personally, while questionaires were mailed to all engineers and teachers whose addresses were available.

The fieldwork was facilitated by the fact that most respondents lived in Lithuanian neighborhoods and usually several of them dwelt within walking distance of one another. All respondents were cooperative, and eventually 146 questionnaires were filled out. According to their profession, 40 respondents were lawyers, 40 were physicians, 36 teachers and 32 engineers, but only the lawyers and physicians constituted probability samples.

Occupational History

Before December 1, 1948, the immigration of refugees was hampered by

173

legal requirements, such as quotas and affidavits. The yearly quotas of most East European countries, including Lithuania, were small; it would have taken many years to bring over the numerous refugees who lived mostly in Germany, in Displaced Persons' Camps. Moreover, most of the so-called "DP's" had no money to pay for transportation. With the passage of the Displaced Persons Act by Congress, the flow of refugees into this country began in December of 1948, ending on January 1, 1952. Out of the sample of 146 persons, 126, or 86.3 per cent, came to the United States between December 1, 1948, and January 1, 1952. Eighteen persons, or 12.5 per cent, came before December 1, 1948, as regular immigrants, and two (1.5 per cent) came after January 1, 1952. The newcomers, arriving almost penniless, had to take any job they could find in order to earn a living. They did not know about life in the United States and usually had nobody to advise them. People they first met were either pre-World War I immigrants from their native country, mostly common laborers, who could only help in getting factory jobs, or their fellow refugees who had arrived some months earlier and were almost as ignorant of the occupational opportunities in the United States as they themselves were. Naturally, after living in Chicago long enough to become acquainted with the opportunities for employment, the refugees started to search for more permanent occupations. After a year or two, this period of searching for a more satisfactory occupation could be considered completed, and the rate of change slowed down markedly.

There were some deviations from this pattern of adjustment. A very small number of persons did not need to start work immediately after arriving, because they were helped by other members of their family and could leisurely look around for a better job. Despite the fact that almost all newcomers tried to obtain employment immediately upon arrival, not all were successful. Several respondents reported that it took them considerable time to get their first job in Chicago. This period encompassed a few weeks or months, and in one case it lasted almost half a year. Outside Chicago, jobs were scarce in the late forties, and some refugees who originally came to other cities eventually moved to Chicago in search of better job opportunities.

Persons belonging to professions that have a special routine for adjustment, such as physicians, engineers, or priests, and those who had good advisors, or were especially lucky, found more satisfactory occupations from the beginning. A number of persons, while working at undesirable jobs, took courses, examinations, studied, and otherwise tried to improve their occupational opportunities. Ninety, or 62 per cent, of the respondents, used this method, and in 62 cases some improvement had already taken place when this study was conducted.

The great majority, 118 respondents, had held two to four jobs since arriving in Chicago. However, the differences between the professions were marked: thirty-six physicians had changed jobs (90 per cent), but only 29 lawyers (72 per cent). This difference can be explained by the institutionalized pattern of occupational mobility of the physicians.

Table 1 gives a concise picture of differences between occupational histories of the four professional groups. Practically no lawyer and no teacher escaped manual work, but almost no physician was ever engaged in this type of occupation. Among the 5 physicians who ever worked as manual laborers, 2 switched to labor in order to earn money while preparing for the Medical State Board examination, when all other introductory steps leading to the resumption of their professional work were already completed. Hence, only three physicians out of 40 started their career as laborers, while 37 started either as white collar workers or in an occupation

TABLE 1. TYPES OF OCCUPATION EVER HELD BY THE RESPONDENTS: SAMPLE OF FOUR PROFESSIONAL GROUPS, CHICAGO, 1954

(All jobs of the same type held by the same respondent are counted as one. Percentages indicate the number of respondents who ever held one or more jobs belonging to a given type, and do not necessarily add up to 100.0 per cent.)

Profession	Persons in the Sample		TYPE OF OCCUPATION										
	No.	%	Laborers		White Collar		Semi-Professional		Professional		Self-Employed	
			No.	%	No.	%	No.	%	No.	%	No.	%
Total	146	100.0	93	63.7	33	22.6	70	47.9	39	26.7	31	21.2
Lawyers	40	100.0	37	92.5	13	32.5	4	10.0	--	--	6	15.0
Teachers	34	100.0	33	97.1	13	38.2	--	--	--	--	1	2.9
Engineers	32	100.0	18	56.2	1	3.1	29	90.6	11	34.4	3	9.4
Physicians	40	100.0	5	12.5	6	15.0	37	92.5	28	70.0	21	52.5

similar to their profession (usually as hospital interns); on the other hand, the first occupation of 37 out of 40 lawyers was manual labor. The engineers were almost exactly half-way between these two extremes. Slightly more than one-half of their group began their work experience in the United States with blue collar work.

White collar work was the peak of the career for teachers and for most lawyers at the time of the investigation, but was quite an unimportant step for most engineers and physicians. No teachers worked in their old profession nor in a semiprofessional occupation, and only four lawyers had an occupation similar to their profession, namely, working as real estate brokers. On the other hand, all but three physicians and all but three engineers had worked in an occupation similar to their profession; for most physicians, this was but a step toward full professional status, already achieved by 70 per cent of the group, and this percentage continued to increase. The engineers were the second best adjusted group, as one-third of them were working in their profession.

The physicians' group included not only the highest proportion of persons professionally employed, but also the highest proportion of self-employed. Twenty-one physicians and 3 3ngineers, working in their respective professions, were self-employed, whereas the only one self-employed teacher was the owner of a grocery store, and among the five self-employed lawyers were three real estate brokers and two grocers.

In conjunction with the discussion of the occupational history of Lithuanian refugee professionals, it must be mentioned that a limited number came to this country in order to occupy various professional jobs that had been offered them while they were still living in Europe. Most of these were teaching positions in colleges and universities. However, only few such persons lived in Chicago and none of these cases were included in the sample.

Variables Associated With Occupational Adjustment

All data indicated that the occupational adjustment of refugee professionals was associated, as expected, with the type of professional skill and, within the limits of each professional group, with age.

Not all professional skills can be transplanted from one country to another; transplanting depends on two main factors: (1) the nature of the skill, and (2) the laws and regulations of each country. Certain professional skills are more culturebound than others. Some professions are entirely dependent on the cultural context in which they arise, whereas others include skills which should, at least theoretically, be the same throughout the world. The possibility of transplanting the first type of profession depends on the cultural similarities between the country in which it was acquired and the country of resettlement; in our case, between Lithuania and the United States. The culturebound professions, as represented in this sample by lawyers and teachers, can be practiced in a country only by persons who know its language almost perfectly and are extremely familiar with the specific social forms conditioning the practical application of the professional skills. To practice law in the U. S., for example, a Lithuanian lawyer must know English well enough to speak it in court and to impress judges and jurors, must know the laws of a given State, and also must acquire all the contacts, learn all the informal ways of behavior and thinking of lawyers in the United States on which professional success may depend.

On the other hand, professions based on the natural sciences should, theoretically, be the same everywhere. It was found, however, that some professional groups of refugees were unable to work in their profession because the practical application of their knowledge differed considerably between the United States and the European countries, including Lithuania. The foresters and the agronomists belonged to this category--they found no opportunity for using their professional skills in this country. More fortunate were those refugees whose professions were more easily transferable, as in the case of physicians. The transplanting of their skills is well institutionalized, since both the nature of their skills and the regulations of most States make it comparatively easy for foreign-educated physicians to practice medicine. However, some closely related professional groups were not as fortunate as the physicians. Though the skills of a dentist do not seem to be more difficult to transfer from one country to another than are those of the physician, regulations made the transfer almost impossible, because dentists are required to complete anew their graduate studies.

The occupational adjustments of the nineteen professional groups living in the Chicago area in the fall of 1954, i.e., 2 to 6 years after arriving to this country, are shown in Table 2.

Further analysis of the data showed great differences in occupational adjustments between age groups (Table 3). Since 1944 was the last year in which the refugees could graduate from institutions of higher learning in their native country and since they usually were in their middle twenties at graduation time, the youngest group among the population investigated was in the middle thirties. In each profession the chances for the younger generation were better than those for the older. It is more difficult for older people to learn, to forget the past, and to get used to new conditions; the ways of behavior, attitudes, and convictions are more difficult to change. Moreover, older persons have presumably less time left to live, and consequently they are less willing to spend time and energy to acquire a position which they are not sure they will be able to enjoy for long. The great stress laid upon youth in the United States makes a more advanced age even more of a handicap.

The percentage of younger persons working in their original profession was much higher than that of older ones. This percentage consistently declined with age, from 27 per cent for persons under 40 to 7 per cent for those over 60. On the other hand, the combined percentage of laborers and owners of small business enterprises increased with age, from 13 per cent for persons under 40 to over 50 per cent for the older age group. The comparison of white collar workers and small businessmen yields an interesting insight into the cultural values held by the refugees, since younger age groups, which had better opportunity to choose their occupation, preferred to do clerical work in offices and stores, while older people, who had poorer occupational opportunities, were more inclined to acquire a grocery store or a similar small business.

A question concerning occupational plans was included in the questionnaire; the replies are summarized in Table 4, where the respondents are classified according to three different criteria, to clarify the differences in the reactions of various subgroups of the population. The distribution of answers indicates that the great majority of respondents answered this question keeping in mind their own occupational potentialities. The percentage of persons planning to achieve a given type of occupation was highly associated with the proportion of the group that had already achieved this occupation. Almost all physicians and two-thirds of the engineers

TABLE 2. OCCUPATIONAL POSITIONS OF LITHUANIAN REFUGEE
PROFESSIONALS: 19 PROFESSIONAL GROUPS, CHICAGO, 1954

Former Profession	Total No.	Total %	Professional No.	Professional %	Semiprofessional No.	Semiprofessional %	White Collar No.	White Collar %	Business No.	Business %	Laborers No.	Laborers %	Housewives No.	Housewives %	Unknown No.	Unknown %
Total	757	100.0	114	15.0	138	18.2	86	11.3	37	5.0	274	36.2	34	4.5	74	9.8
Physicians	78	100.0	36	46.2	34	43.5	5	6.4	--	--	2	2.6	1	1.3	--	--
Priests	40	100.0	26	65.0	11	27.5	--	--	--	--	3	7.5	--	--	--	--
Engineers	60	100.0	19	31.7	30	50.0	--	--	1	1.7	2	3.3	1	1.7	7	11.7
Artist	11	100.0	5	45.5	2	18.2	1	9.1	1	9.1	1	9.1	1	9.1	--	--
Veterinarians	13	100.0	6	46.1	3	23.1	2	15.4	--	--	2	15.4	--	--	--	--
Univ. Professors	31	100.0	7	22.6	9	29.0	6	19.4	1	3.2	5	16.1	--	--	3	9.7
Musicians	17	100.0	8	47.1	3	17.6	1	5.9	--	--	5	29.4	--	--	--	--
Dentists	46	100.0	5	10.9	17	37.0	--	--	4	8.7	10	21.7	10	21.7	--	--
Pharmacists	23	100.0	1	4.3	6	26.1	--	--	2	8.7	4	17.4	1	4.3	9	39.1
Business School Grad.	15	100.0	1	6.7	2	13.3	5	33.3	--	--	2	13.3	--	--	5	33.3
Economists	60	100.0	--	--	12	20.0	9	15.0	5	8.3	20	33.3	2	3.3	12	20.0
Teachers	84	100.0	--	--	--	--	21	25.0	2	2.4	38	45.2	13	15.5	10	11.9
Lawyers	111	100.0	--	--	9	8.1	14	12.6	10	9.0	66	59.5	--	--	12	10.8
Actors	14	100.0	--	--	--	--	3	21.4	--	--	8	57.1	3	21.4	--	--
Agronomists	46	100.0	--	--	--	--	10	21.7	2	4.3	34	73.9	--	--	--	--
Foresters	10	100.0	--	--	--	--	2	20.0	--	--	8	80.0	--	--	--	--
Army Officers	82	100.0	--	--	--	--	6	7.3	9	11.0	51	62.2	--	--	16	19.5
Writers	14	100.0	--	--	--	--	--	--	1	7.1	11	78.6	2	14.3	--	--
Ship Captains	2	100.0	--	--	--	--	--	--	--	--	2	100.0	--	--	--	--

TABLE 3. OCCUPATION OF RESPONDENTS BY AGE:
TOTAL OF 9 SELECTED PROFESSIONAL GROUPS, CHICAGO, 1954

(Data include only 9 more numerous professional groups: army officers, agronomists, lawyers, teachers, economists, university professors, engineers, priests, and physicians. Therefore, percentages differ slightly from those in Table 2.)

Age	Total		OCCUPATION													
			Profes-sional		Semipro-fessional		White Collar		Business		Laborers		House-wives		Unknown	
	No.	%	No.	%	No.	%	No.	%	No.	%	No.	%	No.	%	No.	%
Total	592	100.0	86	14.5	104	17.6	70	11.8	31	5.2	221	37.3	16	2.7	64	10.8
Under 40	71	100.0	19	26.8	18	25.3	6	8.4	--	--	9	12.7	7	9.9	12	16.9
40-49	257	100	40	15.6	45	17.5	50	19.4	9	3.5	97	37.7	4	1.6	12	4.7
50-59	169	100.0	22	13.0	21	12.4	8	4.7	16	9.5	84	49.7	4	2.4	14	8.3
60 and over	61	100.0	4	6.6	13	21.3	6	9.8	5	8.2	28	45.9	--	--	5	8.2
Unknown	34	100.0	1	2.9	7	20.6	--	--	1	2.9	3	8.8	1	2.9	21	61.7

179

TABLE 4. OCCUPATIONAL PLANS: SAMPLE OF FOUR PROFESSIONAL GROUPS, CHICAGO, 1954

OCCUPATIONAL PLANS

Subgroup	Total		Old Profession		New Specialty		Better and/or Easier Job		Self-employment		To Continue in Present Occupation		None	
	No.	%	No.	%	No.	%	No.	%	No.	%	No.	%	No.	%
Total	146	100.0	65	44.5	14	9.6	8	5.5	3	2.1	25	17.1	31	21.2
Former Profession														
Lawyers	40	100.0	2	5.0	10	25.0	5	12.5	2	5.0	9	22.5	12	30.0
Teachers	34	100.0	4	11.8	4	11.8	3	8.8	1	2.9	8	23.5	14	41.2
Engineers	32	100.0	21	65.6	--	--	--	--	--	--	6	18.8	5	15.6
Physicians	40	100.0	38	95.0	--	--	--	--	--	--	2	5.0	--	--
Age														
Under 50	94	100.0	53	56.4	10	10.6	3	3.2	1	1.1	9	9.6	18	19.1
Over 50	52	100.0	12	23.1	4	7.7	5	9.6	2	3.8	16	30.8	13	25.0
Present Occupation														
Professional	39	100.0	39	100.0	--	--	--	--	--	--	--	--	--	--
Semiprofessional	32	100.0	20	62.5	2	6.2	--	--	--	--	5	15.6	5	15.6
White Collar	23	100.0	4	17.4	5	21.7	2	8.7	--	--	8	34.8	4	17.4
Labor	52	100.0	2	3.8	7	13.5	6	11.5	3	5.8	12	23.1	22	42.3

planned to resume their old profession or to continue working in that profession, but only a small proportion of lawyers and teachers did so. This answer was given by more than one-half of the younger age group, but by less than one-fourth of the older one; by 100.0 per cent of those who were already working in their original profession, but by less than 4 per cent of those working as laborers.

At the other extreme we find two closely related response categories: those who planned to continue indefinitely in their present nonprofessional occupation and those who made no plans for the future. Almost 40 per cent of all respondents belonged to these two combined categories, including almost two-thirds of the teachers and of the laborers, more than one-half of the lawyers, of persons over 50 years old, and of the white collar workers. On the other hand, only two physicians gave this response.

The Economic Situation

Most former Displaced Persons arrived in the United States penniless, for they were not permitted to bring into this country any German marks, the only European currency most refugees had. The agency sponsoring their immigration (most Lithuanians were sponsored by the National Catholic Welfare Conference) provided small loans enabling the immigrants to reach their places of destination and to survive for a few days, until they would obtain work; these loans, of course, had to be repaid as soon as possible. It follows that all refugees had to start a new economic life, based entirely on what they were able to earn in this country. Almost without exception, all previous achievements had to be discounted. During the first years after coming to this country, both husbands and wives usually were gainfully employed. In our sample of 146 refugees there were 95 married men living with their wives, and of these, 61 wives (64.1 per cent) were working at the time the study was conducted. Childless wives were employed almost without exception, 19 out of 23, but the majority of mothers also helped to support the family--40 worked outside of their homes, but 30 did not. All husbands of the women included in our sample worked. Consequently, in many cases the economic status of the family depended on the earnings of two persons. While discussing their economic status, some respondents pointed out that their economic position in the United States was achieved as a result of earnings by both the husband and the wife, whereas their former position in Lithuania was due to the earnings of the husband alone.

The respondents were asked to compare their economic status in the United States with that in the native country. Many of them pointed out that such a question was impossible to answer, since the official value of the currencies differed from their real buying power, various commodities varied in price, and symbols of economic status were different. For example, only a few of the respondents had owned a car in their native country, or had various other technological appliances so popular in the United States, but all those who had their own household had been able to hire a full-time maid. The youngest age group among the respondents presented a special case. These individuals had acquired their professional status only a short time before leaving Lithuania. There they had been beginners, single, living in a country under an economically disastrous foreign occupation, usually sharing the household with their parents or other people. In Chicago, most of them had a family and a household of their own and were living in a prosperous country. It was not easy for them to give meaningful replies. The respondents were right in pointing out these difficulties, but the purpose of the question was to elicit information about their attitudes rather than about objective facts.

Each of the ten subgroups listed in Table 5 had at least a few members indicating that their economic situation was "much worse" than it had been in Lithuania, while 6 subgroups had not one single member stating that he was financially in a "much better" situation. Persons working in their profession comprised, as expected, the highest percentage stating that their economic position had improved--36 per cent of this group said so; however, exactly the same percentage, 36, felt that their economic situation had deteriorated, while 28 per cent claimed no change. At the other extreme, 79 per cent of the professionals employed as manual laborers claimed that they were less well off at the time of the survey than they had been before leaving Lithuania, and only one individual out of 52 claimed that his financial position had slightly improved. Marked differences were also found between the different professional groups and between age groups.

In Lithuania, older professionals were, as a rule, economically better situated than younger ones, while in the United States, this older group held less well-paid jobs; hence, the difference between their former economic level and that in 1954 was extremely pronounced. This applied especially to the formerly most successful group, such as full professors, justices of various higher courts, army generals, etc. At the time of the survey many of them were employed as janitors in various Chicago factories.

Several factors tended to diminish the impact of the changes in the lives of refugees, particularly changes in their occupational and economic level. For the former displaced persons, the end of their old life in Lithuania and the beginning of the new one in the United States were separated by several years spent in Germany, first as foreign workers during the war and later as residents of Displaced Persons' Camps. The memories of these years were still vivid in the minds of the respondents, and the overwhelming majority felt that any free occupation, any work, was preferable to the dreary life in the camps. Hence, the jobs they were able to obtain in the United States, though often much lower than their former professional work, were still felt to be a great improvement when compared with camp life. Consequently, the attitude of the refugee professionals towards their new occupation and their new social setting as a whole was quite different from what it would have been if the less rewarding new jobs had immediately followed the better old ones, i.e., if the refugees had come to Chicago immediately after the first Soviet invasion of Lithuania, without the interlude in post-war Germany.

The second factor was an economic one. The difference between the standard of living in this country and that in most other civilized countries before World War II is difficult to describe. The Lithuanian professional class had been rather poor by American standards. Consequently, it was impossible to compare the financial rewards of an occupation in Lithuania and in the United States. Because of the high pay received by the American manual workers, the decline of the social and occupational status was felt less strongly than it would have been if the economic status had declined in the same proportion as the occupational one. The extreme indigence of the life in the camps made the American prosperity even more strongly appreciated.

The third factor helping to facilitate the adjustment to the new circumstances was the large number of Lithuanians already living in Chicago and in most other large American cities, and the important role played by the better-educated stratum of refugees in the Lithuanian-American commu-

TABLE 5. PRESENT AND FORMER ECONOMIC STATUS COMPARED: SAMPLE OF FOUR PROFESSIONAL GROUPS, CHICAGO, 1954

| | Total | | PRESENT STATUS | | | | | | | | |
| | | | Much Better | | Better | | Same | | Worse | | Much Worse | |
Subgroup	No.	%	No.	%	No.	%	No.	%	No.	%	No.	%
Total	146	100.0	4	2.7	24	16.4	35	24.0	54	37.0	29	19.9
Former Profession												
Lawyers	40	100.0	--	--	1	2.5	5	12.5	19	47.5	15	37.5
Teachers	34	100.0	--	--	1	2.9	10	29.4	18	52.9	5	14.7
Engineers	32	100.0	--	--	15	46.9	8	25.0	5	15.6	4	12.5
Physicians	40	100.0	4	10.0	7	17.5	12	30.0	12	30.0	5	12.5
Age												
Under 50	94	100.0	4	4.3	23	24.5	27	28.7	31	33.0	9	9.6
50 and more	52	100.5	--	--	1	1.9	8	15.4	23	44.2	20	38.5
Present Occupation												
Professional	39	100.0	3	7.7	11	28.2	11	28.2	11	28.2	3	7.7
Semiprofessional	32	100.0	1	3.1	10	31.3	9	28.1	9	28.1	3	9.4
White Collar	23	100.0	--	--	2	8.7	5	21.7	10	43.5	6	26.1
Laborers	52	100.0	--	--	1	1.9	10	19.2	24	46.2	17	32.7

nity. In Chicago, there are extensive areas where a person can live for years using a minimum of any language other than Lithuanian. The refugees transplanted to the United States many voluntary Lithuanian organizations and formed new ones. Almost all professional groups set-up their own organizations which united fellow members of their original profession. Since the decline in occupational status was a mass phenomenon due to political causes and not something for which the individual could be blamed even indirectly, a person's status within the refugee group depended mostly on achievements in Lithuania rather than on his occupation in the United States.

Another factor was the ability to provide higher education for the young generation. People who are unable to achieve their goals frequently transfer their frustrated hopes to their children and try to make possible for them what they themselves were unable to attain. The prestige of education was high in Lithuania and it continued to be so among the refugees. Professional persons were at least as eager to educate their children as the rest of the refugee population, and probably more so. Since Illinois law requires all youngsters to attend school up to the age of 16, the occupation of young people over that age is of interest in this connection. The respondents reported 31 children over 16 years of age, living in the same household with their parents. Of this number, 3 individuals had already acquired a profession, 29 were students, 4 were white collar workers, and 1 was a manual laborer. Thus, almost 90 per cent of the children of refugee professionals had either already achieved professional status or were in the process of achieving it. A very high percentage of the children of Lithuanian refugees seek college education, irrespective of the actual occupation of their parents.

All the above factors facilitated the transition of refugee professionals to their new way of life.

Lithuanians and Other Refugees

What has been said about the life of Lithuanian refugees could be repeated with little change to describe the adjustments of political refugees belonging to other national groups, who left their countries because of the establishment of Communist tyranny during and after World War II: the Latvians, Estonians, Poles, Hungarians, Ukrainians, and others. The fate of this broad group of refugees may be compared with that of refugees who fled from the domination of National Socialism in various countries, primarily in Germany and Austria. Several books have been written about anti-Nazi refugees.[3] The occupational attainments of professional persons belonging to this group, when compared with what has been said about the Lithuanian professionals, indicates that Germans and Austrians made better adjustments than did Lithuanians of the same professions. This is especially conspicuous in the case of culture-bound professions difficult to transplant to a foreign country, such as those of lawyers and teachers. The percentage of persons belonging to these two professions who made successful occupational adjustments, as given by Davie and Kent,[4] was many times higher than that of their Lithuanian fellows. This difference can be explained by 1) the higher prestige of the culture of German-speaking countries as compared with that of other Middle and East European nations; 2) better connections and influential protection of the German-speaking groups; 3) more sympathy shown by influential persons in America to the anti-Nazi than to anti-Communist refugees.

FOOTNOTES

[1] Reprinted by the permission of the author and the publisher, _Lituanus_, Lithuanian Quarterly Journal of Arts and Sciences. In a letter to the compiler and editor January 25, 1977, the author stated: "Please feel free to include in your forthcoming book my article," Occupational Adjustments of Refugee Professionals," originally published in the _Lituanus_. The title was changed without my knowledge to "Occupational Adjustments of Professional Refugees," and I would appreciate your using the original title."

[2] The materials of this article are derived from a study which was submitted as a Master's Thesis to the University of Chicago.

[3] Davie, Maurice R., _Refugees in America_, New York: Harper and Bros., 1947.
Fields, Harold, _The Refugee in the United States_, New York: Oxford University Press, 1938.
Kent, Donald Peterson, _The Refugee Intellectual--the Americanization of Immigrants of 1933-1941_, New York, Columbia University Press, 1953.

[4] Davie, _op cit._, pp. 278, 299 and 320; Kent, _op. cit._, p. 301.